Evolving Perspectives on Computers and Composition Studies

D1210116

Advances in Computers and Composition Studies

Series Editors:

Gail E. Hawisher
University of Illinois at Urbana-Champaign

Cynthia L. Selfe
Michigan Technological University

Series Design Editor:

James R. Kalmbach
Illinois State University

Creating a Computer-Supported Writing Facility:
A Blueprint for Action

Evolving Perspectives on Computers and Composition Studies:
Questions for the 1990s

Evolving Perspectives on Computers and Composition Studies

Questions for the 1990s

Edited by
Gail E. Hawisher
University of Illinois at Urbana-Champaign

Cynthia L. Selfe
Michigan Technological University

With a foreword by
Edmund J. Farrell
The University of Texas at Austin

NCTE

Computers and Composition

ELMHURST COLLEGE LIBRARY

NCTE Editorial Board: Richard Abrahamson, Celia Genishi, Joyce Kinkead, Richard Lloyd-Jones, Gladys V. Veidemanis; Charles Suhor, *chair*, ex officio; Michael Spooner, ex officio

Interior Design: Adapted from James R. Kalmbach

Cover Design: Joellen Bryant

NCTE Stock Number: 11661-3020

© 1991 by the National Council of Teachers of English, 1111 Kenyon Road, Urbana, IL 61801, and by *Computers and Composition*, Michigan Technological University, Houghton, MI 49931, University of Illinois at Urbana-Champaign, Urbana, IL 61801. All rights reserved. Printed in the United States of America.

Michigan Technological University and the University of Illinois at Urbana-Champaign are equal opportunity educational institutions/ equal opportunity employers.

It is the policy of NCTE in its journals and other publications to provide a forum for the open discussion of ideas concerning the content and the teaching of English and the language arts. Publicity accorded to any particular point of view does not imply endorsement by the Executive Committee, the Board of Directors, or the membership at large, except in announcements of policy, where such endorsement is clearly specified.

Library of Congress Cataloging-in-Publication Data

Evolving perspectives on computers and composition studies: questions for the 1990s/edited by Gail E. Hawisher, Cynthia L. Selfe; with a foreword by Edmund J. Farrell.
    p.   cm.—(Advances in computers and composition studies)
    Includes bibliographical references and index.
    ISBN 0-8141-1166-1 (NCTE). —ISBN 0-9623392-1-0 (Computers and composition)
    1. English language—Composition and exercises—Study and teaching (Secondary) 2. English language—Computer-assisted instruction. 3. Word processing in education. I. Hawisher, Gail E. II. Selfe, Cynthia L., 1951– . III. National Council of Teachers of English. IV. Computers and composition. V. Series.
LB1631.E94 1991
808'.042'0712—dc20   91-13514
                                                CIP

ELMHURST COLLEGE LIBRARY

Consulting Editors:

Hugh Burns
The University of Texas at Austin

James Collins
State University of New York, Buffalo

Ron Fortune
Illinois State University

Lisa Gerrard
University of California at Los Angeles

Dawn Rodrigues
Colorado State University

Pat Sullivan
Purdue University

Assistant Volume Editors:

Alicia K. Haley
Michigan Technological University

Mary C. Graham
Michigan Technological University

NCTE Project Editor:

Timothy "Boet" Bryant

*To our colleagues and students,
for all their support, companionship,
and inspiration*

Contents

Foreword

Evolving Perspectives on Computers and Composition Studies is a remarkable volume: despite its chapters having been authored by different individuals with strong points of view, it nevertheless manages to present a harmonic, albeit at times disturbing, overview of what we now know, and may yet discover during this premillenial decade, about the complex relationships between computing and composing.

Though highly informative, the volume is, as its title implies, intentionally provocative, raising far more questions than it answers. This is as it should be, for to recast Browning for academe, scholars' inquiries should exceed their knowledge, or what's research for? Frankly, I find refreshing the amplitude of questions posed by contributors, since it was not long ago historically that the profession was unsophisticated about research in both composition and computers. For the former, as *Research in Written Composition* (NCTE, 1963) revealed, it too often employed crude or inappropriate methodologies to explore the questions it did raise; for the latter, until quite recently, it understandably did not even know what questions to ask.

Unlike the rich history of rhetoric, spanning from antiquity to present, the history of electronic computing is a phenomenon of recent decades, one which has evolved and continues to evolve with stunning rapidity. Using thousands of electronic tubes, the first electronic digital computer—the Electronic Numerical Integrator and Computer, or ENIAC—appeared in 1946, fewer than five decades ago. Two years later, Bell Telephone Laboratories announced that American physicists John Bardeen, Walter Brattain, and William Shockley had invented the transistor. It was not until the late 1950s, however, that transistors replaced electron tubes in computers, thereby reducing both the size and the power consumption of components. Transistors gave rise to the semiconductor industry, to microelectronics, to the wedding of transistors into integrated circuits, or chips, and to the rapid development of mini- and microcomputers, machines far smaller than mainframes, the big computers that preceded them.

In 1967 when I wrote *English, Education, and the Electronic Revolution*, I failed to foresee the development and increasing ubiquity in the 1980s of personal computers, let alone the possibility of students using the computer to compose, revise, edit, and confer with each other and the instructor. Beyond the realm of imagination—at least mine—was the possibility, now the reality, of linking classrooms around the globe through such national and international networks as ARPA, Internet, BITNET, USENET, and CSNET. Available in some schools in 1967 were a modest number of programs, mainly drill exercises in grammar and usage ("programmed instruction"), tied to mainframes. I find scant comfort in knowing that Alvin Toffler in *Future Shock* (1970) proved no more prescient than I: in that work he devoted a paltry five pages to computers and classrooms, with nary a word said about the educational implications of microcomputers.

As Donald Ross makes evident in chapter 4 of the present volume, current hardware and software make the computer technology of two decades ago seem antediluvian. For example,

> For the writer, the NeXT [a machine which became available in 1989] includes full desktop publishing, the WRITENOW word-processing software, a 256-megabyte removable optically read disk with an indexed dictionary and thesaurus, windows for screen management, digital voice recording, a compact-disk-quality stereo sound system, a million-pixel high-resolution screen, and a laser printer. This complete system costs about $7,500.

Still on the horizon is the possibility of optical computing, which would replace electrons with photons and render future computers one hundred to one thousand times more powerful than present supercomputers. In *Time*, February 12, 1990, Thomas McCarroll glowingly forecast the possible uses of computing machines based on optics:

> . . . robots that can see; computers that can design aircraft from scratch; processors that can swiftly convert spoken

words into written text and vice versa. Such practical optical computers are still years—some would say light-years— away. Yet many scientists are already predicting that the device will have an impact similar to that of the integrated circuit, which made small personal computers possible. (p. 71)

The promises of optical computing aside, present technology— desktop publishing and the use of hypertext/hypermedia and other electronic writing systems (see, in particular, chapters 8– 11)—now threatens traditional relationships in discourse: between writers and the "ownership" of their written "properties"; between writers and their editors, layout designers, and publishers; between writers and their audiences; between teachers of writing and their students. As Patricia Sullivan suggests in chapter 2, teachers may find themselves increasingly responsible for helping students recognize the possible rhetorical effects that the interplay of typeface, spacing, graphics, and even sound and animation— not verbal language alone—has upon designated audiences. In light of the myriad scholarly books, textbooks, articles, collections of essays, and dissertations related to composition and to computing now being published annually, these new responsibilities may not be eagerly borne by teachers, at least not initially. The integrated circuit has released the genie from the bottle, and it threatens to drown us all in blizzards of information and advice—a modicum of it essential, a fair amount of it noteworthy, much of it trivial. Sifting, sorting, and scanning have become professional life skills, and those among us who still aspire for omniscience in our fields also hanker for breakdowns.

If there is one motif or overarching concern in *Evolving Perspectives*, it has to do with access, with the realization that the computer empowers only those to whom it is available. In their concluding paragraph to chapter 6, Klem and Moran comment, "Access is, it seems to us, the issue that drives all before it. Who has access, and to what?" In chapter 8, Shirk poses the question "Is there the potential for modifying the distribution of knowledge (and therefore social and political power) in our society through the use of the vast hypertextual bodies of information which will become available to those who have access to this technology?" McDaid asks in chapter 9, "How can inequalities of access . . . be addressed? What forms of activism are appropriate and necessary? What do we want? Who gets it? Who controls it? Who pays, and how?" In chapter 12, Ray and Barton raise a flurry of questions, among them these: "Who decides who uses computers and on what basis? How are computers used to exclude or include groups, or to deny or permit access to information? How are computers used to strengthen existing lines of authority? How might broadened access threaten these lines of authority?" In her abstract of chapter 14, Gomez inquires, "How can we move beyond equality of opportunity to equity of opportunity to learn with and about computers?"

The questions raised here are pertinent, the responses to them critical. As the authors of this soundly conceived and richly rewarding volume make clear, computer technology indeed has the power to democratize existing power relationships, to broaden the base of privilege by opening discourse communities to those formerly barred access by gender, class, or race. Whether it will do so remains highly problematic. But the goal is one that should fully engage the best in us all in the decade ahead, for upon it rest the strength and well-being of the society—and with it, education.

Edmund J. Farrell
The University of Texas at Austin
Austin, Texas
March 1991

Introduction

Questions for the 1990s: Setting an Agenda

Questions make the frame in which its picture of facts is plotted. They make more than the frame; they give the angle of perspective.

—Suzanne Langer,
Philosophy in a New Key

With this volume, we seek to identify some of the important questions that scholars, teachers, and researchers in the field of computers and composition must address to develop new perspectives on technology and advance confidently into the twenty-first century. The competition for the manuscripts that appear in this book of questions for the 1990s was held in the spring of 1989. From over fifty proposals, eight editors (the volume editors and the consulting editors) carefully selected the twenty or so that we thought best represented important issues shaping the profession and invited the authors to submit full manuscripts. From those manuscripts, we then chose only those that we agreed might lead to significant new contributions in the field. The final collection is comprised of fifteen chapters, each identifying and defining a particular area of exploration that needs to be undertaken by scholars and researchers. The chapters do not describe a specific, localized study, lab, classroom, or program. Rather they examine generalized areas of study that are important within broad educational contexts, that encourage other researchers and scholars to realize the importance of further work in the field, and that sketch some of the directions that such work might take. In other words, the chapters in this book are focused in such a way as to set an agenda of scholarship and research for the next decade.

During the past decade, profound changes have occurred in writing instruction, many of which have been directly influenced by the arrival of microcomputer technology. Increasingly, teachers of English have come to rely on computers for instruction, research, and professional preparation. With this new reliance on electronic technology, responsibilities too have changed. Not only must members of our profession keep abreast of theoretical perspectives on teaching and learning, but also they must attend to new hardware and software developments as well. Other, more subtle changes have also occurred as technology has become an integral part of our curricula. Teaching in computer-supported classrooms has helped English composition instructors see themselves not primarily as dispensers of advice to students, but rather as fellow students in the position of learning with—and from—those we teach. Computer technology, many teachers feel, provides much needed help in creating fertile sites for the creation and cultivation of knowledge within classrooms.

Such change is all about us. We can see it in the very nature of the discipline itself: in the changing ways in which writers can now construct and assemble texts using computers, in the changing concepts of authorship and ownership within electronically based publishing environments, and in the changing nature of media and hypermedia. Even our attitudes have changed. Teachers of English composition have progressed from skepticism to enthusiastic acceptance, and finally to healthy criticism of what computers can and cannot do for writing classes. The next step must be to plan strategies for the future that are responsive to these changes, that are informed by careful research and by theoretically sound pedagogy.

To conduct an *informed* debate about how electronic technology can—and cannot—serve writing instruction effectively, we must gather two kinds of information, complete two kinds of scholarly tasks: we have to look to the past to review what we have learned through research completed in the last ten years; we have to look to the future, the 1990s, to set forth a continuing scholarly agenda. By examining questions that must still be answered and by exploring ways in which we might begin to gather needed information, we avoid the danger of using electronic technology haphazardly. We avoid making decisions without carefully considering the issues affecting our students and ourselves: how, for example, we can provide equitable access to technology for all students in our classes regardless of such factors as gender, race, handicap, or socioeconomic status; how we can prevent plans to use computers as inappropriate and ineffective teacher substitutes; how we can ensure the adequate and competent preparation of teachers who will be using computers; how we can fulfill the promise of hypertext; and how we can meet the challenges presented by the changing nature of literacy in the electronic age.

The year 2000 will soon be upon us, and much work remains to be done. For this reason, we see this book as indispensable to writing teachers, researchers, and theoreticians interested in literacy issues in the electronic age. Readers will also come from the ranks of professional educators who train teachers and who want to add computer-based learning to their curricula. In addition, this collection will appeal to administrators who are considering the possibility of integrating computers into an educational setting. Finally, the book is invaluable to graduate students in computers and composition studies, for the questions posed by the contributors are aimed at those interested in pursuing research and scholarship in the field.

In presenting this collection to readers, we have divided it into four sections, each outlining an agenda of scholarship and research. The sections are focused on primary areas of change that have determined our efforts in the past decade and that hold great promise for future investigations. Within these sections, each of the consulting editors, a nationally recognized scholar in computers and composition studies, has worked individually with the authors to ensure a coherent yet far-reaching perspective of the particular area under study. Part 1, "Research and Scholarship: The Changing Discipline," examines how electronic writing has profoundly influenced our work in and out of the classroom. Part 2, "Classroom Contexts: The Changing Responsibilities of Students and Teachers," focuses on the new dynamics within writing classes and calls for exemplary training of teachers, for carefully considered instructional strategies, and for a close examination of assessment procedures for students writing in electronic environments. Part 3, "The Promise of Hypertext: Changing Instructional Media," turns to a new development, the creation of hypertexts, a completely on-line instructional medium that promises to transform our notions of textuality and teaching. Hypertext environments, instead of presenting information linearly and sequentially as in books, permit student readers to organize on-line material according to their own constructing perceptions and understandings. Part 4, "The Politics of Computers: Changing Hierarchies," examines how the use of electronic technology presents new opportunities for shifting traditional authority structures in classrooms, in writing programs, and even in our educational system itself. The authors warn, however, that unless we remain aware of the transformative power of any new technology, we may unwittingly use it in ways that contribute neither to learning nor to teaching. The overall purpose of the chapters in this volume is to help us, as scholars and teachers, to understand how learning and, more specifically, writing, are changed by electronic environments and to question future directions in computers and composition studies.

Reference

Langer, S. (1957). *Philosophy in a new key.* Cambridge, MA: Harvard University Press.

Part One

Research and Scholarship: The Changing Discipline

Introduction

Certainly the effect of the typewriter on composition deserves careful investigation. . . . The ease with which kindergarten and primary school children seem to be able to operate portable electric typewriters argues especially for a careful investigation . . . to determine whether or not the typewriter can increase the fluency of writing in general.

—Braddock, Lloyd-Jones, & Schoer,
Research in Written Composition

Early research and scholarship in computers and composition studies captured the spirit of the above quotation taken from Braddock, Lloyd-Jones, and Schoer's groundbreaking monograph *Research in Written Composition* (1963). Like the electric typewriter before it, the microcomputer was thought to make writing "easier" in important ways. Thus studies examined the influence of technology on writers' processes and products, often hypothesizing that the writing, the revision, or the mechanics of particular populations of writers would improve when computers were used as writing tools. Although some of the writers that were studied included professional and experienced writers, most of the research was aimed at various populations of student writers: first-year college students, basic writers, graduate students, advanced students, high school and elementary school students, or some combination of the above. Good-looking, clearly printed texts; ease of revision; and improved attitudes toward composing were some of the reasons given as to why some groups' writing might improve when it took advantage of electronic technology. Like other researchers, we too conducted these sorts of studies in hopes of finding how the use of computers might develop our students' writing abilities. Twenty years after the 1963 *Research in Written Composition*, we had shifted our gaze from the electric typewriter to the microcomputer, but we were still asking the same questions.

These research questions seem outdated and naive to those of us working in computers and composition studies today. In just several short years, we have come to realize that, when a whole society is moving to electronic writing, comparing products and judging them superior or inferior in one medium or another yields little fruitful information. Indeed, our notions of quality are probably changing as inevitably as those changes in standards that accompanied the transition from hand-inscribed manuscripts to printed texts.

In part 1, we look to changes in computers and composition studies that have altered our teaching of writing and, thus, our professional lives. Even those of us who do not teach writing with computers are likely to use word processing, laser printers, and other computer assistance for our own writing. Nancy Kaplan, in chapter 1, argues that electronic tools are so powerful that they indeed may change the tasks that they were assigned to tackle—that their transformative capabilities are likely to lead to new methods of teaching that capture more fully our theories of writing. In emphasizing the profound disciplinary changes taking place all around us, Kaplan sets the stage for the whole of the book. Patricia Sullivan, in chapter 2, then looks at the relationship of author to text in electronic environments. If Kaplan shows us how pervasive and widespread the influence of electronic technology is within our society, Sullivan extends this argument by showing us how electronic technology in the hands of authors blurs the cultures of print and electronic delivery, of assembly and production. In fact, Sullivan maintains that the new media call for new theories of electronic writing and pedagogy as writers begin to take back control of the page from publishers. In chapter 3, Janis Forman moves on to software, specifically to the new groupware packages, that facilitate collaborative writing. She argues that interdisciplinary research teams must be assembled to examine fully the many activities of electronic collaborative writing. And, finally, in chapter 4, Donald Ross examines the concept of an electronic workstation and scrutinizes its relation to those of us working in computer writing classes. In effect, electronic workstations provide students and instructors multiple tools with which to research, create, assemble, share, and assess writing. "Intelligent" systems may yet offer help to electronic writing classes if we integrate them wisely into our classes. These four opening chapters pave the way to the next three sections, in which other kinds of changes are explored and analyzed—changes in responsibilities, instructional media, and political hierarchies.

Reference

Braddock, R., Lloyd-Jones, R., & Schoer, L. (1963). *Research in written composition*. Urbana, IL: National Council of Teachers of English.

Chapter 1

Ideology, Technology, and the Future of Writing Instruction

Nancy Kaplan
Cornell University

Tools work for users, but they also influence the shape of users' work, affecting how users understand their world and their scope of action within it. As electronic writing tools augment and, in some instances, replace older technologies of writing and publishing, writing teachers face a myriad of ideological issues. What effects might electronic textuality have on the economic and social relations among writers, texts, readers, and the institutions traditionally in control of textual distribution? How do existing economic, social, and political formations affect which tools become available and for whose use? What notions of writing processes and products do electronic tools support and what understandings do they occlude or proscribe? And how do new tools interact with existing ideological formations in the writing classroom? At stake is nothing less than the shape of our work and our world.

Curriculum in the most fundamental sense is a battleground over whose forms of knowledge, history, visions, language, culture, and authority will prevail as a legitimate object of learning and analysis.

—Henry Giroux,
Introduction to Literacy:
Reading the Word and the World

Machines have enabled man to transform his physical environment. With their aid he has plowed the land and built cities and dug great canals. These transformations of man's habitat have

11

necessarily induced mutations in his social arrangements.
But even more crucially, the machines of man have strongly
determined his very understanding of his world and hence of
himself.

—Joseph Weizenbaum,
Computer Power and Human Reason:
From Judgment to Calculation

At all levels of formal education, the reading and writing
curriculum immediately raises deeply ideological issues: literacy
is, after all, both a technology and a privileged form of knowledge,
a practice whose history inevitably embodies its culture's deepest
social, political, and economic arrangements (Clanchy, 1979;
Ohmann, 1985). The current debate over "cultural literacy" merely
focuses national attention on the ideological conflicts inherent in
the formation of every educational practice and institution (see
Hirsch, 1987, 1988; Sledd & Sledd, 1988a, 1988b, 1989). As Paulo
Freire (Friere & Macedo, 1987) cautions, "It is impossible to
understand education as an autonomous or neutral practice" (p.
39).

As a profession, rhetoricians and writing teachers have long
recognized that the composition curriculum works self-consciously
to replicate dominant ideologies but that it can be constructed to
resist and reform them as well: even before ideology became a
fashionable topic among literary scholars or social historians, the
tension between replicating and resisting was a hot professional
topic. Exploring the multifaceted connections between the rise of
monopoly capital and the "invention" of composition as a course
of study in the modern American university, Richard Ohmann
(1976) concludes that

> the proliferation of freshman English around the country, as
> the most inevitable part of the whole college curriculum,
> owed to the university's newly assigned task of training
> American professional and managerial elites. (p. 134)

More recently, James Berlin (1988) has argued that no rhetoric
can act "as the transcendental recorder or arbiter of competing
ideological claims, [for every] rhetoric is . . . always already
ideological" (p. 477) even if a particular rhetoric refuses the

ideological question by "claiming for itself the transcendent neu-trality of science" (p. 478). As many practitioners remind teachers of writing, the textbooks we assign (Rose, 1983; Welch, 1987), the theories of writing and cognition they espouse and we endorse (Berlin, 1988; Bizzell, 1982), the particular institutional practices within which we work, the structure of expectations and the social roles our students have constructed or acquired (Perelman, 1986)—all of our practices are shot through with ideological statements.

Like the elements and the physical laws of the natural world, ideology surrounds, permeates, and constitutes the conceptual world we inhabit. In *The Ideology of Power and the Power of Ideology,* Therborn (1980) defines ideology, simply and capaciously, as discourses embodying what exists, what is good, and what is possible. In defining "what exists, and its corollary, what does not exist," ideology speaks of "who we are, what the world is, what nature, society, men and women are like" (p. 18). Similarly, it structures and normalizes human aspirations and desires, shap-ing our conceptions of "what is good, right, just, beautiful, attractive, enjoyable, and its opposites" (p. 18). And most important, Therborn concludes, ideology delineates and constrains human expectations, circumscribing what can be done about what exists and by whom: it outlines what we understand to be possible and what we consider impossible (p. 18). But ideology is in fact always poly-phonic, for the discursive practices shaping human institutions, actions, and beliefs—and the tools human beings develop and use—always present multiple and conflicting meanings and val-ues.

Although composition researchers have been swift to study certain effects of computers as writing tools and as pedagogical delivery systems, the profession as a whole largely lacks a full and ideologically informed account of *all* the tools with which we have taught and are teaching: pens and paper; printed books; black-boards; ditto- or photo-duplicated sheets; and most recently, computers, with their attendant software, projection devices, and networks. No empirical studies, to my knowledge, assess the textbook as a pedagogic delivery system, let alone analyze its ideological implications. Studies focused on computer writing tools, though certainly numerous enough, typically arise from questions that Gail Hawisher (1989), borrowing a term from

Seymour Papert, terms "technocentric" (p. 44): they have attempted to isolate *the* effects of *the* computer or word-processing program on *the* cognitive processes of writers, both novice and expert. A mixed lot, both in their methodologies and in their theoretical foundations, these studies nevertheless share two unexamined assumptions: that although the means of text production changes, the meaning of the term *writing* remains constant and that although the tool may interact with cognitive or social processes, it is itself value-free and neutral. Whether the research subjects in these studies were creating narratives or arguments or explanations, their objective, or output, if you will, was print—words on paper governed by and conforming to the rhetorical conventions of print. Those conventions, as this chapter shows, are imbued with ideological positions: they construct a matrix of relations among writers, texts, readers, and knowledge, a matrix that patterns authority, power, and scope of action in a particular way and thereby excludes other patterns. In the coming decade, as electronic texts, hypertexts, and hypermedia texts proliferate and as our pedagogical practices add electronic discussion to the oral dialogues that have been the staple of the classroom, writing instruction can no longer concern itself exclusively with words on paper. Nor can writing instruction continue to ignore the ways tools implicate and are implicated in the power relations, or more broadly the ideologies, permeating reading and writing acts.

Ideologies and Technologies

As the material instantiations of discursive practices, tools or technologies necessarily embody ideologies and ideological conflict. Tools or technologies enable, but also disable: they expand conceptions of what exists and what is possible, but also contract the field of potentialities. Tools or technologies validate some practices as natural and right, but proscribe others as deviant, impractical, or simply unthinkable. They accord power and privilege to some and exclude others. When a technology is as pervasive and as profoundly shaping as print has been, it is often difficult to perceive the full extent of its entitlements and exclusions. Its formations and empowerments seem simply natural and right. When a new tool emerges, however, the conflict engendered by its emergence can illuminate previously obscured relations.

As McLuhan (1967), Goody (1977), and Ong (1982) have argued, the conventions of the book have organized not simply the text but the world: what we can know and how that knowledge is organized for retrieval. The subject index, largely unknown before the printed book, not only maps the terrain of a book's contents, but also creates ways of conceptualizing the world. Drawing from the work of these theorists, Cynthia Selfe (1989a) recounts Goody's example that "because indexes have no equivalent in the natural world, until we created the print medium and the convention of 'index,' we had no way of envisioning, or even thinking of, systematic information storage and retrieval based on spatial location" (p. 6). Once indexing was firmly established, it came to seem the "natural" organization for information, not only charting books but also systematizing knowledge about the world.

Now the emerging conventions of databases, the digital version of the book's index, are rewriting the world, restructuring what is knowable, by whom, and for what purposes. The database's underlying structure, usually invisible to the user, shapes both the forms inquiry can take and and the forms it cannot take. Anyone first encountering an electronic cataloging system bumps up hard against such reality as he or she struggles to transform strategies appropriate for a system of card files into new mental habits for a system dependent on Boolean techniques. And the nature of those habits depends on the software's data structure and on the user interface constructed by the software's designers. Some databases access information only through keywords, much like the subject headings on index cards, while others permit searches through the full texts of, say, professional journals. The differences between such searches are profound.

Even before the tool's full potential has been realized, it has restructured some of our fundamental ways of thinking about and understanding the world, shifts traceable in our language habits, the metaphors with which we create and express the world (Turkle, 1984; Weizenbaum, 1976). Thus, new techniques for organizing knowledge highlight what has been lurking in the shadows for five hundred years: the index is no more "natural" than the memory palace that preceded it; both heuristics create orders that their users internalize. The new heuristics, the algorithms of electronic search and retrieval, will surely do so as well.

The conceptual fields that computers and their applications create differ profoundly from the potentialities offered by a world constituted primarily through the printed word, rapidly reconstituting what can be said to exist and what human beings can effect with the tools of the age of electronic information. The computing revolution, which above all else is a writing revolution, shifts the forms that recorded thought can take; expands the reach that a text can attain; and, unnervingly, reorders the way that producers, distributors, and consumers of texts conduct their literary and economic relations.

A New Heaven and Earth?

Many have been swift to identify ideological shifts promised by the intrinsic properties of these new tools, highlighting a panoply of revolutionary outcomes in the wake of digitizing the word. In one formulation, analysts predict new entitlements flowing from a hybrid: electronic equipment, in this strain, distributes the power associated with command of the printed word more widely and democratically. John Ruskiewicz (1988), for example, has claimed that

> In extending the enhanced word to the great masses of writers we . . . also enormously democratize the power of the printed word. The undeniable authority and prestige of typeset copy is now within the grasp of the smallest group, the least powerful institutions. I do not think this is a minor point, but one that may ultimately change our notions of publication, power, and prestige and significantly alter the nature of scholarly and political communication. (p. 15)

In a second, more radical formulation, purely electronic information entirely re-forms the landscape of literacy. As Richard Lanham (1989) contemplates swiftly approaching shifts in the forms of recorded thought, he predicts that "electronic 'texts' [in which he includes "interactive multimedia delivery systems"] will redefine the writing, reading, and professing of literature" (p.

265). Lanham's exuberant predictions emanate from perceived differences between print and electronic textuality, differences whose ideological tendencies we need to understand and to examine critically.

Electronic encoding profoundly changes the textual environment. In the medium of print, each verbal work seems to have clear boundaries to distinguish definitively between itself—its marks fixed upon a finite number of pages—and other texts fixed upon their own, separate pages. The meanings that a work conveys seem similarly fixed: they emanate directly from the words immutably recorded on the paper. The bound volume's materiality, as Stanley Fish (1980) points out, invites misunderstanding:

> A line of print or a page of a book is so obviously there—it can be handled, photographed, or put away—that it seems to be the sole repository of whatever value and meaning we associate with it. (p. 43)

In the past two decades, reading theorists (Bleich, 1980; Holland, 1980; Iser, 1980) have argued that fixed boundaries among texts and between texts and their readers are illusions. But theory notwithstanding, the immutable marks on the page in a reader's hand seem to establish a visible gulf between a given verbal work and its reading or at least its reader, as well as between the work in hand and all other works. At least until the sixties, few people had much trouble establishing a text's limits—determining just where it began and where it ended, what was "in" it and what was not.

To be sure, post-structuralism long ago declared the literary work (and by extension all other verbal works) inextricable from the whole fabric of texts surrounding it. "A specific piece of writing," Eagleton (1983) explains, "has no clearly defined boundaries: it spills over constantly into the works clustered around it" (p. 138). Such texts cannot be "totalized," cannot yield a final, unified coherence, and, therefore, cannot set forth or represent immutable truths. But these declarations, focusing on language as a sign-system, are constantly threatened by the material presence of the text on its page. By writing *S/Z*, Barthes *metaphorically* reinscribed Balzac's text, creating another—a separate—text. As Eagleton relates, this text then transposes Balzac's "into different discourses, [and] produces his . . . semi-arbitrary play of meaning athwart the work itself" (p. 137). In an electronic environment, metaphor leaps into action: any reader/writer can literally do what Barthes metaphorically accomplished, reinscribing the text not by constructing a separate, albeit intertextual, text but by altering the material form of the prior text itself.

Although all electronic texts—even those destined for the inflexible structures of the printed page—are constantly open to such reinscriptions, new and intrinsically unprintable forms of nonlinear discourse, or hypertexts, manifest these transformations most clearly. According to Moulthrop (1989), hypertext is essentially "a matrix of information or 'random-access database' enabling readers to retrieve and assemble the texts as they please" (p. 18). In many cases, a hypertext enables readers to add to the database and to the structure of connecting links (pointers leading to and from other sections of the construct) by which other readers access the textual nodes. The instantaneous presence of a multitude of connected texts subverts print technology's hierarchy of relationships between central text and annotations. As Moulthrop continues,

> In printed works, notes and bibliography give writings outside the current text a presence on the page, but that presence is metaphoric. Hypertext abolishes this metaphor: the other writings actually become present when the reader activates a link. (p. 19)

Thus, as a reader alters or adds either to the linking structure or to the nodes of text, the reader/writer's new text dissolves the old within it.

To demonstrate the radical results, Moulthrop used a hypertext writing system, STORYSPACE, to construct an interactive fiction incorporating Borges's story "The Garden of the Forking Paths." Moulthrop's story, "forking paths," undoes the linearity of Borges's narrative and interpolates new text undifferentiated from the "original." This text's reader can not only reorder his or her encounter with the text each time he or she reads; he or she can also add or delete text and create new links to offer yet other paths through the story's spaces. The resulting "solution" radically redefines the notion of intertextuality, which acknowledges an abstract interconnectedness among texts but which has never envisioned a collapse of several texts into a new entity that digests the old within it. This new, electronic intertextuality shifts power from writer to reader/writer, radically altering the world as we have known and accessed it.

In the digitized world, texts are intrinsically fluid, malleable, protean (Balestri, 1988). And it is no longer possible—even for a naive, atheoretical reader—to understand or even to approach them as fixed, stable, linear objects. Key papers delivered at the Hypertext '87 conference vividly demonstrate the transformation. The Association of Computing Machinery (ACM) published these papers in two formats: as a set of traditional printed papers (*Communications of the ACM*, 1988) and as hypertext documents constructed by means of three widely available hypertext writing systems. In a sense, the printed and the hypertextual embodiments merely offer "the same thing" in two different packages. But in fact, these two kinds of objects dramatize profoundly altered relations between the reading and writing spaces that the two technologies create. According to John Smith and Stephen Weiss (1988), a printed text's physical structure recapitulates its logical structure: both are inherently linear. This congruence shapes the reader's traversal of the work. Smith and Weiss state that "such documents encourage readers to read them linearly, from beginning to end following the same sequence" (stack *ACM*. eds, cards 5–6) embodied within the physical structure.

As readers interpret or make sense of a printed work, they can, of course, mutter and muse in the margins of the page, can (in memory at least) produce sets of conceptual links that obliquely traverse the whole collection, representing their constructions of the text's meaning, as the theorists would have it, against the strictly linear tug of the work's representation on the page. Readers' annotations and their conceptual representation of the text's meanings comprise the reinscription or understanding of the work. If readers choose, they can photocopy "their" versions, complete with their commentaries, or write, on separate pieces of paper, rejoinders or reinterpretations. And readers can distribute the new document. But the traces that originate with these readers always remain distinct and visually differentiable from the "primary" text.

The hypertextual embodiment, in contrast, dissociates the text's physical structure from the monological structure of its discourse. It offers readers alternative traversals, multiple and branching paths, from the start. Readers can follow the editor's connections, rather than the authors' linear pieces, through the composite space constituted by the totality of the individual contributions, refusing even for a first reading the linearity of a single essay and overleaping the boundaries that print constructs between various pieces. With the appropriate piece of software at hand, readers may decide to construct new links or add their own comments within the body of the existing text. Once readers have done so, their words and links merge into the whole so that if they distribute a copy of their version, the next reader can no longer distinguish between a primary text and an ancillary text, between the state of the text before and its state after an act of reading/writing. Both in theory and in action, the boundary dividing reader from text and writer, as well as the division between primary text and secondary annotation, simply dissolves.

The scope or field of action implied by the electronic redefinition of a text expands not just conceptually but spatially when it can be distributed quickly and widely through an electronic network. Networks expand an author's potential audience and, therefore, his or her power. Moreover, texts distributed electronically can bypass traditional publishers, and, therefore, bypass entrenched "gate-keeping" communities at least one of whose effects has been to silence or mute nontraditional voices and points of view (Spender, 1981). The printed word has, in fact, created an extensive and powerful system of privilege. In itself hierarchical, it is also the material sign of an author's status within the social system. Because it is fixed and stable it can acquire economic value; it can be copyrighted and owned by its producer or publisher. The printed word can be easily channeled and controlled by the few who have access to the machinery for formalizing and distributing texts. To "achieve" publication, an author must first be author-ized by many institutions, each of which has literally stamped the work and implicitly the writer with the imprimatur of those privileged to judge a text's value. The publisher, in effect, authenticates the value of the text, especially in academic presses and journals, by guaranteeing the text's authoritative origins and its intrinsic value. Electronic production and distribution of texts, as Wahlstrom (1989) notes, "is potentially an enfranchising technology, opening the door for more people to a powerful technology" (p. 176).

The power of these new tools of publication leads to hopeful, even utopian, visions: in a brave new electronic world, anyone with access to the right technology will be able to produce and distribute texts, both in print and in electronic form, which cannot be easily distinguished by visual signs from those which have issued from the keyboards of highly acclaimed authors and which have been privileged by the process of "official" publication. In theory, at least, electronic environments potentially offer a free flow of information and ideas from all to all.

The Fallen World Once More?

Tools of inscription embody and construct ideological practices, redefining what exists, what is good, and what it is possible to do. But understanding the opportunities and transformations that the tools themselves may offer cannot fully explain or predict their effects on the world. Technologies, after all, arise out of and operate within already existing social, political, and economic relations, practices already imbued with ideology. In the tension between the new potentialities they offer and the ideological formations within which they have been created, new tools, especially those Michael Joyce (1988) terms "cardinal technologies" (p. 10), often foreground ideological conflicts.

Like other scholars, historians of technology and social change are never of one mind about these complex interactions. Eisenstein's powerful and much cited study, *The Printing Press as an Agent of Change* (1979), gives primacy to the technology: as the title announces, this study traces how the inherent properties of the press informed and profoundly restructured economic, political, and social relations. In a less well-known work comparing how television was invented, developed, and deployed in two highly industrialized nations, Raymond Williams (1975) calls into question such determinist positions. He begins by challenging the notion that

> television was invented as a result of scientific and technical research [and that] its power as a medium of social communication was then so great that it altered many of our institutions and forms of social relationships. (p. 14)

Instead of privileging the inherent properties of the technology, Williams systematically locates both the research that "discovered" the technologies and the subsequent decisions about their combinations that determined their uses within broader social, political, and economic practices.

From Williams's perspective, it is the existing ideological practices that envision, shape, and control tools. And that bar other innovations. As Weizenbaum (1976) argues, we tend to see the invention of large computer systems as *the* necessary solution to a post–World War II realization "that existing human organizations were approaching certain limits to their ability to cope with the ever faster pace of modern life" (p. 29). But such an interpretation, Weizenbaum submits, insistently denies the presence of alternative solutions to problems such as the growing complexity of air warfare or burgeoning welfare systems. Those other solutions, he contends, might have prompted "modifying the task to be accomplished ... or ... restructuring the human organizations whose inherent limitations were, after all, seen as the root of the trouble" (p. 30). With the aid of historical insight but ideological blindness, we see that the computer arrived "just in time." Weizenbaum asks,

> But in time for what? In time to save—and save very nearly intact, indeed, to entrench and stabilize—social and political structures that otherwise might have been either radically renovated or allowed to totter under the demands that were sure to be made on them. The computer, then, was used to conserve America's social and political institutions. It buttressed them and immunized them, at least temporarily, against enormous pressures for change. (p. 31)

Far from incidental or accidental, a complex technology like television or computers comes into being and takes its "natural" form because, as Ohmann (1985) contends, "those with the vision, the needs, the money, and the power gradually [make] it what they [want]" (p. 681).

The tools' intrinsic qualities may tend toward distributing information and power widely, but those who design these tools and profit from their sales may have other ends in mind. In "Literacy, Technology, and Monopoly Capitalism," Richard Ohmann (1985) rightly objects to assertions that "the computer" will, by itself, effect certain transformations—cognitive or social or political. He takes aim at Ong's (1977) famous claim that "writing and print and the computer enable the mind to constitute within itself . . . new ways of thinking" (p. 44), as if "the technology somehow came before *someone's* intention to enable *some* minds to do *some* things" (p. 681). As the computer revolution unfolds, Ohmann reminds teachers of English that literacy has a history imbricated with ideology and that "technology . . . is itself a social process, saturated with the power relations around it, continually reshaped according to some people's *intentions*" (p. 681). From his vantage point, Ohmann can observe the operation of late-monopoly capitalism serenely at work:

> Graduates of MIT will get the challenging jobs; community college grads will be technicians; those who do no more than acquire basic skills and computer literacy in high school will probably find their way to electronic workstations at McDonald's. I see every reason to expect that the computer revolution, like other revolutions from the top down, will indeed expand the minds and the freedom of an elite, meanwhile facilitating the degradation of labor and the stratification of the workforce that have been the hallmarks of monopoly capitalism from its onset. (p. 683)

In an even darker vein, Andrew Sledd (1988) declares that

> schemes to educate young people in the latest technology of communication, the computer, are not intended to enlighten or empower them all in its use. Rather the plan is to produce a few experts in the service of established power who will refine and program the technology, often for surveillance, plunder and massacre. (p. 499)

The aim of established power, Sledd predicts, is a

> two-tiered educational system producing at the top a minority of over-paid engineers and managers to design the technology

and provide the supervision for a majority of docile data processors and underpaid burger burners on the bottom. (p. 506)

Sledd's grim view turns its gaze not on the media but on the economic and political forces that have "chosen" to design the technology in this way and not some other and which are deploying it to enhance the power and wealth of those already dominant in the culture. An article generously titled "Access for All" in a recent issue of *Macworld* (Levy, 1989) inadvertently highlights the complex tensions between technology's promise and its circumscribed actualization. Describing several small efforts "to assure that technology will work for human beings and not against them, that it will work for the good of a unified society and not aggravate an already splintered community" (p. 43), Steven Levy concludes his article with a vignette. As he observed "a black young man" in East Harlem encountering computers and networks for the first time, Levy was impressed with the way the novice scrolled avidly through the flight listings from the Online Airline Guide available through COMPUSERVE. "For a moment," Levy marvels, "the world was at his fingertips" (p. 52). But, cruelly, not within his economic grasp.

Even as he is introduced to a powerful tool, the young man is reminded that he lacks the means to buy one of those tickets to Paris, or the computers, modems, and networking services that have shown him this shimmering glimpse of the unattainable. Richard Ohmann might see the very fact that the young man was taught to use COMPUSERVE, a commercial network offering—among other things—on-line shopping, as an ominous but thoroughly predictable stratagem of late-monopoly capitalism. As Louie Crew (1989) soberly reminded a group of writing teachers who regularly discuss professional topics through an electronic conference, "billions of exclusions have been effected long before one of us applies for [an electronic] 'mail address.' " Among those excluded, Crew numbers not just the dozens of colleagues employed at institutions that do not subscribe (that is, financially contribute) to national networks like Bitnet, but also and especially the even more numerous denizens of a boarded-up housing project visible from his office window. Not everyone, not even among the highly privileged employees of institutions of higher education, has access to the medium. Those of us with easy access and the requisite know-how simply constitute a new elite. Far from unshackling readers, transforming them into writers, critics, and shapers of knowledge, the electronic revolution, in this view, is simply a hoax, a consolidation of existing power in the hands of an ever-more-elite group (see Gomez in this collection).

For the sake of argument, though, we might think of these privileges simply as the tools enabling pioneering efforts, helping us to actualize for all what the few now possess. For those empowered to utilize electronic textuality's full powers, surely, the new medium allows unconstrained exploration. Yet even the new elites often find themselves hemmed in and hampered in ways they can't predict. Whatever powers may be imputed to their ideal forms, electronic texts don't simply materialize out of thin air; they must be created, housed, and displayed by means of systems—hardware and soft. Those structures and interfaces affect users' expectations and aspirations, shape our values and our sense of our own potential. As Christina Haas (1989) has shown, hardware has a direct impact on a writer/reader's abilities to comprehend texts: the power of the text editor may affect a writer's willingness to communicate at all; a clumsy writing environment, which unfortunately describes most mainframe electronic mail systems at present, discourages its use. The organization of networks to support the touted empowerment of readers and writers immediately constrains and circumscribes that power.

National networks supply a ready example of these differences between conceptual freedom and actual constraint. Many universities, though by no means all, subscribe to Bitnet, a system of hardware, software, and telephone lines supported financially by the subscribing institutions and managed by EDUCOM, a non-profit consortium of academic institutions and hardware and software vendors. Bitnet allows academics to communicate electronically with colleagues around the world. It also links its members to other national and international networks, such as Arpanet and Usenet. The links among the various independent networks provide apparently seamless mail transfer: users are often unaware of the complex systems underlying the whole structure. But electronic mail favors short messages; it cannot easily be used to transfer more than a few pages or kilobytes of text. Collaborative research or scholarship generally requires more latitude. Electronic file transfer, a different set of procedures for electronic transmission of texts across a network, offers that greater latitude—but only some of the time. Although a user at one Bitnet host can easily transfer a large text file to a user at another Bitnet host without using the mail system, it is not currently possible to transfer such a file from a Bitnet host to an Arpanet host. That function has simply not been implemented, I suppose. Moreover, these networks generally support texts only when they are stripped of their formatting. And they certainly cannot easily carry multimedia or hypertext documents.

The limitations of these networks do not derive from insurmountable problems of current technological know-how any more than inequitable access to technology does. Both problems are grounded in the political and economic arrangements within which systems are designed, developed, and disseminated. Someone somewhere, or more likely whole congeries of managers and systems designers, has materially determined what is and what ought to be possible. The motives and interests of these technology managers, whether they are in the employ of colleges and universities or of consortia like EDUCOM or of commercial enterprises like Apple Computer, Inc., structure the electronic environment not just for themselves but for all of us who use it. The bewildering incompatibilities between operating systems, various software packages for writing, drawing, animating, or storing and retrieving information similarly defeat the "inherent" possibilities of the electronic environment. These barriers by and large arise out of the economic practices of the companies that produce them: quite simply, the profit for Microsoft lies in the differences (and incompatibilities) between its products and those of its competitors. Much economic power and computing wizardry go into sustaining these proprietary boundaries.

In theory, then, digitizing offers almost unlimited power. In particular practices, however, the possibilities it offers are always limited by the material and social conditions in which it arises and within which it operates. Only when hardware, software, and the multiple literacies enabling their use are available equally to all, of course, can the "free" information flow freely, and even then only as freely as systems designers and the companies who own the software will allow.

Ideologies, Technologies, Teaching: Implications for Writing Instruction

I have been arguing that no tool can be innocent, free of ideological constructions. And nowhere is that charge more evident than when teachers bring tools into formal educational structures that are already ideologically laden. Each tool brings into the classroom embedded conceptions of what exists, what is good or useful or profitable, and what is possible with its help. Teaching agendas, however, are already informed by ideologies. Just as the new technology opens up conflicts with older tools, so too does it sometimes clash with already existing institutional conceptions of power and possibility. Ultimately, the wider social, political, and economic practices within which teachers work also constrain and shape the ideologies of the tools and of the instruction supported by those tools.

As a simple and quick illustration of the relationship between a tool and its pedagogical uses, consider the blackboard, a ubiquitous technology for teaching, perhaps as old as the clay tablet. While it has a range of utility, and every classroom has one, the blackboard limits the conceptions of writing and revising that it can serve. Many teachers use one to demonstrate revisions because nothing inscribed on it is necessarily fixed or final: as with a word-processing program, anything written on it can be changed. But the blackboard favors certain transformations and discourages others: for example, the blackboard is best at word-for-word substitutions—erase one word, write in another—worst at a complete reordering that would require erasing everything and starting again. Even the amount of text the blackboard will hold conveys messages about the scope revision might or should take. As a tool for teaching revision, the blackboard subtly constructs limits of possibilities.

The classroom equipped with a microcomputer attached to a projection device may expand the blackboard's boundaries—it may offer a more capacious view of revision, but it may still construct lines of authority in the classroom that subvert the tool's "intrinsic" powers. Texts in electronic form can be readily duplicated and shared—and from that property derive many claims about their potential to decenter authority in the classroom. But if the only machine, or the key machine, remains in the hands of the teacher, if the teacher's fingers are the ones on the keyboard, control over the production and reformation of text remains the teacher's. The inherent malleability and "coauthor-ability" of electronic text clash with the hierarchic position of the machine in the classroom. In much the same way, the size of a computer's monitor or display, the degree of its resolution, the power and ease of the word-processing software, its ability to incorporate graphics on the screen as well as on the printed page, and countless other features of the total system—all these elements together shape users' perceptions of what texts are and can become: who can write them, read them, distribute them and to whom.

Introducing computers into the writing curriculum, then, reintroduces old and familiar issues in new, and sometimes unrecognizable, forms. Usage-checking programs, an early and widely used pedagogical application of computers to writing instruction, offer an obvious example of a familiar ideological issue in a new guise. These programs search a text, matching suspect or problematic words and phrases stored in the program's database against instances of such words or phrases in the author's text. Generally, usage-checking programs are designed to be called into play after the "draft" of the text is complete or nearly so. The feedback which these programs supply, some more prescriptively than others, recommends changes for correctness, readability, and so forth, either implicitly or explicitly. Although a few of these programs allow the writer to edit the text while they are still within the domain of the usage-checking software, most "diagnose" a text's ills and then refer writers back to a word-processing program for treatment.

Whether these usage-checking programs fulfill their promise to liberate writers from tedious tasks and reduce the cognitive load for novices is still open to debate. My inquiry here does not examine how accurately these programs perform or how well they instruct (see Collins, 1989; Thiesmeyer, 1989), but rather analyzes how the design of these programs privileges a specific understanding of writing processes, to the exclusion of competing understandings. Such a question redirects attention to covert messages encoded not in the tool's explicit pedagogy but in its very structure. When it operates *after* composing is complete, a program for checking style and usage implicitly enacts a model of the writing process that distances editing and polishing from composing, from the essence of meaning-making. By extracting a particular locution from its semantic context, the tool's design in effect plays out a model of language that divorces style or code from content or meaning. Tools of this type retain and reinforce an orientation toward writing as a product. The tool's structure, then, can subvert or at least conflict with other ideological strands of writing instruction.

This boundary condition is not confined to usage-checking and style-checking software. Both textbooks and the panoply of other software—word-processing programs, hypertext writing programs, and networking configurations—structure an understanding of what writing is and who does or can do it; in short, within the structures of these pedagogical tools lurk messages about "whose forms of knowledge, history, visions, language, culture, and authority will prevail" (Giroux, 1987, p. 20) in our courses and classrooms.

Books, which Marshall McLuhan called the first teaching machine, favor or foreground certain kinds of information, almost certainly at the expense of others. The attributes of books—their ability to "fix" language and ideas, their preference for sequences and hierarchies—make them especially adept at conveying abstract, mediated information about the world. They expatiate, drawing out and expounding on ideas and processes at length, turning events-in-time into spatially arrayed sequences of parts. Such a vehicle may implicitly conflict with the current theories of writing, either those that focus on writing as a recursive cognitive process or those more concerned with reading and writing as social and collaborative acts.

To be sure, conveying knowledge about cognition does not violate the aims of a course grounded in cognitive theories. It has been argued that students need to become more conscious of the processes they use—and such meta-cognitive awareness may be fostered by giving names to various parts and by expatiating on each part's role in the whole activity. That educational objective is certainly well served by textbooks like Flower's (1985) *Problem-Solving Strategies for Writing*. But the more pressing goal, to improve cognitive procedures, may not be so well served. As Mike Rose (1983) has noted,

> We have good reason to suspect that knowledge of any complex process—like knowledge about composing—cannot be adequately conveyed via static print. As soon as such knowledge hits the page of a text, its rich possibilities are narrowed and sometimes rigidified. (p. 208)

Because its representations tend to spatialize, fragment, and sequence processes in ways that distort and undermine them, a book can only *represent* the full flow of the process: the book cannot *perform* it.[1] Because the textbook cannot enact the processes it describes, the textbook's structure covertly works against its content and against the theoretical grounding of the many composition courses that call themselves "process-oriented."

Similarly, the textbook struggles in other ways to perform the complex social and cultural processes articulated in Karen Burke LeFevre's *Writing as a Social Act* (1988). With its hierarchical authority, its apparently closed and monologic structure, the book works against the theory, as Stuart Moulthrop argues (see Moulthrop in this collection). Quite simply, it is difficult for readers to see, let alone experience, the traces of social interactions in a medium which has traditionally validated the author's univocal view. It is hard, especially for a novice, to conceive of talking back to a book; it is hard to imagine contributing anything to a volume already bound and "complete." So the book can assert a claim, can describe an intricate social web, but it cannot offer a demonstration: it cannot do as it says. Insofar as the book's structure encodes stasis rather than kinesis, individuality rather than community, it materially opposes itself to competing theories of what writing is.

Exploiting the processing capabilities of computers, some electronic writing tools have promised to improve on the book's limited performance of cognitive and process-oriented theories. Programs like HBJ WRITER and WRITER'S HELPER, for example, seem designed to facilitate the performance of writing processes, rather than to teach students about them. Each program is an integrated package with components for planning, composing, revising, and editing. HBJ WRITER's and WRITER's HELPER's heuristics programs pace students through systematic routines, presumably to stimulate memory, to generate "content," and to prompt global plans, analysis of an audience, or general awareness of the rhetorical situation. (See Ohmann, 1976, though, for a prescient discussion of the ideological assumptions these programs surely share with the textbooks he analyzes.) The word-processing programs that are part of these software packages facilitate text production. The style and usage components of these software packages offer the usual sorts of advice about the passive voice, nominalizations, sexist language, and so on.

Many tools of this sort try to permit users to begin the writing process anywhere and to loop recursively through the subprocesses in any order. Like textbooks, however, these tools in practice have generally fragmented, staged, and separated one writing activity from another. Although such programs gesture toward enacting, rather than merely representing, the model, they still closely resemble the textbook's chapters: "pre-writing" followed by writing followed by editing. Although the process model would have writers switching easily and rapidly from planning subgoals to searching long-term memory while holding in mind schemas for discourse, these computer programs, and a host of others like them, make swift segués among their components out of the question: such software tools make it operationally difficult to switch from producing text to planning or setting goals. They discourage writers from reassessing their plans while the writers are struggling to produce or to revise, for example, the third paragraph of their texts. No doubt the designers of these tools envisioned a flexible environment; what they actualized, however, was a succession of stages.

It would be a good idea, however, not to point an accusing finger at the people who conceived of these tools. The "flaws" in the software packages I have briefly discussed derive not from the authors' misconceptions about what they were trying to achieve but from the limitations of the hardware available when these software packages were conceived and written, and even from the limitations of the programming languages of their codes. (For a fuller discussion of this problem, see LeBlanc, 1990.) Developing a pedagogical tool always necessitates compromise between the full glory of the vision and the dimmer reality of its instantiation. In this, authors of software programs face difficulties different in kind, but no different in effect, from those the authors of textbooks face. And these factors, rather than the particular pieces of software currently available, underscore my point.

The designers of pedagogical tools necessarily inhabit a world of possibilities and impossibilities constructed by the systems available to them. Authoring systems (COURSE OF ACTION or HYPERCARD, to name only two of many) similarly circumscribe the possibilities open to designers of electronic educational materials. In other words, the struggle to create tools that embody a particular conception of what writing entails may be considerably more difficult than it at first appears. Thus, a particular tool—John Smith's WRITING ENVIRONMENT is a good example of the phenomenon—may turn out to privilege those who write "top-down" while hampering writers who draft and plan simultaneously (or nearly so). Nor do ideological limitations end with the privileging of some composing styles over others: such limits constrain teachers' ability to design the full range of pedagogical tools we might imagine. Lanham's (1989) sweeping enthusiasm notwithstanding, the tools to create the tools with which to teach can yield only some manifestations of their full potential: even if, in theory, these tools offer a very wide field for actualization, in practice they do not fulfill this promise.

Composition courses that foreground the social context for writing have occasionally inspired new tools—chiefly ones that invite dialogue, such as the various tools supporting both synchronous and asynchronous electronic conversations. More often, instructors trying to integrate technology into a social-constructionist pedagogy have easily exploited the generic writing and computer tools commercially available. Off-the-shelf word-processing programs, networks, and hypertext tools seem ready-made to address writing as a social process and therefore seem to avoid some of the difficulties encountered by those creating tools to support cognitive-process pedagogy. As many have noted, the computer screen seems far more public and collaborative from the outset than pens and paper or typewriters, tools associated with the private and solitary activities of individuals. The ease with which word-processed texts can be exchanged and distributed, the accessibility of electronic texts to multiple and multiply-authored revisions (especially in hypertext systems like INTERMEDIA), the inherently dialogic and nonhierarchical space of a network can bring into full view the social context in which texts are formed and reformed. And these tools may address other social and political problems of the literacy curriculum as well. Michael Spitzer (1989) notes, for example, that communication through a network can extend educational opportunities to the handicapped, the elderly, the part-time student who cannot easily take time off from work to travel to campus (p. 188). In networked communications, Spitzer observes, "no one can notice an individual's age, sex, race, dress style, hair length, or other distinguishing characteristics" (p. 195).

Whether these uses of computers in fact remove markers of class, gender, and race, or decenter authority in the classroom, or encourage writers to see their work as social and collaborative, remains to be seen. But Cynthia Selfe (1989b) cautions practitioners not to assume that because the devices can in theory lead to such practices, they necessarily will. In some networked environments, only the instructor or administrator can initiate a dialogue. Unselfconsciously revealing its unequal distribution of power, LIVEWRITER, a networking tool designed specifically for the writing classroom, terms the teacher's activity "snooping" when he or she tunes in on a writer at work. LeBlanc (1990) calls attention to the unabashed marketing strategy of a similar system, Robotel's MICROSELECT video network: the brochure claims that the tool offers teachers "better . . . control over student work" through their ability to "end the class's work at any point by preempting their screens" (pp. 171–172). Such devices affirm the teacher's strict control over the discourse and may even extend the teacher's power well beyond its habitual domain, the completed essay, into the composing process itself. But even in systems where students can initiate discussion as well as respond without the mediation or the interference of the teacher, Selfe reminds us, invisible and therefore all the more powerful forms of discipline and repression may be at work. Embedded as they are within other educational practices (grading comes readily to mind), the texts that students produce in an electronic discussion may not free either teachers or their students from the imprisoning context of classroom writing (Perelman, 1986).

Nor are teachers of writing themselves free from ideological forces constructing their working environment. Software development yields few professional rewards. It may even penalize those trying to achieve tenure if they devote time to development projects instead of producing scholarly books or research. Moreover, software development remains resource-intensive. Thus, even if developing software were not a professionally risky business, it still lies beyond the economic reach of most faculty. In effect, teachers' choices of hardware and software may be narrowed to those products that large corporations or what LeBlanc (1990) terms "research design teams" choose to design and disseminate. And those instantiations of electronic writing tools may not serve all our ends equally well. In the conclusion of his probing analysis of the social, political, and economic forces at work behind the scenes of software development, LeBlanc notes that

> Marxist theorists like Henry Giroux and Richard Ohmann argue that corporate based computer manufacturers...create products that serve to control users and preserve the "instrumental ideology" from which they themselves emerged. (pp. 171–172)

In the marketplace for educational materials, many tools deeply rooted in our best understandings of writing and reading, and especially those tools challenging the ideological assumptions behind programs like IBM's CRITIQUE or John Smith's WE (WRITING ENVIRONMENT), may never come into being.

Questions for the 1990s and Beyond

New technological conditions offer educators a multitude of opportunities, not least among them the invitation to examine the ideological systems within which formal education operates. Two opposing views of our technological future have presented themselves. The technological determinists, those who argue that the tool's properties and functions ultimately configure the environment, tend to envision a bright, democratic, participatory world. The social determinists, those who argue that entrenched political and economic practices inexorably shape the tool to their ends, tend to forecast a deepening rift between those who control tools and those who are merely their users or their victims. There may be no unclouded vision to be had here: certainly, the historians of technology and social change have yet to declare the truth. But while we are awaiting clearer insight, it behooves teachers to act as if the real relationship between them and their tools issued in some dialectical outcome—a future "determined" by working against either form of determinism. In practice, this means conscious and deliberate scrutiny of ideological pedagogical formations in all of our work. For teachers of writing, electronic tools promise much: powerful enactments of cognitive and social theories of reading and writing and rich extensions of privilege to those who have been excluded from public discourse. As teachers experiment with these systems and study their impact on writers, however, they have an obligation to confront the not-always-benign implications of choices foisted upon them and of choices they themselves initiate.

Several questions deserve greater consideration. Most immediate are those that foreground the tension between what teachers teach and what teachers use to teach with:

- What statements do a particular tool—a stylistic program or a complete "writing environment"—make about the nature, function, and power of the writer, the text, the reader? And how do these messages "fit" with the other ideological strains of contemporary writing instruction?

- When teachers or researchers study the effects of word processing, desktop publishing, electronic communications, and so on—we must ask, what is the relationship between the conceptual fields a particular configuration of hardware and software opens and those it obscures or proscribes? Claims that networks redistribute authority and encourage wider and freer participation, for example, need to specify which network, according which privileges, to which participants, and under what circumstances. What privileges and prohibitions are embedded in the design of the particular tools used in the studies? How are writers' behaviors, and even their desires, affected by the workings of those tools' deepest structures?

- How do alternative modes of discourse—the new possibilities of hypertexts and hypermedia structures—work, rhetorically and ideologically? Whose interests and visions, whose realities, do these structures serve, can they be made to serve?

- Ought teachers to foster awareness of the ideological constructs tools imply among students learning to write? How?

Teachers' concerns, however, should extend well beyond the confines of their daily work, leading them to examine their situatedness in a full field of ideological constructions, for theorists and practitioners alike need to understand that both the tools that come to hand and those they seek to create may come with ideological price tags.

- To what extent are the tools teachers are using shaped by composition theory, and to what extent are they the products of technological and economic forces blind or even hostile to their theories? In other words, can we discover and disclose the difference between a reactive agenda—teaching and research responsive to what happens to be available—and a constitutive one—teaching and research enacting their best theories and therefore capable of influencing their technological environment?

- What forces at work in teachers' economic, social, and political environment privilege the development of some kinds of software and discourage other directions, other imaginings of what is and what is not possible?

- What role does the structure of the institution—its budgeting priorities or its decisions about student and faculty access to various technologies—play in determining what tools can be created, what tools can be used?

- How do professional rewards encourage or discourage faculty development and use of emerging technologies in their teaching and research practices?

- What impact will electronic "publishing" have on the political structure of various professional communities? On the construction of knowledge in composition, rhetoric, and other fields?

- What part does the emerging networking environment play in the process of forming and validating discourse communities? Are hardware and software configurations working toward the maintenance and the perpetuation of existing hierarchies of privilege, as Weizenbaum (1976) and others have predicted? And what alternatives can teachers imagine and create?

Many of these are not merely abstract, academic questions. They are deeply political, engaging teachers daily in struggles for power and control of resources within their educational institutions. If others outside the academic institution have the political and economic power to determine what hardware and software become available, who decides what hardware and software enters writing courses and classrooms? Decisions about what hardware will be accessible to students in this field are often made without direct input from teachers of writing, who, in most institutions of higher education, are marginal in any case (see Strickland in this collection). Therefore, the political and economic arrangements preexisting this new struggle for control of expensive and still-scarce equipment tip the balance in favor of the "haves" and against the "have-nots." It is not unusual to find that the most powerful and enabling computing environments are distributed first to the sciences while humanists and writing programs often make do with the very equipment ideological analysis suggests is least appropriate for the revolutionary and liberatory purposes they often envision. In many institutions, perhaps in most, teachers of writing may have considerable autonomy in determining what theory of writing will inform their teaching. But if they have little or no say in constructing the technological environment, their autonomy may not even reach as far as the classroom door.

Engaging the sorts of questions I have raised may seem to take teachers far afield from our customary activities. It may not help them write tomorrow's assignment or construct next term's syllabus. But it is nevertheless crucial if they seek to empower themselves or to foster the conditions within which students can empower themselves. Andrew Sledd (1988) and others have issued dire warnings about complicit acts, but teachers need not accept such condemnations; they need subscribe neither to the determinism of technology nor to the determinism of political and economic power. Instead of construing the domain of their work as a battlefield where these two positions can fight it out, as Giroux (1987) does, we can instead treat it as Freire (Freire & Macedo, 1987) does—as a text which we are in a sense given to read but one which we are also enjoined to rewrite:

> Reading the world always precedes reading the word, and reading the word implies continually reading the world.... In a way, however, we can go further and say that reading the word is not preceded merely by reading the world, but by a certain form of *writing* it or *rewriting* it, that is, of transforming it by means of conscious, practical work. (p. 35)

Reading ourselves, as teachers of English in a technological world, awakens us to our roles, and our complicity, in the world. To foster the liberatory education Freire advocates, our practical work must begin with reading the world, but it must not end there, acquiescing to that apparently authoritative text in front of us. Rather, teachers must actively appropriate the world-text, and thus reinscribe—re-vision—the technology of the word.

Note

1. I am not suggesting that the pedagogy of Flower's text represents the pedagogy of all textbooks, but only that all textbooks attempting to foreground writing processes encounter the same resistance from the medium. Susan Horton's (1982) *Thinking Through Writing*, an equally good example, never mentions cognitive processes and does not divide writing into named stages—planning, composing, revising, and the like. Still, it concerns itself chiefly with invention heuristics. Only at the end does it discuss writing a complete essay. By then the semester in which the text is used must be nearly over.

References

Balestri, D. (1988, February). Softcopy and hard: Wordprocessing and writing process. *Academic Computing*, 14ff.

Berlin, J. (1988). Rhetoric and ideology in the writing class. *College English, 50*, 477–494.

Bizzell, P. (1982). Cognition, convention, and certainty: What we need to know about writing. *PreText, 3*, 214–243.

Bleich, D. (1980). Epistemological assumptions in the study of response. In J. P. Tompkins (Ed.), *Reader-response criticism: From formalism to poststructuralism* (pp. 134–163). Baltimore: The Johns Hopkins University Press.

Clanchy, M. T. (1979). *From memory to written record: England, 1066–1307.* Cambridge, MA: Harvard University Press.

Collins, J. L. (1989). Computerized text analysis and the teaching of writing. In G. E. Hawisher and C. L. Selfe (Eds.), *Critical perspectives on computers and composition instruction* (pp. 30–43). New York: Teachers College Press.

Communications of the ACM. (1988, July). *31*(7).

Crew, L. (1989). Megabyte University, September 9, 1989. [Megabyte University is an electronic discussion group. For texts, contact Fred Kemp, YKFOK@TTACS.BITNET].

Eagleton, T. (1983). *Literary theory: An introduction.* Minneapolis: University of Minnesota Press.

Eisenstein, E. (1979). *The printing press as an agent of change.* Cambridge, England: Cambridge University Press.

Fish, S. (1980). *Is there a text in this class?: The authority of interpretive communities.* Cambridge, MA: Harvard University Press.

Flower, L. (1985). *Problem-solving strategies for writing.* (2nd ed.). San Diego: Harcourt.

Freire, P., & Macedo, D. (1987). *Literacy: Reading the word and the world.* Granby, MA: Bergin & Garvey.

Giroux, H.(1987). Introduction. In P. Freire & D. Macedo (Eds.), *Literacy: Reading the word and the world* (pp. 1–27). Granby MA: Bergin & Garvey.

Goody, J. (1977). *The domestication of the savage mind.* Cambridge, England: Cambridge University Press.

Haas, C. (1989). "Seeing it on the screen isn't really seeing it": Computer writers' reading problems. In G. E. Hawisher and C. L. Selfe (Eds.), *Critical perspectives on computers and composition instruction* (pp. 16–29). New York: Teachers College Press.

Hawisher, G. E. (1989). Research and recommendations for computers and composition. In G. E. Hawisher and C. L. Selfe (Eds.), *Critical perspectives on computers and composition instruction* (pp. 44-69). New York: Teachers College Press.

Hirsch, E. D., Jr. (1987). *Cultural literacy: What every American needs to know.* Boston: Houghton Mifflin.

Hirsch, E. D., Jr. (1988). Comments. *Profession, 88,* 77–80.

Holland, N. N. (1980). Unity identity text self. In J. P. Tompkins (Ed.), *Reader-response criticism: From formalism to post-structuralism* (pp. 118–133). Baltimore: The Johns Hopkins University Press.

Horton, S. (1982). *Thinking through writing.* Baltimore: The Johns Hopkins University Press.

Iser, W. (1980). The reading process: A phenomenological approach. In J. P. Tompkins (Ed.), *Reader-response criticism: From formalism to post-structuralism* (pp. 50–69). Baltimore: The Johns Hopkins University Press.

Joyce, M. (1988, November). Siren shapes: Exploratory and constructive hypertexts. *Academic Computing,* 10–14, 37–42.

Lanham, R. (1989). The electronic word: Literary study and the digital revolution. *New Literary History, 20,* 265–290.

LeBlanc, P. (1990). The development of computer-aided composition software and its implications for composition. Doctoral dissertation, University of Massachusetts, Amherst, 1980.

LeFevre, K. (1987). *Invention as a social act.* Carbondale: Southern Illinois University Press.

Levy, S. (1989, August). Access for all. *Macworld*, 43–52.

McLuhan, M., & Fiore, Q. (1967). *The medium is the massage: An inventory of effects*. New York: Random House.

Moulthrop, S. (1989). In the zones: Hypertext and the politics of interpretation. *Writing on the Edge 1*(1), 18–27.

Ohmann, R. (1976). *English in America: A radical view of the profession*. New York: Oxford University Press.

Ohmann, R. (1985). Literacy, technology, and monopoly capital. *College English, 47*, 675–689.

Ong, W. J. (1977). *Interfaces of the word: Studies in the evolution of consciousness and culture*. Ithaca: Cornell University Press.

Ong, W. J. (1982). *Orality and literacy: The technologizing of the word*. London: Methuen.

Perelman, L. (1986). The context of classroom writing. *College English, 48*, 471–479.

Rose, M. (1983). Speculations on process knowledge and the textbook's static page. *College Composition and Communication, 34*, 208–213.

Ruskiewicz, J. (1988). Word and image: The next revolution. *Computers & Composition, 5*(3), 9–15.

Selfe, C. (1989a). Redefining literacy: The multilayered grammars of computers. In G. E. Hawisher and C. L. Selfe (Eds.), *Critical perspectives on computers and composition instruction* (pp. 3–15). New York: Teachers College Press.

Selfe, C. (1989b). *Notes from the margin*. Paper presented at the Fifth Computers and Writing Conference, Minneapolis.

Sledd, A. E. (1988). Readin' not riotin': The politics of literacy. *College English, 50*, 495–508.

Sledd, A. E., & Sledd, J. H. (1988a). Hirsch's use of his sources in *Cultural literacy*: A critique. *Profession, 88*, 33–39.

Sledd, A. E., & Sledd, J. H. (1988b). Replies to E. D. Hirsch, Jr. *Profession, 88*, 80–81.

Sledd, A. E., & Sledd, J. H. (1989). Success as failure and failure as success: The cultural literacy of E. D. Hirsch, Jr. *Written Communication, 6*, 364–389.

Smith, J., & Weiss, S. (1988). Hypertext: An overview. In Yankelovich, N. (Ed.), *Hypertext on hypertext* [Hypercard stacks] (stack *ACM*. eds). New York: ACM Press Database and Electronic Products.

Spender, D. (1981). The gatekeepers: A feminist critique of academic publishing. In H. Roberts (Ed.), *Doing feminist research* (pp. 186–202). London: Routledge & Kegan Paul.

Spitzer, M. (1989). Computer conferencing: An emerging technology. In G. E. Hawisher and C. L. Selfe (Eds.), *Critical perspectives on computers and composition instruction* (pp. 187–200). New York: Teachers College Press.

Therborn, G. (1980). *The ideology of power and the power of ideology.* London: Verso.

Thiesmeyer, J. (1989). Should we do what we can? In G. E. Hawisher and C. L. Selfe (Eds.), *Critical perspectives on computers and composition instruction* (pp. 75–93). New York: Teachers College Press.

Turkle, S. (1984). *The second self: Computers and the human spirit.* New York: Simon & Schuster.

Wahlstrom, B. (1989). Desktop publishing: Perspectives, potentials, and politics. In G. E. Hawisher and C. L. Selfe (Eds.), *Critical perspectives on computers and composition instruction* (pp. 162–186). New York: Teachers College Press.

Weizenbaum, J. (1976). *Computer power and human reason: From judgment to calculation.* New York: W. H. Freeman and Company.

Welch, K. E. (1987). Ideology and freshman textbook production: The place of theory in writing pedagogy. *College Composition and Communication, 38*, 269–282.

Williams, R. (1975). *Television: Technology and cultural form.* New York: Schocken.

Chapter 2

Taking Control of the Page: Electronic Writing and Word Publishing

Patricia Sullivan
Purdue University

Traditionally, writers have given manuscripts to publishers, and publishers have had control of the printed page. But changes in computer technology are now offering the control of the page to writers. What are the consequences of this gift of technology: for writers, for the page, for readers, for computer classrooms, for teachers, for theories of teaching electronic writing? What elements of visual meaning need to be incorporated into our theories of electronic writing? How do new production processes for the page open up new processes for electronic writing? And how do we introduce this technological development into our theoretical and curricular discussions about electronic writing in the nineties? Or, put another way, how do we take control of the page?

Through most of printing history, the creation of text and the publication of text have been handled by separate groups, at the very least since the abbess handed her devotionals to the convent scribes. The gap has widened since the steam press further specialized the production process into a factory activity. Thus, many of today's publishing writers have been well insulated from the process of producing the published text and from designing pages, activities now carried out by editors and graphic artists who interface with the typographers and production personnel. As a result, writers have not needed to think carefully about how the look of the page will affect the meaning of the text. For them, the meaning of the text has resided *solely* in the content of the words.

But the gap between the manuscript and the printed page is closing. Through the technology, first through the development of the desktop publishing software and now, increasingly, through the standard word-processing package, the writer is entering an era where the published page is more directly under her or his control. This innovation has profound implications for writers, for writing, for the teaching of writing with computers, and for theories of electronic writing. Thus, weighing the consequences of "taking control of the page"[1] needs to be placed on our agenda for the nineties.

What will happen in the 1990s as the gap between the manuscript and the printed page closes in a new and interesting way? The title of this essay expresses the possibilities of this technology positively—focusing on the challenges we face as we seize control of the page, sensing the possible reorganization of the age-old form/content debate. But the title also accommodates a darker reading of the impact of the technology on writing: the page controls the text when authors fail to seize control themselves and integrate the published page into their approach to electronic writing. This essay, then, aims to explore the possible impacts of publishing the visual page on writers, teachers, classrooms, curricular theories, and readers.

The Relationship of Electronic Publishing and Theories of Writing

The theory connecting the computer to writing and learning to write has essentially been one built out of accommodation to the dominant forces on the writing scene. During the past decade, for various economic and cultural reasons, all teachers of writing did not wholeheartedly embrace the computer as an instrument for writing and teaching (Schwartz, 1984). Hence, the proponents of using computers in writing and the teaching of writing have had to demonstrate that computers "fit in," "were better," or "were at least as good" as traditional methods of teaching composition. Typically, early research was taken up with these curricular battles, and framed its research questions to examine whether "writing at the computer improved X," where X was writing, or drafting, or revising, or "something else of interest"(Hawisher, 1988). And, as Hawisher points out in her review of empirical research on computers and composing, the results of these studies have been mixed. Word processing has not inspired many new wrinkles in writing theories either. That fact is clearly reflected in the index of *Teaching Composition: Twelve Bibliographic Essays* (Tate, 1987). True, the second edition of this work includes an essay by Hugh Burns on "Computers and Composition," but the only entries for *computer* or *word processing* in the index refer to Burns's essay. Writing theories, by and large, have not embraced the computer and woven it into their conceptions of writing and its teaching.

Ironically, one reason the dominant forces have not confronted the consequences of electronic writing for composition theory (and its teaching) can be traced to the accommodation strategies used by advocates of computers in the English curriculum. Many proponents of computers have introduced them as tools for the writer's arsenal. By focusing on the "toolness" of writing with computers, discussions of computers and composition have promoted an image of the computer as a "helpmate" or "assistant" to writers and teachers rather that as an agent of change. From the first, most computer-writing discussions have sought to fit electronic writing into currently accepted writing theories. If we look, for example, at Wresch's early collection (1984), we find that three sections discuss programs for "prewriting," "editing and grammar," and the "writing process," and that the section on word processing research also focuses on the writing process. Miller (1986) pursues a similar strategy when he compares writing processes to software engineering processes and critiques how the computer can "assist in text composition" (p.188). Certainly, discussions continue along these lines, framing the issues in ways that identify computer-assisted instruction or word processing as aids to writers engaged in composing.

Although theory-makers continue these attempts to accommodate electronic writing to theories of composition, they resist change in the opposite direction. Walter J. Ong (1977), however, reminds us that technology constantly remakes the way in which we communicate and even think. In discussing how technological innovations affect the process of communication and of thinking, Ong cautioned that

> It can be misleading, encouraging us to think of writing, print, and electronic devices as ways of "moving information" over some sort of space intermediate between one person and another. In fact, each of the so-called "media" does far more than this: it makes possible thought processes that were inconceivable before. The media are more significantly within the mind than outside it. (p. 46)

We need to confront the possibility, even the probability, that present and future technology may well "threaten" some aspects of writing theory and writing pedagogy. The threat certainly exists with the coming era of word publishing. A separation of the production of words and the publication of words is reflected in our current theories of writing and its teaching. As the two processes merge and become simplified in the word-publishing milieu, we must expect adjustments of theory to follow.

As an illustration, consider the impact of word publishing, and its enticement to take control of the page, on the relationships among writers, texts, and readers played out in most contemporary theories of writing. To identify these relationships, we must first construct an abstract, if overly simple, depiction that situates writer, reader, and text in relation to one another and inside some milieu (Fig. 1).

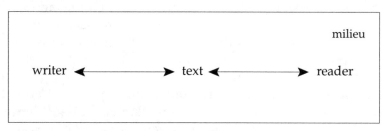

Figure 1. An abstraction of the elements of writing

Viewing this abstraction can draw out one possible tension between electronic writing and textually based writing theories. Textually based theories, often called current-traditional pedagogies (Young, 1987), focus primarily on the text and only secondarily on the reader of the text. But, because one strength of electronic writing is in the bond of writer and text, a natural conflict emerges between the pedagogies of electronic writing and current-traditional writing. The theories favored by electronic writing have focused on two areas: detailing the interaction of the writer and the text as it is taking shape, and on imagining or in some other way handling writing for a reader. Though naturally drawn to the writer-text relationship, scholars who work with theories of electronic writing and programs for teaching writing on the computer (Burns, 1979; VonBlum & Cohen, 1984; Schwartz, 1984; Selfe, 1984; Wresch, 1984) have wisely resisted collapsing their work to that writer-text relationship. Interestingly enough, the move toward a holistic view of the electronic writing process has grown out of these efforts to resist a focus on the writer-text relationship or on a text-based approach to electronic error correction.

If we extend the discussion of this abstraction to the classroom, we can see natural differences emerging between pedagogical approaches in conventional versus electronic classrooms. Figure 2 shows a typical picture of the relationship among writer-text-reader that informs the "text-making" in a conventional (non-electronic) classroom. Drafts of texts are coherent products with which the writer (or writers) and reader (or readers) interact. They are typed, reviewed, notated, revised, and then retyped. It often takes several hours to produce a final text draft.

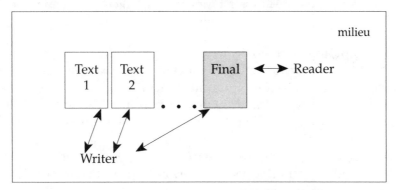

Figure 2: The writer-text-reader relationship in a conventional class

Because theories of electronic writing to date have been enhancements of the theories of writing advanced in composition studies, they have not seen the computer adding a significant component to the writer-text-reader relationship. Instead, most theories have tended to treat the computer as an aid or a tool, at times even calling it an "electronic pencil." Yet, as Figure 3 depicts, the electronic drafting process could be seen to make the distinction between early and late drafts increasingly seamless and less distinctive. Writers and readers often interact with segments of an emerging draft, a draft that becomes final only in those minutes before it is printed or mailed to the teacher. In this way, the segmented stages that have contributed to our linear writing paradigm of prewriting, writing, and rewriting begin to dissolve in the electronic classroom.

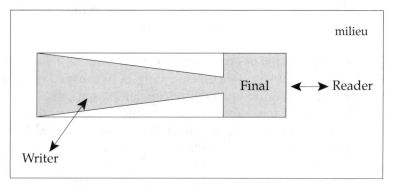

Figure 3: The writer-text-reader relationship in an electronic class. There are no distinct drafts; rather, there is a seamless flow of prose culminating in a final piece.

Many of the discussions of what writing-at-the-computer adds and subtracts to writing processes focus on the *making* of text. These discussions point to how computers facilitate revision, the hastiness of making text, the difficulty of parting with text, and the reuse of text that exists in other documents (see Hawisher, 1988). All of these activities reveal the writing processes in ways that teachers can see as we peer over the shoulders of students who write at the computer, ways that were not so easy to observe when students scribbled away in their garrets.

Perhaps just as important as the effects computers have on composing processes in the classroom are the changes computers encourage in the processes of text publication. Traditionally, in text publication, writers interact primarily with their manuscripts, and audiences never see manuscripts in the process of evolution (Fig. 4). If we envision this process of publishing as it happens within the context of professional writing classrooms, we can also imagine a reorientation of composing processes and the relationships among writers, readers, and texts. In fact, such a reorientation brings text publishing into the same electronic environment used for text production (Fig. 5). Significantly, this integration allows and even invites the writer to take control of the page.

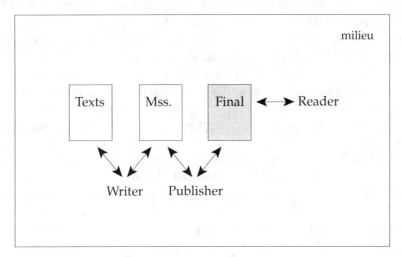

Figure 4: The traditional publishing process

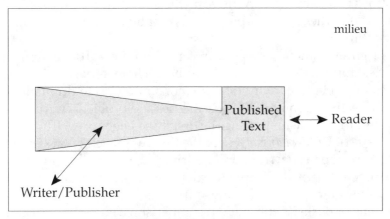

Figure 5: The electronic word-publishing process

The writer can choose the margin settings, the layout of lists, the typeface, the type size, the special fonts, the use of rules, the boxing, and on and on. The writer can draw, find, develop, or scan artwork, icons, illustrations, and visual abstractions into the text. The writer can see how all of these componenets look before the publication is set and make changes up until minutes (instead of weeks) before the deadline. The writer can control most aspects of the publication, within the limits of available equipment.

The preceding discussion has framed the development of computer-assisted word publishing in a positive way; however, two critiques of this position need to be aired: a work-economy critique and an aesthetic critique. In an industrial setting, it is just as easy to see the flip side of the writers' new power over publishing: more and more frequently a company envisions computer-supported word publishing equipment as a way to make the writers take on the job of designers and publication producers. Such actions are likely to restrict the time writers have to give actual writing tasks and devalue writing within a corporate setting. Writers have frequently complained about just such situations (Sullivan, 1988). At the same time, electronic publishing equipment rearranges a whole range of publication production jobs, with the possible effect of "de-skilling" the whole process of publishing (Aller, 1988). The skills of professionals in typography, design, layout, keylining, and so on are jeopardized by the innovations in technology. Writers, furthermore, are asked to take on the tasks of these other professionals without adequate training or recognition.

From an aesthetic viewpoint, recent technological developments in desktop publishing often have been characterized by design eyesores. Hana Barker (1988) demonstrates, quite dramatically and effectively, some of the possibilities and problems introduced by desktop publishing using the first three pages of each article in an issue of *Visible Language*. For the first two articles, Barker compares plainer typewriter manuscripts to more exciting manuscripts created on dedicated word processors, demonstrating that the computer-generated manuscripts were more richly designed. In some of Barker's subsequent comparisons, however, desktop-designed articles (sporting multiple typefaces, inappropriate type sizes, and irrelevant boxes) are equally as off-putting as typewriter manuscripts. Barker's point, which is echoing across the academy, is that electronic publishing is not so easy as it looks, particularly if publications are to be both attractive and readable. Her critique is made through the established aesthetic realm. We can take Barker's requirements further and claim that rhetorical effectiveness is also a criterion for page design. Such a realization demands an integrated rhetoric/aesthetic of visual meaning.

The Technological Nudge: Word Processing Is Rapidly Becoming Word Publishing

Why should English teachers pay increasing attention to the publishing process at this time? The primary reason lies with the changes being made to word-processing packages. Word processing is currently reshaping itself into word publishing given the support of affordable laser printers, page- description languages, and desktop-publishing programs. As soon as affordable laser printers could produce near-typeset-quality text and bit-mapped reproductions of images at about the same cost as the older technology, the industry standards for "documents" changed. Within two years of 1985, when Apple introduced the Laserwriter, the "look" produced by laser-printed text, multiple fonts, and visuals remade the standard for corporate documents. Further, PostScript, the page-description language developed for laser printers, a language that describes images as well as it describes characters, made possible the desktop-publishing software that has captured the imagination of corporate America. Simultaneously, desktop-publishing programs (PAGEMAKER appeared in 1986) were developed with the ability to place words and images precisely on the same page, to massage both words and images once they were combined, and to preview pages as they would be printed. Desktop publishing became the rage in the corporate world because the entire page (text and graphics) could be reliably communicated to a printer and inexpensively produced in a form that looked nearly as good as commercial printing. Further, a desktop-publishing system could be paid for in a couple of months out of a savings in a commercial printing budget.

Desktop publishing was heralded as the first lateral market since the personal computer. Everyone everywhere wanted to have a desktop-publishing system. Products such as PAGEMAKER, VENTURA, and READYSETGO catapulted to prominence as tools for page processing. These programs made sense as intermediaries between the different parts of publishing because they allowed users to import words and images, lay the mixture out on a page, and export the page to a laser printer or commercial printer. Word-processing packages had already begun in a primitive way to import images into texts, but the desktop-publishing packages made the integrating of text and graphics—a highly complex process—quite seamless, if still complex. Further, desktop systems allowed users to interactively make changes to pages—to actually *see* the effect of changes—as opposed to batch processing, in which changes were not made until a special formatting program was run. But desktop systems did not necessarily consolidate the entire publishing process onto one desktop and certainly not into one program. Writers could still use a word-processing program on their own machine to create text and then give that text to the person who worked with the desktop-publishing software. Even if a writer directed the entire process, the writer probably would create text using a word-processing package and import it into a publishing software file. Hence, this bringing together of writing and publishing still maintained a physical and intellectual distance between the two activities (Fig. 6).

At this point, readers who are *not* teachers of professional writing might ask, "How does this publishing revolution affect the teaching of first-year composition?" Most colleges are not going to purchase expensive publishing packages for their first-year classes. Further, the production process outlined above looks quite complex. The emphasis in most first-year rhetoric courses will stay focused on standard word-processing packages. However, the standard word-processing packages are becoming increasingly complex. More and more desktop-publishing features are incorporated with each new product release. Picturing the changes in word-processing programs between 1986 and 1989 (Fig. 7) illustrates how intensely they have come to focus on features that manipulate the characters and pages. In three years, word-processing packages have become increasingly concerned with features of page layout.

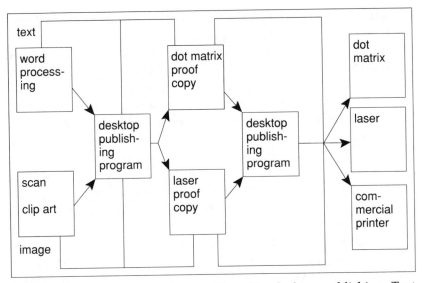

Figure 6: Publishing processes as affected by desktop publishing. Text and image are fed into a publishing program, and from there to a printer for output. After proofing, the file may be outputted from a higher-resolution printer to get "near-type-set-quality" copy.

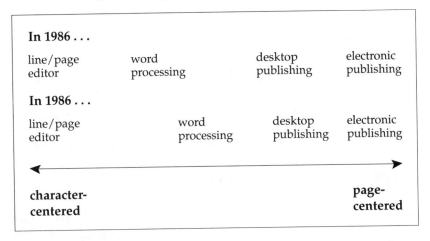

Figure 7. Changing relationships between word-processing packages and publishing packages

In the late eighties, both word-processing and high-end electronic publishing packages (used by professional typesetters) quickly moved into the desktop-publishing market previously controlled by packages such as PAGEMAKER, VENTURA, and READYSETGO). From the word-processing end, the standard word-processing packages such as WORDPERFECT and MICROSOFT WORD have been adding page-layout features to their basic packages. The standard word-processing package can put text in columns, can accept graphics, can accept data from spreadsheets, can make indexes, outlines, and tables of contents, has a spelling checker, has font alternatives, has various rules and boxes, and can show a preview of the actual printed page. New versions of MICROSOFT WORD and WORDPERFECT can flow text around graphics and have sophisticated style options. From the electronic-publishing end, certain high-end packages such as INTERLEAF and FRAMEMAKER have been retooling their programs to run on smaller machines so that they can capture the "home" book-publishing trade. INTERLEAF, for example, can currently run on a mid-range IBM PS2 model (the 55x with 2 Megabytes of RAM and a hard drive). Such a feat moves the power of commercial typesetting machines into the hands of the modest English professors. Although desktop-publishing packages are still distinguishable from word-processing packages by their abilities to manipulate graphics after these have been imported, simple graphics packages are beginning to be bundled with word-processing packages (e.g., SUPERPAINT with MICROSOFT WORD for the Macintosh), and the most common features of these packages are rapidly being incorporated in ways that make desktop-publishing features standard in word-processing packages.

Thus, word processing is quickly becoming word publishing. Word publishing further simplifies the publishing process, and more importantly for the writer, provides the central platform for the paging computers that use word-processing packages. Metaphorically, the word gains the seat of power in production. Figure 8 depicts the word-publishing process.

In the word-publishing process, many of the desktop-publishing activities are in place. Clip art, drawn art, and scanned art can be imported into the word-processing file and manipulated in limited ways. For example, in the 3.02 Macintosh version of MICROSOFT WORD that is recording this text, I can import graphics into a text and move them around in a graphics frame. I can also run text next to them using a column format, but I cannot change the graphics in any substantive way; they are pictures in my text. With text-graphics maneuvers and with a high-end product like INTERLEAF, I would be able to manipulate the images deftly. With a desktop-publishing program, I would be able to accomplish some additional maneuvers. However, for most situations, I do not need more publishing features than word-processing packages afford me.

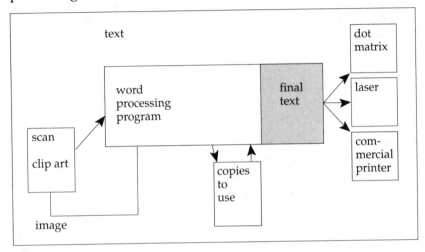

Figure 8:   Publishing process as affected by current word-publishing
            programs

Two points need emphasis here. First, the word-publishing process accomplishes many of the desktop-publishing activities in a simpler, and usually cruder, fashion, but it does not make publishing altogether simple. Although the graphical user interfaces (adopted first by Apple and now by DOS environments) make the entire process seem simple when it is demonstrated, the process is actually far more complicated than typing and appreciably more complex than simple word processing. Second, the word-publishing process collapses the publishing dialectic. In the past when authors wrote books and designers designed books, the words had a fierce advocate and so did the page. Word publishing, in contrast, threatens the aesthetic integrity of the page, if the writer does not internalize the role of the designer. And writers currently are trained to think little about the look of the text. That problem is increasingly important.

The How of Word Publishing: Possible Approaches to "Seeing the Page"

So far I have been arguing that in a published document, both words and images contribute to the meaning of the document, yet usually writers are trained primarily or only in the making of verbal meaning. With word publishing, technology allows writers to take on the work of making both words and images. But to do word publishing successfully, writers must come to terms with the page, as well as with the text, and as well as with the *making* of publications. Writers must become sensitive about how pages look, attuned to how readers will see pages, and able to negotiate a look for pages that supports the aims of texts. Such activities add a new dimension to writing and call for pedagogy supporting the process of seeing the page.

Some work on the pedagogy of the page is underway in composition and in technical and business communication. In 1986, Stephen Bernhardt presented the beginnings of a pedagogy for "seeing the text." He focused on the principles of gestalt (filtered through Arnheim, 1969), searching for a way of reading the visual impact of the page and beginning a vocabulary for speaking about the page. Barton and Barton (1985) have looked more generally to art criticism (primarily the semiotic approach of Bertin, 1983), focusing on exploring general principles and on critiquing how these principles might be assembled into a rhetoric for visuals in texts, but they too are working on language that can be used both for the discussion of visuals and for the pedagogy of teaching visuals.

Also needed for work on the pedagogy of the page is a way to relate texts and images under the umbrella of rhetorical theory. Although we can find texts that teach the aesthetics of a visual literacy (Arnheim, 1969; Dondis, 1973; Bertin, 1983; Tufte, 1983), we have less success finding the *meaning on the page* treated both holistically and specifically from both a visual and a verbal perspective. Although the visual arts have a superior approach to the aesthetic qualities of the page, they are not specific enough about the verbal meaning or the integration of visual and verbal elements. Their questions are different. Researchers such as Bernhardt

(1986), Sullivan (1988), and Kostelnick (1988) have begun to develop a writing-based and rhetorically grounded approach to page design through the notion of a visual-verbal scale or continuum. Bernhardt observes that not all documents are equally visual, nor need they be. Sullivan pictures the relationship as a number of elements ranged over a fulcrum, and focuses discussion on finding an integration point that yields a balance for the type of document being produced (Fig. 9). Kostelnick pictures the relationship as a continuum, a spectrum that ranges from low visual intensity to high visual intensity.

These theoretical models are new and are in need of input from writers and teachers of writing as they work more with publishing in the 1990s. Consider the visual-verbal quality of a document. The basic elements of a document are its words, its sharing of conventions with other documents of its type, its placement of words and images on a page, and the integration of words and images that it manages. To focus theory on the relationship between words and images, writing teachers and scholars need to consider the page as a basic unit of meaning and the place where this type of integration most commonly occurs. Then the integration can be usefully viewed on a continuum from text-based to image-based, with the point of visual-verbal integration as a fulcrum that moves along the continuum depending on the type of document being produced (see again Fig. 9).

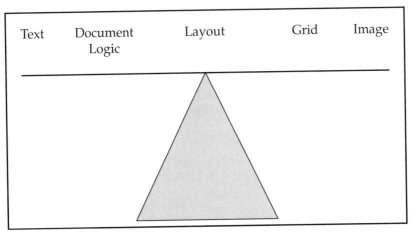

Figure 9. The position of the fulcrum shows the point of visual-verbal integration in a document.

The point of visual-verbal intergration acts as the balancing point for documents, one that shifts according to the rhetorical nature of the document (who the audience is, how the document will be used, what the textual and visual conventions are, what the nature of the content to be conveyed is). To suggest dramatic examples, the concept of the grid becomes more prominent in an advertisement, just as the text assumes more prominence in a traditional essay. In computer documentation, the layout becomes more prominent in texts meant for quick reference, and text becomes more prominent in texts aimed at learning system architecture. Always, however, these components work together to create meaning on the page, and the document is coherent if they also work across pages to create logical patterns and connections.

Word publishing requires developing a vision of the page that implicates production, that implicates rhetorical theory, and that implicates aesthetic issues such as taste. If writers and teachers of writing hope to use computers more effectively in word publishing, we must develop a rhetoric of the page that includes visual dimensions of meaning. The challenges facing word publishing are tied to a user's ability to see the page as a unit of meaning that merges or integrates the visual and verbal meaning in an appropriate way for a document under development. On the skill level, the challenges of word publishing are tied to the abilities of writers to function as publishers. That is, writers must be able to write text, develop a global logic for documents, devise layouts, draw (or procure) suitable artwork, and "see" the grid. And all of these tasks are in addition to the challenges of mastering the computer technology and production process problems. On another level, the real challenge of word publishing is to internalize a dialectic that produces a published book. This dialectic involves the text-driven perspective of a writer and the spatial-aesthetic perspective of a designer.

What Research Agenda Emerges in Word Publishing?

Thus far, this chapter has discussed word-publishing innovations from the public viewpoint (how writers must learn to adjust to the shifts in production processes), and from the aesthetic viewpoint (how writers must become artists who produce and design their own books). This discussion has probably touched readers for whom the visual and visual literacy is vital. Michael Heim (1987) offers another compelling argument for scrutinizing the page more carefully when he contrasts the different psyches associated with the classic book texts and word-processing texts. Heim portrays the book-culture psyche as being characterized by permanence and resistance, as using personal expression, as urging contemplative formulation of ideas, and as capturing a private solitude of reflective reading and writing. The word-processing culture, by contrast, is characterized by automated manipulation, algorithmic logic, and overabundance of dynamic possibilities. This latter culture is tied to a public network where original authorship is challenged. Expanding electronic writing processes into word-publishing processes will engender even futher upheaval.

The original question of this chapter—"How do we take control of the page?"—clearly is a central question for professional writing in the 1990s. But it moves into all areas of electronic composing as the basic software for word processing becomes more sophisticated and more accommodating to texts that integrate words and images. Further, while this argument has focused on the production of the printed page, parallel arguments could be made about advances in electronic facilitation of jointly-authored texts, advances in electronic facilitation of hypermedia and hypertexts, and advances in writers' abilities to gather electronic information from many sources (databases, bulletin boards, clip art, and so on) and weave those texts into a new one. Such composing fluidity suggests that the "control" writers might gain is temporary, situational, and heuristic rather than all-encompassing. It suggests, then, the need for rhetorical theory.

Further, theoretical, pedagogical, and research questions are suggested by the development of word publishing. First, writers face a distinct set of challenges, among them the following:

- How do writers internalize the dialectic relationship of author, who jealously guards the texts, and publisher, who zealously works to produce a page that looks a certain way?

- What do writers need to know about visual components (e.g., graphics principles, two-dimensional layout, aesthetics)?

- As electronically produced texts become more and more intensely visual, can an anti-visual text maintain power and effectiveness?

- Can pictures take a more active role in the making of a text's argument?

- What do writers need to know about how the audience views the visual dimensions of a text?

Second, our currently held explanations of process and electronic writing theory face challenges:

- What explanatory metaphors can be developed to make word-publishing processes understandable? The empowering metaphors for electronic writing, those of "electronic pencil" and "smart(er) typewriter" do not adequately capture the nature of word publishing. What analogical moves do we need to make in theorizing about processes of word publishing?

- Do the increasingly "simple" processes that attend word publishing mask deeper, more complex processes for writing? When writers try to take control of the page, do they end up spending more composing time on production details? Does seeming simplicity suggest embedded processes that we have not yet identified?

- Can word publishing be usefully described as a contemporary resurgence of the ancient rhetorical canon of delivery? Certainly it deals with crafting a message at the point of its delivery to its audience, embellishing it appropriately, shading and nuancing its vehicle. But delivery would have to be recovered or rejuvenated in its most positive light for the association to convey thoughtfulness rather than sleight of hand.

- Can word publishing theory aim to reconfigure the split between rhetoric and poetic? To the extent that aesthetic criteria are introduced into judgments about textual quality, the poetic is more highly valued. There are other ways that poetic craft might become more important: for instance, we might investigate how to keep a composition as fluid as possible for as long as possible (a trait prized in artistic composing processes).

- Does investigating "what the page means to the reader" and "how the writer can manipulate what the page means to the reader" hold implications for new developments in audience theory?

Finally, teachers of electronic writing instruction face challenges:

- What are the components of a teaching theory that explains how the word and the image make the page? In what ways does this shift alter our perspective of the static printed page and the dynamic on-line page?

- In what situations might English teachers want to spend class time teaching students the possibilities of the software, and in what situations might we want to ignore (or disable) such capabilities?

- Can teachers of professional writing use the teaching of "how-to-publish" as a site for the teaching of visual design?

- How will our culture modify the structure of publishing houses in ways that integrate this larger view of writing with an expanded notion of authorship?

In 1980, J. Paul Hunter wrote an essay about revising the English major, asking departments to "face" the eighties. It was a time of great change, and he sounded initially tired, then resolved, then energized by the enormous tasks facing the decade. Following his lead, we must "face" the teaching, research, and theoretical consequences of the electronic innovations that are continuously simplifying and complicating our composing lives. On to the 1990s!

Note

1. This essay focuses on the printed page, even though parallel arguments could and need to be made about the electronic page. This discussion focuses on the static page, the printed page, and uses "the book" as its metaphorical base. I do not consider this argument sufficient to handle the changes introduced by the electronic page, as that "page" is dynamic, inviting of multiple authorship, handicapped by monitors, and potentially linked to other electronic pages in hypertextual ways. I consider this discussion a precursor to one I will soon make about the electronic page.

Acknowledgments

I thank Hugh Burns, Gail Hawisher, and Cynthia Selfe for their perceptive and helpful readings of this essay. It was Hugh who saw this paper as calling for a rethinking of delivery.

References

Aller, B. M. (1988). *Identifying the human factors associated with the corporate implementation of desktop publishing.* Unpublished master's thesis, Michigan Technological University, Houghton, MI.

Arnheim, R. (1969). *Visual thinking.* Berkeley: University of California Press.

Barker, H. (1988). Typographical points on the desktop. *Visible Language, 22* (2/3), 343–367.

Barton, B. F., & Barton, M. S. (1985). Toward a rhetoric of visuals for the computer era. *The Technical Writing Teacher, 12*(2), 126–145.

Bernhardt, S. A. (1986). Seeing the text. *College Composition and Communication, 37,* 66–78.

Bertin, J. (1983). *Semiology of graphics: Diagrams, networks, maps* (W. J. Berg, trans.). Madison, WI: University of Wisconsin Press.

Burns, H. (1979). *Stimulating invention in English composition through computer-assisted instruction.* (ERIC Document Reproduction Service No. 188 245).

Dondis, D. (1973). *A primer of visual literacy.* Cambridge, MA: The Massachusetts Institute of Technology Press.

Hawisher, G. E. (1988, April). *Research in computers and writing: Findings and implications.* Paper presented at the American Educational Research Association Convention, New Orleans.

Heim, M. (1987). *Electric language: A philosophical study of word processing.* New Haven: Yale University Press.

Hunter, J. P. (1980). Facing the eighties. In D. Fisher & R. I. Brod (Eds.), *Profession 80* (pp. 1–9). New York: Modern Language Association of America.

Kostelnick, C. (1988). A systematic approach to visual language in business communication. *The Journal of Business Communication, 25*(3), 29–48.

Miller, L. (1986). Computers for composition: A stage model approach to helping. *Visible Language, 20*(2), 188–218.

Ong, W. J. (1977). *Interfaces of the word.* Ithaca: Cornell University Press.

Schwartz, H. (1984). SEEN: A tutorial and user network for hypothesis testing. In W. Wresch (Ed.), *The computer in composition instruction* (pp. 47–62). Urbana, IL: National Council of Teachers of English.

Selfe, C. L. (1984). Wordsworth II: Process-based CAI for college composition teachers. In W. Wresch (Ed.), *The computer in composition instruction* (pp. 174–190). Urbana, IL: National Council of Teachers of English.

Sullivan, P. (1988). Writers as total desktop publishers: Developing a conceptual approach to training. In E. Barrett (Ed.), *Text, context, and hypertext* (pp. 265–278). Cambridge, MA: The Massachusetts Institute of Technology Press.

Tate, Gary (Ed.). (1987). *Teaching composition: Twelve bibliographical essays* (2nd ed., rev.). Fort Worth, TX: Texas Christian University Press.

Tufte, E. R. (1983). *The visual display of quantitative information.* Cheshire, CT: Graphics Press.

VonBlum, R., & Cohen, M. E. (1984). WANDAH: Writing-aid AND author's helper. In W. Wresch (Ed.), *The computer in composition instruction: A writer's tool* (pp. 154–173). Urbana, IL: National Council of Teachers of English.

Wresch, W. (Ed.). (1984). *The computer in composition instruction: A writer's tool.* Urbana, IL: National Council of Teachers of English.

Young, Richard. (1987). Recent developments in rhetorical theory. In G. Tate (Ed.), *Teaching composition: Twelve bibliographical essays* (2nd ed., rev.) (pp. 1–38). Fort Worth, TX: Texas Christian University Press.

Chapter 3

Computing and Collaborative Writing

Janis Forman
Anderson Graduate School of Management at UCLA

Software is increasingly available to facilitate collaborative writing, but most of the research on groupware is carried out by social scientists who lack training in the study of texts and their production—composition specialists' area of expertise. How is groupware used to handle collaborative writing? Why do groups use the technology they do? What are the advantages and disadvantages of using technology for collaborative writing? These are questions best addressed by interdisciplinary teams composed of social scientists and composition specialists.

Last year, a software vendor stopped by my office at the Anderson Graduate School of Management at UCLA to demonstrate a new product intended to enhance collaborative revision of documents. The product had a number of attractive features, but as I looked at the options for inserting readers' comments, I realized that the software would place serious constraints on the kinds of suggestions for revision that readers could make. For example, at no point did the software prompt or allow for holistic comments, the implicit assumption being that all revision is local revision of paragraphs and sentences. The package was, in fact, adapted from groupware[1] used in the production of highly compartmentalized legal documents which lend themselves exclusively to local revision. If my school were to adopt this software, I realized, the technology would work against all my efforts to teach MBA students about revision at the discourse level—the composing activity they need to focus upon.[2]

This vendor's demonstration was revealing to me in two ways. It foreshadowed the increasing presense of groupware in the marketplace of the 1990s, and hence in the schools. It also served as a warning: if composition specialists do not become more actively involved in research on and creation of such software, we may end up with products that can do more harm than good. This essay argues for such involvement in a specific way, in composition specialists' cross-disciplinary research on computing and collaborative writing. The essay then sketches a research agenda, discusses the challenges of the agenda, speculates about the impact of the agenda upon our teaching, and suggests questions for further research.

Even if we, as composition specialists, had not already developed an interest in collaborative writing[3] and were concerned only about how technology affects composition, the increasing market presence of groupware would force us to think about how these new computer tools may influence collaborative writing. Researchers at the Institute for the Future predict growth in this segment of the software industry, and have identified numerous scenarios in which groupware would be applicable to team activities, including collaborative writing, in particular, and activities often considered part of this process—scheduling, record keeping, synchronous and asynchronous communication,[4] and decision making. Vendors are actively involved in designing and marketing these groupware products (Johansen, 1988).

Research on Computing and Collaboration

In addition to the increased availability of groupware, the study of computers and collaborative writing *by composition specialists* will have even greater urgency as our colleagues in social psychology and in the management of information systems (MIS) continue their research on groupware. Some promising research on computing and collaboration has recently been conducted by composition specialists, especially about how groupware may affect the authority structure in the classroom (Jennings, 1987, p.17), and the extent to which communal writing spaces with computers intensify collaborative writing habits among faculty and student technology users (Selfe & Wahlstrom, 1985, p. 1; Rodrigues, 1985). Anecdotal and descriptive reports of successful uses of groupware (e.g., electronic mail, computer conferencing) for writing instruction have also appeared (Spitzer, 1989; Batson, 1988; Levin, Riel, Rowe, & Boruta, 1985). But our profession still knows relatively little about how groupware might affect collaborative writing; on balance, most of the research is occurring outside of composition.

Valuable and substantial research has been done on collaborative work and groupware by social psychologists and MIS specialists. Commonly absent in published findings of social psychology and MIS is a discussion of the unique features of collaborative writing as *writing*, as the creation of *texts*. This situation is, of course, understandable. Social scientists are not often trained in the study of texts and their production, which is generally the unique province of humanists. When collaborative writing is discussed in the social science research on computers and collaborative work, it is discussed as a task indistinguishable from other forms of collaborative work.

There is every reason to believe that our colleagues in social psychology and in MIS will continue their research on computing and group work.[5] Our concern as composition specialists is how to join forces with them to study collaborative writing jointly. In sum, this chapter argues for our involvement in research, product design, and theory of computing and collaborative writing, and for our participation on interdisciplinary teams—preferably composed of social psychologists and specialists in MIS—because thus far researchers in these disciplines have been responsible for the major findings about collaborative work and technology. With composition specialists on such teams, there will be a place for consideration of texts and group composing; at the same time, composition specialists will gain a better understanding of collaborative composing from the perspectives offered by other disciplines. It is only through collaborative cross-disciplinary research that we will be able to answer basic questions about the uses of groupware for collaborative writing and the relative merits of such uses.

I argue for collaborative cross-disciplinary efforts from personal experience as well as from reviews of the social-psychological and MIS literatures. From 1985 to 1989, I worked with a colleague in MIS on a study of students using groupware to collaborate on the writing of group reports. Without the perspectives she brought to our study, I would have been unable to formulate questions about writing and computing that I sensed to be important but, as a composition specialist, could not identify. These questions concerned how the computing policies and practices of groups contribute to their use of technology for report writing, how the social dynamics of groups influence their choice and use of groupware, and how the geographical proximity of group members may enter their decisions about which technology to use and when to use it (Forman, 1991; Markus and Forman, 1989). Working with an MIS specialist also helped correct some of my misconceptions about technology and writing. For example, when I began the project I regarded the computer as a machine that writers use. As I worked more closely with the MIS specialist, I learned that the technology is regarded more accurately as a set of options or tools that writing groups manage or mismanage. My "gestalt switch" enabled me to focus on how and why students choose to use or not to use groupware for writing and revising rather than to focus on software and hardware per se as elements of the writing process. As an additional benefit of cross-disciplinary collaborative research, I was forced to look critically at my own research assumptions and questions whenever translating concepts and methods from composition for my MIS colleague (Forman, 1988).

Assuming that we can be involved on interdisciplinary research teams, what then are the key issues for the 1990s?

Issues for the 1990s

Our research agenda might center around three key questions:

- Why do groups use groupware to handle collaborative writing?
- Why do writing groups use technology?
- How do groups use groupware when they write?

- What are the advantages and disadvantages of using technology for collaborative writing?

Why Do Groups Use Groupware for Collaborative Writing?

One aspect of our research agenda should be descriptive, answering the question of how collaborative writing groups use software. Thus far, composition research has shown that collaborative composing processes can involve several communication media: face-to-face discussions, telephone conversations, written communications. With the introduction of groupware, composition teachers and scholars will want to investigate the place of the new technology in the mix of communication media. At which points in composing do teams prefer to work face-to-face or by phone? When do they choose to communicate and compose using computer technology? When do they write, read, and revise online, and when do they work with hard copy?

Several factors which may influence how groupware is used should be included in our research agenda: group characteristics (size, age, gender); task characteristics (type of document, task familiarity); and technology environment (computer facilities, uses of groupware beyond the writing course).

Group characteristics. Research in MIS, social science, and composition suggests that group size, age, and gender may influence the use of groupware for writing. In their conceptual review of research on groupware, MIS experts argue that group size significantly affects how teams use the technology:

> As membership increases, the number of potential information exchanges rises geometrically, and the frequency, duration, and intimacy of information exchange all decline. Consensus becomes harder to achieve, and affectional ties and satisfaction with the group decline. . . . There is greater interest in giving information and suggestions and less interest in asking opinion, giving opinion, or showing agreement. Smaller groups are more likely to actively attempt to resolve opinion differences, whereas larger groups tend to use humor as a tension-reducing mechanism. . . . (DeSanctis & Gallupe, 1987, p. 598)

Although this overview does not concern collaborative writing tasks per se, it suggests extension of the research to include how members feel about the collaborative writing process. As group size varies, do speculative thinking and negotiation of ideas take place on- or off-line? Do the characteristics of such groupwork vary depending upon technology use?

From composition research on collaborative writing, we can also hypothesize that age influences groupware use. In a study of writing groups at the fifth-, eighth-, and eleventh/twelfth-grade levels, Gere and Abbott (1985) found that a group's talk about writing and their written products changed as a function of the group's grade level. For instance, older students paid more attention to form than to content and wrote longer texts than did younger students (p. 369, 371). Do we see changes in the uses of groupware for collaborative writing on the basis of users' ages? Do younger students using technology write more than their peers who write without technology? Do younger students, because they are exposed to the technology's capabilities at increasingly younger ages, write more than older students who have just recently been exposed to the technology?

From social science research, we have learned that the gender composition of groups influences team motivation, the kind of team leadership that emerges, and the team's effectiveness in accomplishing a task (Craig & Sherif, 1986; Kerr & Sullaway, 1983). In addition, recent work on collaborative writing by composition specialists suggests that a student's gender identity affects his or her behavior and attitude toward interpersonal conflict. Behavior and attitude in turn affect how well a group manages the collaborative writing process (Lay, 1989). Does gender affect *computer-mediated* collaborative writing, and, if so, how? Which teams using technology—all male, all female, mixed—manage conflict most creatively and produce writing of the highest quality?

Task characteristics. We will also want to investigate how the *type* of collaborative writing task and the *frequency* with which groups write in a particular genre influence groupware choice and use. The term *collaborative writing* is used in composition circles to encompass more than one kind of group writing activity. For instance, collaborative writing can mean peer review of a text ultimately attributed to a single author or, less often, to several individuals' drafting and revising of a single document attributed to all group members. What is the role of technology in different kinds of collaborative writing activities? Is groupware most effective for revising activities, thus facilitating collaboration as peer review? How useful is the technology for collaborative invention, a central activity in the composition of multi-authored texts?

Genre may also influence students' choice and use of groupware. Does technology use vary depending upon whether a group writes a short story, an essay, or a research report? The group revision package mentioned at the beginning of this essay was adequate for highly compartmentalized documents requiring local revision. Is there a preferred groupware package for narrative, for argument supported by details, or for analysis, integration of data, and visual display of quantitative information? In sum, does the type of document that students are asked to write influence their selection and use of groupware?

Besides the particular genre, the frequency with which teams work in a genre might influence their selection and use of groupware. Preliminary composition research in industry shows that the *routine* of managers' writing assignments (e.g., several proposals a month) contributed to the frequency and ease with which managers used technology (Forman, 1987). Conversely, a preliminary composition study of students' use of technology to write a consulting report indicated that the *novelty* of the assignment contributed to students' inefficient use of groupware: teams had so much difficulty organizing, drafting, and revising a report that the use of groupware proved to be an impediment to their task rather than an aid (Forman, 1991). We need verification and extension of this preliminary work.

Technology environment. As schools increasingly acquire computer technology, we will want to know what influence the "networked community" of the school has on the use of groupware for writing. In other words, does the overall technological environment of an institution affect the use of groupware for writing? For instance, if messaging and document transfer are common throughout a school, do students use this technology for collaborative writing? Conversely, how effective is groupware if used solely in the writing class? Historians in our profession will also want to trace the links between computing and literacy, between the growth of institutions' computer resources and instruction, on the one hand, and the ways in which collaborative writing is taught and conducted, on the other.

Why Do Writing Groups Use Technology?

Preliminary research in composition and in social psychology suggests that several factors may enter students' decision about whether to use technology: teams' and individuals' methods for learning groupware; the relative ease or difficulty of compliance in usage; and "technology leadership" within a group.

Learning. Recent investigations in composition demonstrate that students' decisions to use groupware to accomplish their writing tasks and the kinds of software they select may depend, in part, upon their learning experience, their incentives and disincentives to use groupware, and the technological leadership that emerges in teams (Forman, 1990). From these findings, questions have emerged for future research: How do student groups best learn groupware that can assist them in writing collaboratively? Do they learn best by taking formal classes, observing others using groupware, receiving instruction from fellow team members, working with a tutor, reading printed or on-line documentation, using simplified versions of manuals tailored to their needs, using a trial-and-error method, or attending group meetings to identify and solve learning problems? Is a combination of methods best for different individuals and different groups? Does the group, as well as individuals on the team, have a "learning style" and, if so, how is it defined? Further, do students' prior experiences learning technology and their attitudes toward learning affect their acquisition of a new set of computer skills?

Thus far, the computer literature on learning technology cannot help us much in answering these questions because it focuses upon different populations—secretaries and office temporary personnel learning simple operations such as word processing.[6] Although composition research on learning technology has focused on student populations, it concerns the acquisition of word-processing technologies rather than of more sophisticated technologies (Selfe, Ruehr, & Johnson, 1986; Wagner, O'Toole, & Kazelskis,1985).

If we assume that most students have little or no experience using groupware before college, we will also need to investigate the incentives and disincentives for learning and using groupware. Preliminary research in composition suggests that students are reluctant to learn and to use new software if its benefits are not immediate and obvious, and if using the technology for collaborative writing is not built into a reward structure (for instance, included in their grades for the writing course). Incentives for learning and using new technology may include students' recognizing that the "short-term pain" of learning the technology leads to the "long-term gain" of a more efficient and effective group writing process, that technology usage will influence their grade, and that groupware will have applications beyond the writing course (Forman, 1990). This preliminary identification of possible incentives and disincentives for groupware use warrants further investigation.

Compliance. Studies of compliance follow logically from investigations of learning. Once groupware is learned, what factors affect teams' willingness to use technology throughout the writing process? Does compliance depend upon whether student teams develop an "etiquette," a set of formal or informal rules for using groupware? Social-psychological studies of electronic messaging indicate that no strong etiquette as yet applies to how electronic communication should be used. A few user manuals devote a paragraph to appropriate uses of a computer network, but, generally speaking, people do not receive either formal or informal instruction in an etiquette of electronic communication (Kiesler, Siegel, & McGuire, 1984, p. 1125). With the increasing availability of groupware in university settings, what kind of etiquette emerges in student writing teams?

Leadership. Compliance may be influenced by group leadership (Forman, 1990). Thus, team leadership in the learning, choice, and use of technology will also warrant our attention. How does leadership in the use of technology emerge? Under what conditions does the "technology expert"—the student who knows the most about computing—support the team's use of groupware? Under what conditions do technology novices champion the use of new technology? Perhaps more fundamentally, how do student technology leaders exert influence on team decisions about technology use for collaborative writing when such leaders have no formal authority?

What are the Advantages and Disadvantages of Groupware Choices?

In addition to identifying the changes in composing that groupware influences, we will want to judge the benefits and liabilities of these changes in order to develop an effective pedagogy. For instance, since talk about writing is important to collaborative composing (Gere & Abbott, 1985, p. 375), does partial or complete replacement of talk by electronic communication help or hinder collaborative writing processes and the quality of written products? And does the introduction of technology into the collaborative writing process make reading and writing more important than talking and listening currently are in collaborative composing? Further, does the quality of group decision making involved in collaborative writing improve or decline with the introduction of groupware? In their study of group decision making with and without groupware, social psychologists at Carnegie-Mellon found "differences in participation, decisions, and interaction among groups meeting face to face and in simultaneous computer-linked discourse and communication by electronic mail" (Kiesler, Siegel, & McGuire, 1984, p. 1123). Team members using groupware participated more equally in decisions, were more likely to change their initial opinions in the course of discussion, were more uninhibited in expressing hostile feelings, and took longer to reach consensus (pp. 1128–1129). Do the same changes occur if the group's primary task is writing? And, if so, are these changes beneficial or harmful to collaborative writing?

The Agenda's Challenges

The wide-ranging agenda for research in computing and collaborative writing makes it difficult to determine clearly defined limits to studies in each of the two disciplines. In my four-year experience of interdisciplinary research on computer-mediated collaborative writing, my collaborator and I struggled with defining questions about a complex subject viewed from several disciplinary perspectives. As specialists in different disciplines, we faced difficulties in understanding different epistemological and methodological frameworks, in grappling with their potential irreconcilable differences, and in coming to terms with the expectations that each of our discourse communities had about what constitutes publishable work and what form it should take. As researchers investigating a complex subject, we experienced a magnified version of the dangers every researcher faces—fuzzy, unfocused thinking and a Rabelaisian enumeration of poorly defined research questions. We had to learn to define smaller pieces of the subject, and, in this defining process, have just begun to map the territory of our investigations.

Our contribution as composition specialists to such interdisciplinary research is our knowledge of texts and of collaborative writing processes. But here again, as with the difficulties of defining interdisciplinary research questions, challenges abound. The study of collaborative writing is—alone—relatively new, and there are many unanswered, complex questions in this domain. In a preconvention workshop at the 1988 meeting of the Conference on College Composition and Communication, "What Are We Doing as a Research Community?" George Hillocks pointed out some of the complexity:

> We do not know how prior knowledge affects the course of group discussion or how knowledge changes as a result of discussion. And we do not know as much as we need to know about the strategies themselves and how they are used in the composing process. (p. 1)

In addition to the need to know about the role of students' knowledge and strategies for composing collaboratively, composition specialists need to consider more fully the varied contexts for and aims of collaborative writing—before or along with our study of *computer-mediated* collaborative writing. Collaborative writing in the classroom generally operates under far different assumptions and with radically different models than does collaborative writing in corporate settings. (Nor is collaborative

writing uniform across classrooms or across organizations.)
"School collaborative writing" generally assumes nonhierarchical
student groups using peer review to produce documents ultimately attributed to a single author. Goals of such writing may
include anything from the development of team building skills to
the social construction of knowledge. In business settings, collaborative writing often operates within a strict hierarchy. Subordi-
nates write documents for their superior's signature. Ultimate
ownership and responsibility for the document belongs to the
superior who reviews rather than drafts the document. In general,
the goal of the collaborative effort is a product that accomplishes
a specific task such as informing or persuading clients or employees. As these writing situations differ, so might technology use.

As composition specialists, we have yet to answer fundamental
questions about collaborative writing; at the same time, our colleagues in MIS are investigating another emerging field, increasingly sophisticated groupware technology. Thus, both elements of
our study—collaborative writing and computing—are in need of
further investigation. The challenges for interdisciplinary research
teams will therefore be numerous and exciting.

Impact of the Research Agenda on Teaching

As composition instructors, we want answers to two questions:
How can groupware be successfully used for collaborative writing? How will the technology affect collaborative learning as well
as the writing that results from the collaborative process? At one
extreme, we can imagine a technology-based utopia: the computer
becomes a "composition workplace"—a depository for group
memory (a place where team members store and share new
information); a tool for managing writing schedules and for
thinking about and allocating different power relations in the
group writing process (for instance, who has access to what drafts,
who can read, who can write, who has final editorial control); a
common system for generating, organizing, changing, and sharing texts; and an aid promoting students' and instructors' sharing

of authority and development of other new patterns of interaction. At the other extreme—the failed version—we might find students using a hodgepodge of hardware and software poorly suited for collaborative tasks, and wrestling unsuccessfully with problems of integrating technology into their collaborative writing efforts. Moreover, in the absence of our involvement in research on computing and collaborative writing, we can imagine students being forced to work with groupware that handicaps their efforts and limits their growth as writers.[7]

Whether groupware is successfully integrated into a collaborative writing process depends, partially, I think, upon our success in conducting a series of systematic investigations of computing and collaborative writing and in translating our findings to the classroom. The outcomes of the research agenda proposed here should yield valuable lessons for the classroom about the most effective ways that students learn to use and continue to use groupware; the roles of talking, listening, reading, and writing on computer-mediated collaborative writing processes; and the best matches between technology and a particular writing group and task.

Questions for Further Research

As this essay has argued, research on computing and collaborative writing will depend upon our successful partnership with researchers in the social sciences, namely social psychologists and specialists in MIS. Social psychologists will have much to contribute about how computer-mediated collaborative writing may be influenced by group processes, group structures (e.g., hierarchical versus nonhierarchical, project versus functional groups), motivation, leadership, and other group characteristics (e.g., age, size, gender). Specialists in MIS will be able to provide insights about how organizational policies and practices may affect computer-mediated collaborative writing. Questions for further research listed here will, then, require us to enlist the assistance of these experts.

To review, we need answers to a wide range of questions:

- What is the place of new technology in the mix of communication media used for collaborative writing? In other words, at which points do teams prefer to work face-to-face, by phone, or by electronic communication?

- Does groupware use for collaborative writing differ on the basis of group characteristics such as size, age, and gender?

- What is the role of technology in different kinds of collaborative writing activities? For instance, is groupware most effective for revising, thus facilitating collaboration as peer review, or is it especially useful for collaborative invention, a central activity in the composition of multiauthored texts?

- Does genre influence a group's choice and use of groupware?

- Does the frequency with which a group writes in a genre influence the group's choice and use of technology?

- How does the overall technological environment of an organization affect the choice and use of groupware for writing?

- How do student groups best learn groupware that can assist them in writing collaboratively?

- Do groups as well as individuals on teams have a "learning style," and, if so, how is it defined?

- Does prior experience learning technology and attitudes toward learning affect acquisition of skills in using groupware for collaborative writing?

- What kind of etiquette for using groupware emerges on writing teams?

- What factors influence a team's willingness to use technology throughout the writing process?

- How does leadership in the use of technology emerge in collaborative writing?

- Under what conditions do technology experts on a team support the team's use of groupware for collaborative writing?

- Under what conditions do technology novices champion the use of groupware for collaborative writing?

- How do student leaders exert influence on team decisions about technology use for collaborative writing when such leaders have no formal authority?

- Because talk about writing is important to collaborative composing, does the partial or complete replacement of talk by electronic communication help or hinder collaborative writing processes and the quality of written documents?

- Does technology used for collaborative writing make reading and writing more important than talking and listening?

- Does the quality of group decision making in a collaborative writing effort improve or decline with the introduction of groupware?

Notes

1. Like Johansen (1988), I choose the term *groupware* over several possible synonyms that appear in the computer literature. Johansen has identified several synonyms, including "computer-supported cooperative work" (CSCW), "technological support for workgroup collaboration," "workgroup computing," "collaborative computing," "interpersonal computing," "coordination technology," "decision conferences," "computer conferencing," "computer-supported groups" (CSG), "group decision support systems" (GDSS), "group process support systems," "computer-assisted communication" (CAC), "augmented knowledge workshops," "interfunctional coordination," and "flexible interactive technologies for multiperson tasks." The proliferation of synonyms is symptomatic of technology in its early stages. Subsumed under the term *groupware* are electronic messaging, computer conferencing, document transfer, and tools for group project management (e.g., for scheduling and outlining tasks). Groupware does not refer to stand-alone technology—technology intended for use by a single individual—even if such technology is used by groups, such as a group of students composing at a single terminal. Like Johansen, I also use "groupware" to refer to technology that assists small groups rather than large organizations (pp. 10–11).

2. Only about 5 to 10 % of the MBAs have problems with grammar and usage.

3. Here I assume that collaborative writing refers to both multiple authorship of a text and to peer "intervention" (for example, brainstorming, critiquing) in the writing of a text ultimately attributed to a single individual.

4. Synchronous communication refers to communication in which parties exchange information at the same time. Asynchronous communication refers to communication in which parties exchange information at different times.

5. See especially Siegel, Dubrovsky, Kiesler, and McGuire (1986) for a social-psychological perspective, and special sections devoted to groupware issues in *MIS Quarterly* beginning in 1988 for MIS perspectives.

6. See, for example, M. K. Singley and J. R. Anderson (1985), "The Transfer of Text-Editing Skills" in *International Journal of Man-Machine Studies* (pp. 403–423). Subjects were students in a secretarial school, none with prior computer experience. The researchers looked at whether or not, and in what manner, the subjects' learning line editors transferred to their learning of screen editors. See also L. M. Gomez, D. E. Egan, and C. Bowers's (1986), "Learning to Use a Text Editor: Some Learner Characteristics that Predict Success" in *Human-Computer Interaction*, (pp.1–23). Researchers observed first-time users of computers as they learned to use a computer text editor. Thirty-three adult women were the subjects.

7. Debs (1989) warns of the current tyranny of certain word-processing packages that impose counterproductive constraints on business writers:

> . . . a number of companies are requiring writers to meet their style specifications dictated by these [poorly conceived] software programs; they must rewrite any text which exceeds the programmed sentence length or readability level. Other companies . . . have set up controlled or limited vocabulary programs. Writers must produce text using no more than the accepted 1,000 to 3,000 word vocabularies approved by the company and programmed in the computer. . . . (p. 4)

References

Batson, T. (1988, February). The ENFI project: A networked classroom approach to writing instruction. *Academic Computing,* 32–33 and 55–56.

Craig, J. M., & Sherif, C. W. (1986, April). The effectiveness of men and women in problem-solving groups as a function of group gender composition. *Sex Roles, 14,* 453–466.

Debs, M. B. (1989). *A different collaboration—word processing in the workplace.* Unpublished manuscript. University of Cincinnati.

DeSanctis, G., & Gallupe, R. B. (1987, May). A foundation for the study of group decision support systems. *Management Science, 33 ,* 589–609.

Forman, J. (1987, November). Computer-mediated group writing in the workplace. *Computers and Composition, 5*(1), 19–30.

Forman, J. (1990). Leadership dynamics of computer-supported writing groups. *Computers and Composition, 7*(2), 35–46.

Forman, J. (1988, October). What are the advantages and disadvantages of collaborative cross-disciplinary research on collaborative writing? Presentation at the International Conference for the Association of Business Communication, Indianapolis, IN.

Forman, J. (1991). Novices work on group reports: Problems in group writing and in computer-supported group writing. *Journal of Business and Technical Communication, 5*(1), 48–75

Gere, A. R., & Abbott, R. D. (1985, December). Talking about writing: The language of writing groups. *Research in the Teaching of English, 19,* 362–385.

Gomez, L. M., Egan, D. E., & Bowers, C. (1986). Learning to use a text editor: Some learner characteristics that predict success. *Human-Computer Interaction, 2,* 1–23.

Hillocks, G. (1988, March). The need for interdisciplinary studies on the teaching of writing. Presented at preconvention workshop ("What are we doing as a research community?") conducted at the annual meeting of the Conference on College Composition and Communication, St. Louis, MO.

Jennings, Edward M. (1987). Paperless writing: Boundary conditions and their implications. In L. Gerrard (Ed.), *Writing at century's end: Essays on computer-assisted composition* (pp. 11–20). New York: Random House.

Johansen, R. (1988). *Groupware: Computer support for business teams.* New York: The Free Press.

Kerr, N. L., & Sullaway, M. E. (1983). Group sex composition and member task motivation. *Sex Roles, 9*(3), 403–17.

Kiesler, S., Siegel, J., & McGuire, T.W. (1984, October). Social psychological aspects of computer-mediated communication. *American Psychologist, 39*, 1123–1134.

Lay, M. M. (1989, September). Interpersonal conflict in collaborative writing: What we can learn from gender studies. *Journal of Business and Technical Communication, 3*(2), 5–28.

Levin, J. A., Riel, M. M., Rowe, R. D., & Boruta, M. J. (1985). Muktuk meets jacuzzi: Networks and elementary school writers. In S. W. Freedman (Ed.), *The acquisition of written language: Response and revision* (pp.160–171). Norwood, NJ: Ablex.

Markus, M. L., & Forman, J. (1989). *The social dynamics of computer-supported groups.* Unpublished manuscript, UCLA.

Rodrigues, D. (1985, October). Computers and basic writers. *College Composition and Communication, 36*, 336–339.

Selfe, C. L., Ruehr, R. R., & Johnson, K. A. (1986). Teaching word processing in composition courses: Age, gender, computer experience, and instructional method. *The Computer-Assisted Composition Journal, 2*(2), 75–88.

Selfe, C. L., & Wahlstrom, B. J. (1985, October). An emerging rhetoric of collaboration: Computers, collaboration, and the composing process. *Collegiate Microcomputer, 4*, 289–295.

Siegel, J., Dubrovsky, V., Kiesler, S., & McGuire, T. W. (1986). Group processes in computer-mediated communication. *Organizational Behavior and Human Decision Processes, 37*, 157–87.

Singley, M. K., & Anderson, J. R. (1985). The transfer of text-editing skill. *International Journal of Man-Machine Studies, 22*, 403–423.

Spitzer, M. (1989). Computer conferencing: An emerging technology. In G. Hawisher and C. L. Selfe (Eds.), *Critical perspectives on computers and composition* (pp. 187–200). New York: Teachers College Press.

Wagner, W. G., O'Toole, W. M., & Kazelskis, R. (1985). Learning word-processing skills with limited instruction: An exploratory study with college students. *Educational Technology, 25*(2), 26–28.

Chapter 4

Prospects for Writers' Workstations in the Coming Decade

Donald Ross
University of Minnesota

After a decade of comfortable struggle, writers, composition teachers, and students have become familiar with word-processing software. Along the way, we have become aware of software that analyzes ordinary English prose. We have accepted some of these approaches, notably spell-checking programs, quite well. Others have caused more skepticism. This survey covers a wide range of computer programs that might possibly become relevant to the writer, ranging from ordinary tools such as a thesaurus to more complex programs that attempt syntactic or discourse analysis. Our profession needs to move toward showing students how to use as many of these tools as possible and teaching students to become "post editors," who evaluate recommendations that will inevitably be imperfect and imprecise. Emerging computer systems, i.e., the ones that will replace those on our desks, will present the writer with multiple windows into the writing process. This new hardware and software "architecture" should better model the experienced writer who sees a writing task as having multiple, parallel, and interacting dimensions. Assuming that composition specialists are able to influence the design of this writer's workstation, will we be more successful than we have been in the past in guiding our students to realize the full potential of the technology?

As teachers of English composition, we have enjoyed a decade of becoming familiar with computer-based writing environments for ourselves and, increasingly, for all of our students. All along we have accepted gradual changes, many of them significant improvements, in word-processing software. Some early struggles with hostile mainframe systems have given way to local networks with writer-centered interfaces that have been developed by composition teachers. Although it is easier to learn to use some programs than others, the extra hour or so doesn't seem to bother students or teachers, and typing speed is no longer seen as a major barrier to using the software. The spell-checking program, once a controversial feature that students learned about on the side, is now built into nearly every program.

However, as our profession has become more experienced, our equipment has aged as well. Currently, many teachers of composition are riveted to screens that are five years old or older, bought at a university discount, obsolete upon purchase. The universities' computer labs are also aging, and the increasing presence of students who have some kind of machine at home makes it harder to argue for replacing technology on campus. So we covet a hard disk, a modem, or a modest software upgrade. In the meantime, hardware has improved significantly, and, more important for educational purposes, totally new kinds of software that can benefit both experienced writers and student writers is starting to emerge for middle-priced and expensive systems known as "advanced workstations."

This chapter focuses on the features our profession can hope for, lobby for, and, ultimately expect to find on the computers that will replace those on our desks and in our labs by the end of the decade.

The bulk of this chapter is a survey of approaches to the analysis of texts, because our success in enhancing text-analysis software is most likely to affect writers' environments in the future. Most current text-analysis software responds simply to a single word or brief phrase. Even within this narrow compass, these programs make egregious mistakes–audio replay systems sound like a record going at the wrong speed, spell-checking programs miss all words not in their dictionaries, and style-checking programs identify whole groups of supposed errors that are indeed correct. This survey also, however, covers research involving progressively larger portions of the text paragraphs, sometimes entire essays. The further software designers go down this line of linguistic complexity, the more likely it is that they must ask the "users," i.e., writers, to check on how things are going. The final sections of the chapter's software survey, on machine-translation projects, start out with the assumption that people will be involved all the way along. Whether such software is used in a teaching context or by a writer at home, this is the interactive working environment writers need and expect.

The workstation itself, as it is described in this chapter, is an imaginary construction based on current trends in hardware and software; it offers a convergence of information about the text on a single screen and supports several "windows" in addition to the window for the writing itself. Developers of commercial word-processing programs are beginning to bring some of these tools together, at least on the same hard disk.

Finally, this chapter addresses the issue of writing teachers' embracing and resisting these new technologies. Many teachers have resisted endorsing the software that students use regularly on their own–a thesaurus is considered by some teachers and students to be on a par with *Cliffs Notes*. In a curious countertrend, nearly a decade after the introduction of style-checking programs into some classrooms, recent reports indicate that they are linguistically naive and pedagogically unsound. Somehow, teachers of English composition need to do a much better job of deciding what support software to sponsor, and, more important, how to use it. Workstations are going to be interesting, complex, and powerful; we should ensure that they will become useful as well.

A Survey of Software Trends

A number of trends are evident in the development of software functions: spell-checking programs, style-checking and usage-checking programs, audio replay of text, text-analyzing programs, and programs especially relevant to literary studies.

Spell-Checking Programs

Spell-checking programs compare each word in the text with a dictionary and point out which text words cannot be found. The linguistic sophistication of these dictionaries varies—some involve reasonably complex morphological rules although most just have the individual word forms (Miller, 1986; McIlroy, 1982; Nix, 1981; Peterson, 1980). Except for search speed and the size of the dictionary, the technical approaches used by these programs do not seem to matter to the writer. Dobrin (in press) compares some of the approaches these programs use to suggest which dictionary entry comes closest to what the writer typed.

Style-Checking Programs and Usage-Checking Programs

The next most familiar program is often called the "usage cop," or style-checking program (Ross, 1985). The number of such programs has increased in the past five years. These programs are best represented by Bell Lab's WRITER'S WORKBENCH (Macdonald, Frase, Gingrich, & Keenan, 1982; Kiefer & Smith, 1984; see also Cherry, 1981 and Cherry & Vesterman, 1980). Cohen and Lanham (1984) outline the style-analysis program in the H[ARCOURT] B[RACE] J[OVANOVICH] WRITER. (See also Thury's, 1987, TOOLS FOR WRITERS and Wresch's, 1988b, WRITER'S HELPER II for other recent varients.)

The underlying linguistic and computational sophistication of these style-checking programs, however, has remained fixed. Text is searched for a set list of words or phrases and tied either to an alternative or an explanatory message or both. Thus, *"on account of —> because —> wordiness"* or *"chairman —> chair —> sexist language"* are typical responses of such programs. Although the technical search for these set phrases is bound to be accurate, it is not always true that the writer is well advised to follow the advice given or to make the suggested changes.

Our profession, for instance, no longer considers it acceptable to have the student wade through lists of "mistakes" that are dissociated from their context in an essay (Feldman & Norman, 1987, pp. 40–44, outline some unhappy examples). Nor do we any longer accept that explanations and examples should be worded only in technical, linguistic terms, or that the replacement of problematic words or phrases with the alternative should be accomplished only by multiple key strokes. Syntax at the sentence level is important to some beginning writers, but it must be computed accurately before the writer will trust the system's advice (Thiesmeyer, 1987). The teacher or student should be able to increase or decrease the lists of problematic items.

A new "product" of more recent vintage is the on-line (actually on-disk) handbook from major publishers. The growing list includes W.W. Norton's TEXTRA and Prentice-Hall's COLLEGE WRITER that came out in 1987–88. None of these packages improves significantly on the pedagogical value of the printed handbook—they are not sensitive to the context in the student's essay where problems arise, they focus on errors, and their explanations are usually mediated through linguistic terminology (students must know what a participle is before they can care if their participles dangle). The assumptions that lie behind the program's scolding are often flawed—excellent writing, for *PMLA* or *Scientific American*, for instance, has long sentences and is written for the same college-educated audience that many of our students wish to join (Barker, 1983).

CORRECTEXT, which became commercially available as CORRECT GRAMMAR, can conduct a "full parse" of sentences, rather than using a minimal, surface-structure analysis to arrive at its commentary. In Dobrin's report (in press), the program does quite well on several (technically) difficult sentences taken from an editorial in *The New York Times*. The program does complain if the writer violates some arbitrary rules, such as starting sentences with coordinating conjunctions or using three or more prepositional phrases in a row. Aside from some minor flaws, the program is so much more reliable than others on the market that its real mistakes even baffle a linguist like Dobrin and would surely defy an inexperienced student writer.

The most recent evidence, based on empirical studies of the computer output and students' writing, indicates that current style-checking programs make little positive difference in a writing classroom (Bowyer, 1989; Garvey & Lindstrom, 1989; Mortenson, 1988; Pedersen, 1989; Peek, Eubanks, May & Heil, 1989). Dobrin concludes that even with a better parser than the excellent one offered in CORRECT GRAMMAR, it is still not obvious whether a teacher would find a place for this kind of analysis in a curriculum that encourages students to write and explore their thinking with writing. The presence of normative rules, systematically ignored in prestige writing, are not likely to win favor with experienced writers.

Audio Replay of Text

Lees and Berry have pointed out the potential value to some writers of being able to hear their drafts read aloud (Lees, 1987; Berry, 1989). In their studies, students and teachers found it desirable to have an obviously mechanical voice, because the reading is perceived to be neutral or objective. Lees's particular setting used a Kurzweil machine to translate from the printed page to a spoken version. Future improvements in the hardware for speech synthesis from computer-readable text should let the writer call up an audio replay of the whole text, selected pages, or even a marked block. Obviously, if students' writing is already in the computer, teachers can play selected elements back more easily. Improvements in the technical quality of the speaking voice for this hardware are inevitable, because increased storage will allow the spoken form of each word to be part of a dictionary. Linguists who design the output will then be able to concentrate on speech contours between words in order to make the output sound realistic. If the replay can be put on pause while another tool or the editor is used, writers will be able to interact even more fruitfully with the system.

Analysis of Text Structures

At the whole-text level, programs already exist for switching between an outline, a notepad, or a previous draft. Some software to aid writers has had applications for the entire text, albeit mechanically. The most frequently tried approaches in such work involve what Wresch has called "reformatters" (Wresch, 1988a). Some software programs, for example, isolate the first sentences of paragraphs to see if the writer (or teacher) finds them a satisfactory abstract of the text (Von Blum & Cohen, 1984; Wresch, 1988b). This is a crude way to address concerns of cohesion and organization, especially given the difficulty of making a more persuasive analysis of text structure.

Inexperienced writers often have a mechanical way of organizing their writing. Their opening sentences frequently forecast the contents of paragraphs, are likely to echo key words for the entire essay, and contain explicit transitional devices. However, these features are by no means universal in the work of mature writers; yet they are frequently (and properly) taught as a way for a novice writer to learn how to signal organization.

Programs for outlining are now packaged with ordinary word-processing software, and many provide considerable flexibility for moving paragraphs around, defining levels of subordination, and editing within the outline format. Some early, disembodied outliners, such as THINKTANK, were used briefly in some classes, and then apparently dismissed (Dobrin, 1987), perhaps because students could not write within the outline file. Given the decades-old lore about the value of outlining, espoused by many textbooks, it might be wise to see if outlining as an approach to planning and revising makes any difference to the quality of written products.

Literary Studies: Stylistics, Concordances, and Genres

Researchers in composition studies should also look at the area of literary stylistics for suggestions about how combinations of syntactic features, lengths of words, phrases, and clauses, and vocabulary repetition might be brought together to guide student writers. With the assistance of David Hunter, I am working on a microcomputer version of EYEBALL (Ross & Rasche, 1972), a program that tags each word along with all of the aforementioned dimensions, thus allowing for both statistical generalizations and selective retrieval of cross-classified features. In some preliminary studies, a rather systematic difference has emerged between the style of university seniors and that of excellent journalism and feature writers. However, acceptably accurate parsing is not possible without an interactive step, which takes time and requires fairly detailed linguistic knowledge in order to perform well. Perhaps a future version of a program like CORRECT GRAMMAR will ease this task. William Wresch's WRITER'S HELPER II has taken some tentative steps with an experimental routine that combines features from several linguistic levels in its report on the student's style.

A second area of literary studies that could be relevant for writers is the concordance, or the context-free word index (Burton,

1982). Concordance programs are now available for microcomputers with a hard disk (Boivin & Bratley, 1985; WORDCRUNCHER, 1987; Wobbe, 1987). WRITER'S HELPER II and commercial programs have built vocabulary lists and word counts into their revision routines. The computer procedures to develop the indexed text are now rapid enough that the student need not wait long to use a text-retrieval routine.

It is not yet clear what is the best way to present information about word counts to either expert or students writers. The most obvious difficulty is that the repetition of words is a function of text length—the longer the text, the more likely it is that "function words" (*the, was, from,* and so forth) will be repeated; the same difficulty obtains for "content words" (nouns, verbs, adjectives, and adverbs), whether they are ordinary words of the language (*woman, house, thing*) or thematic words of the particular essay (*student* and *dorms,* or *DNA* and *recombinant*). Thus, in order to use such a program effectively, writers must learn how to interpret quantitative reports against baseline data about texts.

An example here can illustrate this problem. A concordance of the word *computer* for the first sixteen paragraphs of a draft of this essay is represented in Figure 1.

When scholars use concordances for literary analysis, they bring many years of experience to the task. Thus, the Romanticist knows that the vocabulary of Kantian epistemology is important, so he or she looks for words like "imagination" and "reason." The Fitzgerald expert will pay attention to color words, while the Woolf specialist might look at household items for their symbolic values. Learning how to use a concordance or a word index is an acquired skill. Until composition researchers have taken the trouble to deal with the issue of text length and set up an appropriate on-screen working environment, this area is still not ready to go into the hands of teachers or their students.

The final topic of literary studies that merits our attention is that of genre. It turns out that nearly all stylistic features are sensitive to the form of the writing. Some efforts have been made to tailor the presentation of quantitative measures such as sentence length to student writing (Kiefer & Smith, 1984; Barker, 1983), but all the other features need to be "calibrated," as it were, based on a reasonably large sample of students' essays. At one stage of IBM's

EPISTLE/CRITIQUE project, the researchers gathered syntactic and lexical conventions on 250 subgenres each from law and journalism. That level of detail brings stylistic analysis to the level of an expert system that is likely only to be relevant in highly structured genres like constitutional amendments or summonses (Miller, 1986).

Para.	Sent.	Word	Citation
9	1	11	on empirical studies of the **computer** output and students' writing, indicates
10	3	29	hardware for speech synthesis from **computer**-readable text should let the writer
10	4	9	writing is already in the **computer**, we can play it back
13	2	12	we are working on a micro**computer** version of EYEBALL (Ross &
14	2	6	these are now available for micro-**computers** with a hard disk (Boivin
14	2	2	the **computer** procedures to develop the index
16	1	5	a concordance of the word **computer** for the first sixteen paragraphs

Figure 1: Sample concordance output. Each citation provides a partial context for the word's use.

Computational Linguistics

Computational linguistics projects continue to reveal the difficulties of automatic language analysis (see Harris, 1985, for a general introduction). An accurate morphological analysis of English words is a major undertaking in terms of the amount of computer programming involved (Allen, 1977; Kay, 1977); in contrast, a word-processing package's placement-of-hyphen routines shows how much approximation comes with a less elaborate, "low-budget" program. Accurate syntactic analysis, i.e., beyond the crude approximation of WRITER'S HELPER II, still requires a mainframe computer—the syntactic rules are many, complex, and interrelated.

New approaches to what can be called the "style" of inquiry or dialogue systems, however, are relevant to writers in the next decade. Early projects of this type sought to address precise queries of structured databases (e.g., Woods 1973, 1977). Current interest has shifted to less deterministic approaches for "expert" systems; attention has gone to checking questions for "ill-formed input" (reversed or missing letters, inappropriate punctuation, and so forth).

Another important trend in expert systems is that many programs now explain *how* they interpret a user's question. For instance, Berkeley's UMX CONSULTANT, a set of programs that gives information about its operating system, suggests some of the issues (Wilensky, et al., 1988, pp. 40–42). A typical exchange gives both the answer and an example:

#Can you tell me how to move a file?

Use **mv**.
For example, to move the file named foo to the file named fool, type **'mv foo fool'**.

In the following, the consultant changes from the term *protection* in the question to the precise language of the operating system:

#How do I change the protection of a file?

Use **chmod**.
For example, to remove individual read permission from the file named foo, type **'chmod u-r foo'**.

This program also infers something about the user's experience, and gives more information to the (apparent) novice than to the veteran:

#How can I delete a file?

Use **rm**.
For example, to delete the file named foo, type **'rm foo'**.

or

How can I find out the inode of a file?
Use **ls -i**.

Other dialogue systems give feedback before an inquiry goes to the database. For instance, Davidson and Kaplan's "Natural Language Access to Databases: Interpreting Update Requests" (1983) illustrates a typical approach—the computer side of the dialogue responds to a query with several possible interpretations and the effects of each on the database. The user selects the desired interpretation or tries something else. The idea is valuable: The computer program is not going to be accurate all of the time; decisions that matter should be checked with human beings first. Where teachers of English composition wish to teach and to explain, and not to give students bad advice or suggest that the computer can do a better job than it can, this alternative might be emulated by those who design spell-checking and style-checking programs.

Artificial Intelligence

Artificial Intelligence (AI) projects once seemed at odds with computational linguistics. The former did theoretically based work in syntax, while the latter used complex semantic approaches and virtually ignored syntax. More recently, the two groups have seen their work converging as their systems have tried to deal with similar problems (Wilks, 1982; Schank, 1982). So far, the working computer programs have tended to be restricted to semantic "domains" with a fairly narrow, technical scope such as the scheduling of airplanes. Even within those limits, the links between formal syntax and semantic content help to suggest the complexity involved in style or error analysis of student writing.

AI has typically paid special attention to problems of entire texts—stories, paragraphs, letters. This effort has led to the idea of the scene or frame, a set piece that explains the linguistic, physical-world, and cultural presuppositions that lie behind a text. The classic examples include behavior at birthday parties and ordering food in a restaurant. The CRITIQUE system (formerly EPISTLE) under development at IBM is exploring ways in which a computer might read, understand, and even automatically respond to routine business letters (Miller, 1980; Heidorn, Jensen, Miller, Byrd & Chodorow, 1982; Miller, 1986). Such applications can, however, make for additional difficulties in an educational setting. Composition teachers have long since become suspicious of anything resembling a formula, and they do not relish the prospect of students all coming up with clones of a single letter, essay, or even answers to test questions. Fortunately, such concerns are being addressed. Chapelle (1989), in a series of speculations about how intelligent computer-assisted language learning might look, has been concerned with prewriting interaction that focuses on a particular topic, where the knowledge needed has been represented in a system.

As Chapelle notes, "a precise definition of 'intelligent courseware' has not yet emerged" (p. 59). The same could probably be said for the term *artificial intelligence*. For our purposes, it may not matter. The insights into language analysis that have emerged from AI research, along with some of the fruits of computational linguistics, have, unfortunately, yet to be incorporated into the available software.

Machine-Assisted Translation

Some computer-aided composition seems to be moving in directions that come close to "machine translation" (Slocum, 1985a; see also Slocum, 1985b; Kay, 1982; Wilks, 1973). Slocum is careful to explain that most commercial translation involves two people—a junior translator who prepares a working version and a more highly qualified senior translator who post-edits that version. He notes further that the major ongoing production and research projects use computers only to approximate the job done by the team's junior translator. It is important for teachers of English to recognize that machine translation projects are chiefly for technical texts—artistic translation of literary works has never been their goal.

Slocum also develops a taxonomy that ranges from fully automated machine translation to the presence of a Terminological

Data Bank (i.e., a specialized lexicon for the semantic domain of text being translated). The former is as false an ideal for the translator as it is for our colleagues and deans who occasionally talk about taking the teacher "out of the loop" by coming up with automatic essay grading. The on-line handbook comes closest to a data bank of terms.

More relevant for our purposes is the model of Machine-Assisted Human Translation. In this model, a person interacts with a system to recover information from a dictionary, a thesaurus, or a terminological data bank. The alternative model, Human-Assisted Machine Translation, is not what writers need—it is used in a heavily automated setting to resolve syntactic ambiguities and select the appropriate word sense from a lexicon.

On another dimension of Slocum's taxonomy, the needs of writers come close to those of the "indirect" translation, in which analysis of the source language and synthesis of the target language are separate computer processes. In indirect translation, the "meaning" of a source text is determined independently (for example, by a writer) before any possible replacements or other changes take place. Composition teachers need a "transfer" system, in which a writer decides which changes will preserve the intended meaning, rather than the more complicated procedure that tries to represent meaning in a neutral language (such as propositional calculus). Finally, our current knowledge of English grammar only permits "local-scope" analysis, in which the word is the unit to concentrate on, and the program looks to a few words on either side to figure out parts of speech, idiomatic usage, and word sense. "Global" analysis, in which the computer program tries to determine meaning from the context of the whole sentence or larger chunks of text, is not feasible.

In these senses, goals for a writer's workstation are similar to those needed for a translator's workstation (Melby, 1984). Writers need serviceable output that preserves the source's content and explicitly flags areas where decisions are impossible to arrive at automatically. A nice way to characterize the environment is to see writers as expert post-editors who approve, modify, or reject any suggestions the computer programs come up with. If writers feel a stake in overriding the program, they will both pay attention and learn something about their language and about language in general from the experience.

Writers' Workstations—How Should They Be Designed?

Given the preceding discussion and what our profession knows of computer development trends, we can assume the following about "standard" hardware and system software for the 1990s. The monitor will be something like what is available on an IBM/RT, Sun workstation, NeXT, or Macintosh II. Pointing and clicking with a mouse will be possible. Software design will include pull-down menus. Several concurrent windows will be displayed. Large databases such as dictionaries will be instantaneously available through video disk or a similar technology.

In this context, it may be helpful to outline the main features of the NeXT machine that became available in 1989, chiefly because it should set the standard for stand-alone computers for the early 1990s. For the writer, the NeXT includes full desktop publishing, the WRITENOW word-processing software, a 256-megabyte removable optically read disk with an indexed dictionary and thesaurus, windows for screen management, digital voice recording, a compact-disk-quality stereo sound system, a million-pixel high-resolution screen, and a laser printer. This complete system costs about $7,500. As might be expected, given all of these features, the memory is quite large, and input/output speeds are quite rapid. In addition, the "shell" operating system of this machine includes a graphics-based "interface builder" that has at least the functional capability of the Macintosh HYPERCARD software, a capability that people in computer-aided writing instruction have found to be provocative.

In moving toward and beyond such workstations, writing teachers must begin now to encourage software developers to improve the accuracy and technical efficiency of their products and to teach their students how best to use these tools.

For example, most spell-checking programs now suggest alternatives to a misspelled (or missing) word by opening up a dictionary section or by searching a dictionary by consonants (and treating vowels as wild cards), the standard way for telephone operators to search on-line directories. Some programs use morphological rules to expand the basic entry to include plurals, parts of verbs, and so on. The writer can replace the correct word without having to type it. Whether obvious, high-frequency typographical errors, such as *teh* or *adn* should be changed automatically as soon as the space bar is touched is an open question.

Computer versions of dictionaries and thesauruses are already becoming available. For instance, Microsoft's BOOKSHELF, on a compact disk, read-only memory (CD-ROM), includes these aids, as well as a style manual, usage-checking program, and five other book-length reference sources. (See Tanner & Bane, 1988, for an introduction to this technology.) These physically small devices have space to store thousands of pages of text and to retrieve information selectively quite quickly. The NeXT computer's optical disk includes similar resources. Without a hard disk, as the size and complexity of word-processing programs go up, it will not be possible to include these tools and the word-processing program on one floppy disk or in the computer at the same time. However, the current computer versions of these reference sources simply present the published entries intact on the screen, which means that the student writer still needs to learn how to interpret the complex, abbreviated entries.

We can make better use of the technology in designing dictionaries, thesauri, and style-checking aids for on-line display. Menu options for a dictionary entry, for instance, should include definitions, etymology, idiomatic phrases, synonyms and antonyms, and (perhaps) comparable words in other languages (Melby, 1984). A computer thesaurus should include all entries at the target word's category, with the facility to move up or down one category at a time for other levels of generality. For either resource, it would help to use a mouse to move an alternative into the text.

A proper style-checking program should begin a text analysis by highlighting all the phrases or words in its repertoire. In addition to those elements that are currently flagged in commercial programs, some of those noted in the work by Hull and Smith (1984) and their colleagues (Hull, Ball, Fox, Leven & McCutcheon, 1987) on automatic error identification could be taken into account. The menu could also include (successively) a possible revision of each error and an explanation. With this approach, the passive handbook would be replaced with an active look-up procedure sensitive to context, written in nontechnical language, and backed up with examples and tutorials. Take the typical confusion among *its/it's/its'*. The last example is always a mistake. The student, whether on his or her own or at the teacher's prompting, should be able to point to either of the other choices to get a useful explanation.

In a teaching context, Hull and Smith (1984) argue that it is desirable to postpone the exact location of usage, syntax, or spelling errors. The program Hull and Smith have developed first points to a general area of the text where a problem may exist rather than to a specific word or phrase. The student then tries to find and fix the problem, and is given appropriate commentary on his or her success. Only as a last resort does the program identify the problem and make the correction. This approach emphasizes the student's role in finding and correcting errors or problems in his or her writing. For student writers, the approach postpones full understanding of what the software has to offer. And this fact raises another concern.

Students cannot learn how to navigate a complex, computer-based writing environment without help. In the past, many teachers have tended to avoid some of the issues, for example, by not telling students that a commercial on-line thesaurus existed or by prohibiting its use. As teachers, we may need to decide whether it is more important simply to correct a draft or to teach students something about the linguistic bases of their problems. In the next decade, teachers should strive to include the best tools available as part of the computer-based curriculum, rather than placing artificial barriers between students and the medium's potential. As Wresch (1988a) put it recently, "If students will have ready access to such programs as adults, then it is logical to initiate instruction on their use while students are still in school" (p. 17)).

To illustrate how some of these resources might come together, we can look at a single clause from *Moby-Dick* (Fig. 2). At the top is a concordance of the content words through the first two chapters of the novel. The three levels above Melville's words give analysis of clause structure, the syntactic functions of words and phrases, and each word's grammatical category. Below the clause are various ways of looking at individual words—etymology, pronunciation, some echoes in *Bartlett's Familiar Quotations*, and references to a thesaurus. It is arguable, perhaps likely, that experienced writers and readers have at least a sense of much of

Concordance of content words (with references to Bartlett's Familiar Quotations):

man
- Extracts No. 22
- Ch. 1, Para. 10, Sent. 6
- Ch. 1, Para. 10, Sent. 7
- (in Latin, Civites) which is but an artificial **man**
- The urbane activity with which a **man** receives money
- on no account can a monied **man** enter heaven

universe
- Ch. 2, Para. 6, Sent. 8
- the **universe** is finished; the copestone is in

vast
- Extracts No. 32
- Extracts No. 42
- Extracts No. 53
- Extracts No. 62
- besides a **vast** quantity of oil, did affort 500 weight
- and requires **vast** address and boldness in the fishermen
- Not a mightier whale than this / In the **vast** Atlantic is
- they are propelled before him with **vast** swiftness

First sentence of Chapter 49

(SUBORDINATE) CLAUSE — (It begins with "when")

SUBJECT		PREDICATE	DIRECT OBJECT			PREPOSITIONAL PHRASE				
DET	NOUN	VERB	DET	ADJ	NOUN	PREP	DET	ADJ	ADJ	NOUN
a	man	takes	this	whole	universe	for	a	vast	practical	joke
\ā\	\'man\	\'tāks\	\'this\	\'hōl\	\'yü-nə-vərs\	\'far\	\ā\	\'vast\	\'prak-ti-kəl\	\'jōk\
OE	OE	OE	OE	OE	L	OE		L	Fr	L
ān	man(n)	seize, touch	pes	(ge)hāl	ūniversum	charac-ter of		vastus	practicable	jocus
one	vassal	ON	ON	complete amount; all parts	the whole world			waste, immense	useful, opp. to theory	word-play
			pessi		ūnus + versus					Ger
			sdsi		one + turn					jucks
										joke, spree
		TAKER: catch, hook, bag, sack, pocket, receive, accept		WHOLE: total, gross, entire; complete → intact, perfect, full, absolute, thorough	WORLD: creation, nature, universe; earth, globe, sphere; cosmos			SIZE: huge, immense, enormous, vast, (etc.)	EXPEDIENCE: practical, practicable, effective, pragmatic	ABSURDITY: pun sell, catch, verbal quibble, joke
				in a boundless universe is boundless better, boundless worse		ships of this vast and unwieldy burthen			The capitalist himself is a practical man. There is the greatest practical benefit in making a few failures early in life.	

Figure 2. Illustrating successively, a concordance of the sentence's content words; the sentence itself; syntactic analyses at the clause, function, and category levels; the sentence itself; etymological information; pronunciation key; references to *Bartlett's Familiar Quotations*; and references to *Roget's Thesaurus*.

this information, and that they use part of it each time they work actively with language.

Incidentally, this impossibly crowded page may serve as an example of why advanced writer's workstations are needed to convey a sense of the riches of language to our students. Better workstations would present more information in a better format.

How might these resources help students see ways to improve their writing? Several empirical studies have shown that students tend to fix their writing at the word or sentence level, rather than voluntarily revising or rewriting their drafts (see, for example, Hawisher, 1987, 1988; LeBlanc, 1988; Tiechman & Poris, 1989; Bernhardt, Edwards, & Wojahn, 1989). Depending on the circumstances, even practiced writers may elect to do the same. This finding is expressed with some regret by composition teachers who appreciate the "power" of word processing to make comprehensive revising easier. However, it would be helpful if teachers could use the technology to foster extensive rethinking of a draft, if such revision were warranted and fruitful.

It may turn out that having some of the full text analysis routines discussed herein will help student writers see the need for more extensive revisions. For example, if a concordance or word index is "computed" as the writing moves along, rather than as a separate, two-stage process, instructors could teach students how to use the information more effectively. On the local level, accessing a window on the screen that gives, for highlighted words or phrases, regular morphological variants—such as plurals, passives, and possessives—could help maintain consistent terminology for the technical writer, or warn about dreary repetition for the essayist. By using such retrieval software, the writer should be able to specify a handful of key words and phrases to see where they appear in a document and to gauge whether the themes those words represent are appropriately spread throughout an entire text.

Although concordances are the best current approach to displaying semantic information, it may turn out that some kind of schematic display of syntactic patterns would be even more valuable to the writer. This approach would involve going beyond the lists of set phrases that are in style-checking programs, and looking for more abstractly defined patterns. The HBJ WRITER, for example, uses some of Richard Lanham's dicta about inordinately long series of prepositional phrases as a guide to one kind of revision. Many style-checking programs key off the presence of *to be* verbs as a gross indicator of passive voice.

Here, we must proceed cautiously, however, in our instructional applications. Analyzing syntax at the sentence level is important to some beginning writers, but it must be computed accurately before the writer will trust the system's advice (Thiesmeyer, 1987). Although it is nice to think about being able automatically to spot verb-subject agreement problems, the ambiguity and prevalence of the -*s* ending makes this a hard area to work on.

It is possible already to parse most short sentences and ordinary prepositional or noun phrases accurately. Most phrases are fairly regular and continuous—a determiner (article, pronominal adjective, etc.), perhaps some adjectives, and the noun. However, in English (unlike inflected languages such as French or German), the noun phrase is not the source of many mistakes, so it is hard to know how this analysis would help the beginning writer. Finding a verb helps enormously in figuring out the functions of noun phrases—subjects usually come before the verb, direct and indirect objects come after. Whether it is built into a dictionary or is a separate program, morphological analysis can make the parsing more accurate. In principle, then, the combined tools of morphological analysis and parsing can lead to information that will be between 80% and 90% accurate, depending on the regularity of the student's syntax. As might be feared, sentences with syntactic mistakes are most likely to throw a parser off its course. Given that we will have to accept approximation, it seems fruitful to explore ways, at least in a one-on-one coaching environment, where we can help our most skilled students see the value of such analyses.

In describing these features, we are also describing a working environment for writers in the next decade—not an automated editing or proofreading environment, but one that depends on human judgment. Technically, we can bring lexical, syntactic, and content tools to bear on a text as it develops. Each word and sentence can have attached to it a wealth of information in several dimensions, levels, or layers. Real language works by putting these analytical levels together so that the reader makes sense of the composite—i.e., the levels interact. The central point in outlining current trends is to emphasize partnerships in the workstations of the 1990s. They must be designed to expect peoples' active participation in the computer environments they use.

It has become a commonplace to observe that, despite the word-processing program's technical power to aid revision, students do not always leap at the prospect of using these packages. The emerging technology of the "writer's workstation" is also out of phase with our current tutoring and teaching approaches. It seems that teaching effective ways to revise, no matter what technology is involved, will continue to challenge instructors. The same dilemma will hold true as reference materials and other kinds of information move off the shelf and directly onto the visual desktop.

Questions

To affect the design and implementation of new writers' environments in the 1990s, teachers of English composition must do a great deal of thinking and analysis. Among the many questions they must address are the following:

- How do experienced writers work? For over two centuries, we have seen studies, often autobiographies, about the working conditions of famous poets, novelists, and playwrights. More recently, sociologists have observed the working habits of scientific teams (Latour & Woolgar 1979, Gilbert & Mulkay 1984), with special emphasis on the writers' collaboration and social interaction. We have also had a few case studies of how students put texts together, some involving extensive interviews, keystroke or videotape description, and analysis of the minute-by-minute production of characters. Ordinary people, both within and outside the academy, have physical, social, and psychological "corners" where they write. This chapter has discussed the resources an ordinary writer puts together to make the job flow smoothly—especially those resources that can be brought together in a computer.

- Will computer screens with many windows change our model
  of the writing process? If so, how? It has been a hope of many
  in computational linguistics that the properly programmed
  computer can be a testing ground for linguistic theories and
  claims. Word-processing programs, when coupled with
  invention software and style-checking programs, have suggested a linear model of composing. The effect has been
  refreshing, because both the pedagogy and the research that
  computers have encouraged have been process oriented. (A
  contrary approach, which concentrates on the high quality of
  the computer's printed product, has not had a strong impact
  on the research community, although it strongly informs
  television advertisements for all sorts of computers.)

- How can we set up computer hardware and software to help
  writers? In the late 1970s, researchers at the Xerox Palo Alto
  Research Center and IBM Yorktown Heights conducted some
  influential work in the general areas of the ergonomics of
  hardware, screen design, and software engineering (Card,
  1978; Card, 1982; Card, Moran, & Newell, 1980; Gould, 1980;
  Gould, 1981). The PARC studies led to the "mouse" pointing
  device, pull-down menus, and other more subtle features
  that have set industry standards in the past five years. More
  recently, Haas and Hayes (1986) have shown that the color
  and size of the typical computer screen may make it hard for
  students to find typographical and spelling errors. For all we
  know, features of our computer systems are unconsciously
  replicating the disaster of the QWERTY keyboard, which was
  consciously designed to slow typists down.

- Will linguistically sophisticated style-analysis programs make a
  difference in anyone's writing? If such programs become at
  least as reliable and as easy to use as good spelling checkers,
  will experienced writers, teachers, or students use them
  regularly?

- Alternatively, experienced writers work with their own internal style monitors, their intuitive sense of the boundaries
  on sentence length and complexity, vocabulary repetition,
  and so on. Could teachers work with their students to
  develop individualized versions of such programs, and would

students care to maintain them over the years as new stylistic problems replace the older ones?

- Assuming that software developers build tools that analyze the raw data from machine dictionaries, thesauri, and the like, can we effectively show students how to use them? Experienced writers know the value of information such as a word's etymology or its pronunciation; how can we transmit this knowledge to the younger writer?

- Economically and politically, with more sophisticated and useful software tools, how do we ensure that they are available on even the cheapest computer, and that students in all school districts and colleges or universities can learn to use them throughout their writing careers?

While some of this research may already be going on in industry, the reports are not widely circulated. Furthermore, we should remember that earlier research on writing aids was designed to meet the needs of the then-profitable customers of the computer industry: programmers and secretaries. The culture of users has changed, and this means the range of choices in current and future hardware and software should be opening up. Conducting ergonomic research is outside the pale of the writing researcher who has neither corporate sponsorship nor access to prototype designs. The difficulty is further compounded by the need to involve colleagues from such disparate fields as mechanical engineering, cognitive and behavioral psychology, and computer science. Despite these problems, whether working directly with computer companies or indirectly through other kinds of research, we should make some efforts to change and improve the next writers' environments that come from Silicon Valley, Japan, or Europe.

References

Allen, J. (1977). Synthesis of speech from unrestricted text. In A. Zampolli (Ed.), *Linguistic structures processing* (pp. 239–252). Amsterdam: North Holland.

Barker, T. (1983). Using computers in technical writing: A progress report on adapting GRAMMATIK to support composition teaching. *Proceedings of the Texas Popular Culture Association.* Lubbock: Texas Tech University Press.

Bernhardt, S. A., Edwards, P., & Wojahn, P. (1989) Teaching college composition with computers: A program evaluation study. *Written Communication, 6,* 108–133.

Berry, E. (1989). Speech synthesizers as aids to revision. *Computers and Composition, 6(3),* 81–92.

Boivin, L., & Bratley, P. (1985). *FATRAS: A full-text retrieval system.* [Computer program.] Montréal: Université de Montréal.

Bowyer, J. W. (1989). A comparative study of three writing analysis programs. *Literary and Linguistic Computing, 4(2),* 90–98.

Burton, D. (1982). Automated concordances and word-indexes: Machine decisions and editorial revision. *Computers and the Humanities, 16(4),* 195–218.

Card, S. K. (1978). *Studies in the psychology of computer text editing systems.* [SSL-78-1.] Palo Alto, CA: Xerox Palo Alto Research Center.

Card, S. K. (1982). User perception mechanisms in the search of computer command menus. In T. P. Moran (Ed.), *Eight short papers in user psycholog* (pp. 225–231). Palo Alto, CA: Xerox Palo Alto Research Center.

Card, S. K., Moran, T. P., & Newell, A. (1980). Computer text-editing: An information-processing analysis of a routine cognitive skill. *Cognitive Psychology, 12,* 32–74.

Chapelle, C. (1989). Using intelligent computer-assisted language learning. *Computers and the Humanities, 23,* 59–70.

Cherry, L. (1981). Computer aids for writers. *Proceedings of the ACM SIGPLAN, 16(6),* 61–67.

Cherry, L., & Vesterman, W. (1980). *Writing tools—The STYLE and DICTION programs.* Murray Hill, NJ: Bell Laboratories Technical Report.

Cohen, M., & Lanham, R. (1984). HOMER: Teaching style with a micro-computer. In W. Wresch (Ed.), *The computer in composition instruction: A writer's tool* (pp. 83–90). Urbana, IL: National Council of Teachers of English.

Davidson, J., & Kaplan, S. J. (1983). Natural language access to databases: Interpreting update requests. *American Journal of Computational Linguistics, 9,* 57–68.

Dobrin, D.N. (1987). Some ideas about idea processors. In L. Gerrard (Ed.) *Writing at century's end* (pp. 95–107). New York: Random House.

Dobrin, D.N. (in press). A new grammar checker. *Computers and the Humanities.*

Feldman, P. R., & Norman, B. (1987). *The wordsworthy computer: Classroom and research applications in language and literature.* New York: Random House.

Garvey, J. J., & Lindstrom, D. (1989). Pros' prose meets WRITER'S WORKBENCH: Analysis of typical models for first-year writing courses. *Computers and Composition, 6,* 81–109.

Gilbert, C. N., & Mulkay, M. (1984). *Opening Pandora's box: A sociological analysis of scientists' discourse.* Cambridge: Cambridge University Press.

Gould, J. D. (1980). Experiments on composing letters: Some facts, some myths, and some observations. In L. W. Gregg & E. R. Steinberg (Eds.), *Cognitive processes in writing* (pp. 97–127). Hillsdale, NJ: Lawrence Erlbaum.

Gould, J. D. (1981). Composing letters with computer-based text editors. *Human Factors, 23,* 593–606.

Haas, C., & Hayes, J. R. (1986). What did I just say? Reading problems in writing with the machine. *Research in the Teaching of English , 20,* 22–35.

Harris, M. D. (1985). *Introduction to natural language processing.* Reston, VA: Reston Publishing.

Hawisher, G. E. (1987). The effects of word processing on the revision strategies of college freshmen. *Research in the Teaching of English, 21,* 145–59.

Hawisher, G. E. (1988). Research update: Writing and word processing. *Computers and Composition, 5,* 7–28.

Heidorn, G. E., Jensen, K., Miller, L. A., Byrd, R. J., & Chodorow, M. S. (1982). The EPISTLE text-critiquing system. *IBM Systems Journal, 21,* 305–326.

Hull, G. A., Ball, C., Fox, J. L., Levin, L., & McCutchen, D.(1987). Computer detection of errors in natural language texts: Some research on pattern matching. *Computers and the Humanities, 21,* 103–118.

Hull, G. A., & Smith, W. L, (1985). Error correction and computing. In J. L. Collins & E. A. Sommers (Eds.), *Writing on-line: Using computers in the teaching of writing* (pp. 89–104). Upper Montclair, NJ: Boynton/ Cook.

Kay, M. (1977). Morphological and syntactic analysis. In A. Zampolli (Ed.), *Linguistic structures processing* (pp. 131–234). Amsterdam: North Holland.

Kay, M. (1982). Machine translation. *American Journal of Computational Linguistics, 8(2),* 74-78.

Kiefer, K., & Smith, C. R. (1984). Improving students' revising and editing: The WRITER'S WORKBENCH system. In W. Wresch (Ed.), *The computer in composition instruction: A writer's tool* (pp. 65–82). Urbana, IL: National Council of Teachers of English.

Latour, B., & Woolgar, S. (1979). *Laboratory life: The social construction of scientific facts.* Beverly Hills, CA: Sage.

LeBlanc, P. (1988). How to get the words just right: A reappraisal of word processing and revision. *Computers and Composition, 5,* 29–42.

Lees, E. O. (1987). Text-to-voice synthesis: What we can learn by asking writers to proofread with their ears. In L. Gerrard (Ed.), *Writing at century's end: Essays on computer-assisted composition* (pp. 45–54). New York: Random House.

Macdonald, N. H., Frase, L. T., Gingrich, P. S., & Keenan, S. A. (1982). THE WRITER'S WORKBENCH: Computer aids for text analysis. *IEEE Transactions on Communications, 30,* 105–110.

McIlroy, M. D. (1982). Development of a spelling list. *IEEE Transactions on Communications, 30,* 91–99.

Melby, A.K. (1984). Recipe for a translator work station. *Multilingua, 3-4,* 225–228.

Miller, L. A. (1980). Project EPISTLE: A system for the automatic analysis of business correspondence. In *Proceedings of the First Annual National Conference on Artificial Intelligence.* Stanford, CA.

Miller, L. A. (1986). Computers for composition: A stage model approach to helping. *Visible Language, 20,* 188–218.

Mortenson, T. (1988). Writing style/readability checkers to add to word processing. *Computer-Assisted Composition Journal, 2*(2), 66–70.

Nix, R. (1981). Experience with a space efficient way to store a dictionary. *Communications of the ACM, 24*(5), 297–299.

Pedersen, E. L. (1989). The effectiveness of WRITER'S WORKBENCH and MACPROOF. *Computer-Assisted Composition Journal, 3*(3), 92–100.

Peek, G. S., Eubanks, T., May, C., & Heil, P. (1989). The efficacy of syntax checkers on the quality of accounting students' writing. *Computers and Composition, 6,* 47–62.

Peterson, J. L. (1980). Computer programs for detecting and correcting spelling errors. *Communications of the ACM, 23,* 676–687.

Ross, D. (1985). Realities of computer analysis of compositions. In J. L. Collins & E. A. Sommers (Eds.), *Writing on-line: Using computers in the teaching of writing* (pp. 105–113). Upper Montclair, NJ: Boynton/Cook.

Ross, D., & Rasche, R. H. (1972). EYEBALL: A computer program for description of style. *Computers and the Humanities, 6,* 213–221.

Schank, R. C. (1982). Representing meaning: An artificial intelligence perspective. In S. Allen (Ed.), *Text processing: Text analysis and generation, text typology and attribution* (pp. 25–63). Stockholm: Almqvist & Wiksell.

Slocum, J. (1985a). A survey of machine translation: Its history, current status, and future prospects. [Introduction to two special issues on machine translation.] *Computational Linguistics, 11*(1), 1–17.

Slocum, J. (1985b). Machine translation. *Computers and the Humanities, 19,* 109–116.

Tanner, D. F., & Bane, R. K. (August, 1988). CD-ROM: A new technology with promise for education. *T.H.E. Journal, 16,* 57–62.

Teichman, M., & Poris, M. (1989). Initial effects of word processing on writing quality and writing anxiety of freshman writers. *Computers and the Humanities, 23,* 93–103.

Thiesmeyer, J. E. (1987). Expert systems, artificial intelligence, and the teaching of writing. In L. Gerrard (Ed.), *Writing at century's end: Essays on computer-assisted composition* (pp. 108–115). New York: Random House.

Thury, E. M. (1987). TOOLS FOR WRITERS [Computer program]. Santa Barbara, CA: Kinko's Academic Courseware Exchange.

Von Blum, R., & Cohen, M. E. (1984). WANDAH: Writing-aid AND author's helper. In W. Wresch (Ed.), *The computer in composition instruction: A writer's tool* (pp. 154–173). Urbana, IL: National Ccouncil of Teachers of English.

Wilensky, R., Chin, D. N., Luria, M., Martin, J., Mayfield, J., &.Wu, D. (1988). The Berkeley UMX consultant project. *Computational Linguistics, 14*(4), 35–84.

Wilks, Y. (1973). An artificial intelligence approach to machine translation. In R. C. Schank and K. M. Colby (Eds.) *Computer models of thought and language* (pp. 114–151). San Francisco: W. H. Freeman.

Wilks, Y. (1982). Discussion of Roger C. Schank's paper. In S. Allen (Ed.), *Text processing: Text analysis and generation, text typology and attribution* (pp. 65–74). Stockholm: Almqvist & Wiskell.

Wobbe, R.A. (1987). PC-TEXT ANALYSIS TOOLBOX [Computer program]. Institute, WV: West Virginia College of Graduate Studies.

Woods, W. A. (1973). An experimental parsing system for transition network grammars. In R. Rustin (Ed.) *Natural language processing* (pp. 111–154). New York: Algorithmics Press.

Woods, W. A. (1977). Lunar rocks in natural English: Explorations in natural language question answering. In A. Zampolli (Ed.), *Linguistic structures processing* (pp. 512–570). Amsterdam: North Holland.

WORDCRUNCHER (1987). [Computer program]. Provo, UT: Electronic Text Corp.

Wresch, W. (April, 1988a). Six directions for computer analysis of student writing. *The Computing Teacher,* pp. 13–17.

Wresch, W. (1988b). WRITER'S HELPER II [Computer program]. Iowa City: CONDUIT.

Part Two

Classroom Contexts: The Changing Responsibilities of Students and Teachers

Introduction

Instead of rejecting technology, humanists could grasp the
opportunity to make it multiply the good and wondrous in
man. If the output of . . . computers is frightening and
inhumane, to a large extent the fault is ours.

—Ellen W. Nold,
"Fear and Trembling: The Humanist
Approaches the Computer"

A great deal of controversy has accompanied the introduction
of computers into writing classes. Such titles as Ellen Nold's "Fear
and Trembling: A Humanist Approaches the Computer," from
1975, or Helen Schwartz's "Monsters and Mentors: Computer
Applications for Humanistic Education," from 1982, begin to
capture the trepidation and misgivings with which English teachers
greeted electronic technology ten years ago. Computers, even the
"micro" versions, evoked sweaty palms and heart palpitations.
Yet these attitudes changed rapidly. Almost as quickly as microcomputers spread through schools and universities, English
teachers became enthusiasts of computers in writing classes. In
fact, many became such strong advocates that there was danger of
computers being perceived as a panacea for the ills that ailed
writing instruction. Today we realize that neither unquestioning
condemnation nor wholesale acceptance is an appropriate response to computer technology. Often the classroom behavior of
both students and teachers seems to change when computers are
introduced, but we must examine these changes critically so that
we can plan for optimum learning in our writing classes.

Certainly the one change that writing instructors most often talk
about when they discuss computer-supported classrooms is a
shift toward increased participation and collaboration among
students and teachers. Electronic environments often seem to

113

engender new cooperative ventures in which teaching and learning are shared by instructors and students; in such environments traditional notions of teaching are altered. Instead of instructors primarily "instructing," they become collaborators within a group of learners. The new cooperative electronic classroom that instructors describe fits into a theory of teaching in which we understand knowledge as socially constructed.

Why do some instructors come to regard their writing classes so differently with the introduction of technology? The question is an interesting one. When computers were first used in English classrooms, writing teachers had to give up the title of classroom "expert," previously awarded by divine right of tradition, because the majority of instructors were simply not expert enough to "work" the machines. In doing so, however, many teachers noticed a serendipitous effect: giving up one kind of power often generated power from other sources; some teachers found themselves becoming more open to student ideas, student expertise, and student-centered change. Thus, the use of computers acted as a catalyst, instituting changes within our classes by subtly altering the relationship between students and teachers, and among the students themselves. However, these positive changes do not occur automatically.

In part 2, the authors examine the implications of these changes, and with them, the shifting responsibilities of students and teachers. Kate Kiefer, in chapter 5, looks at the relationship between the changing nature of electronic writing and the training of teachers for electronic environments. She argues persuasively that teachers must be prepared for teaching electronic writing across the curriculum in ways that emphasize writing as learning. In chapter 6, Elizabeth Klem and Charles Moran continue the focus on teachers, but in the context of developing new instructional strategies better suited to the electronic environment. By reviewing current research on computer writers and readers, as well as their reactions to heuristic programs, style analyzers, and networked environments, Klem and Moran demonstrate what we have learned in the past ten years. This background knowledge can, in turn, lead us to additional questions whose answers help inform our instructional choices. In chapter 7, Andrea Herrmann turns to questions regarding the evaluation of students and their writing in electronic environments. If writing in electronic classroom contexts is fundamentally different from traditional environments, she asks, shouldn't we change our assessment procedures to include some measure of students' ability to use hardware and software to their own ends?

By emphasizing the changing contexts of teaching, these three chapters prepare us for the next section, in which hypertexts— texts formed within an entirely new instructional medium—are introduced and discussed.

References

Nold, Ellen W. (1975). Fear and trembling: The humanist approaches the computer. *College Composition and Communication, 26,* 269–273.

Schwartz, H. (1982). Monsters and mentors: Computer applications for humanistic education. *College English, 44,* 141–152.

Chapter 5

Computers and Teacher Education in the 1990s and Beyond

Kathleen Kiefer
Colorado State University

As we see that computers fundamentally change writing, and as we recognize the dominant role that writing assumes in the critical thinking that goes on in all disciplines, we must revise the teacher-education curriculum to reflect the importance of the computer for writers. Imagining an electronic writing medium to enhance critical thinking across the curriculum raises practical, pedagogical, and theoretical questions, foremost of which is the appropriate role of the "writing" coach within such an electronic medium and how teachers can best accommodate all their students as writers and thinkers.

In the last twenty years, much has changed in training teachers of writing. Most obvious, teachers and researchers have become convinced of the importance of teaching writing as a process, and because of this, we see an emphasis on writing activities unheard of in most classrooms in the sixties. Students now spend class time writing and engaging in peer critiques; teachers spend class time prewriting with their students and intervening in students' writing processes more often and more profitably than simply correcting surface errors, as they so often did in the past. Surely, this revolution in thinking about writing and writing instruction did not happen easily or quickly. (Some teachers and administrators lament that it has not happened universally even yet.) But it would not have happened at all if the teacher-education curriculum had not focused on writing as process and how to teach such processes.

117

We are facing another revolution in teacher education, not so much because of another major shift in our understanding of writing but because of a new medium for writing. The computer is for some writers no more than a transcription tool: like a pen, pencil, or typewriter, the computer simply lets a writer encode ideas as text. But for other writers, the computer is far more than a transcription tool: the computer helps them generate ideas and text, move text quickly and easily, and revise substantially. As teachers exploit the potential of the computer as a writing tool and as a tutorial medium, the computer can become a window into the writing processes of students learning critical thinking skills and the discourse conventions of various academic and nonacademic writing communities.

Along with the introduction of the computer as a composing tool, teachers in all disciplines are rediscovering the importance of writing as a tool for learning. Moreover, English teachers are re-asserting their crucial role in helping students learn critical thinking skills through reading and writing. According to the NCTE Commission on the English Curriculum,

> Because thinking and language are closely linked, teachers of English have always held that one of their main duties is to teach students *how* to think. Thinking skills, involved in the study of all disciplines, are inherent in the reading, writing, speaking, listening, and observing involved in the study of English. The ability to analyze, classify, compare, formulate hypotheses, make inferences, and draw conclusions is essential to the reasoning processes of all adults. The capacity to solve problems, both rationally and intuitively, is a way to help students cope successfully with the experience of learning within the school setting and outside. (1979)

English teachers are not uniquely qualified to teach critical thinking through reading and writing; we are, however, identified as those teachers having primary responsibility for teaching reading and writing, and hence, critical thinking as it relates to the language arts.

For this reason, English teachers especially have heeded the call to approach reading and writing as crucially important to developing critical thinking. In fact, NCTE in cooperation with ERIC has begun publishing the Monographs on Teaching Critical

Thinking series to foster greater awareness of the various approaches to teaching critical thinking, not simply through analytic argument or attention to logic but also through various inquiry methods and, of course, a wide variety of reading and writing activities. (See, especially, Siegel & Carey, 1989, but also Golub, 1986.)

At the same time, the writing-across-the-curriculum movement is gathering momentum as a viable means of fostering critical thinking in all disciplines. Langer and Applebee (1987) note in *How Writing Shapes Thinking: A Study of Teaching and Learning* that

> Subject-area writing can be used productively in three primary ways: (1) to gain relevant knowledge and experience in preparing for new activities; (2) to review and consolidate what is known or has been learned; and (3) to reformulate and extend ideas and experiences. Our analyses of the students' papers and their self-reports indicated that writing used to reformulate and extend knowledge led to more complex reasoning. (p. 136)

As research continues, and as teachers refine their goals for writing in all classrooms, writing teachers especially need to be open to new ways of using all the tools at hand. The computer creates a unique medium for both writing across the curriculum and critical thinking, if we prepare ourselves to view it as such.

Training Programs and Issues of the 1980s

As teachers have reflected on using computers in the classroom, many have shared their experiences and teaching ideas (see, for instance, Arms, 1983; Bean, 1983; Bullock, 1984; Rodrigues & Rodrigues, 1986; and Holdstein, 1989; among others). By and large, however, teachers have addressed local issues (How do I get all of my students onto the two PC's in the corner? What invention heuristics will work well in this context? How can I get more out of a spell-checking program? a sentence-combining program?) or immediate concerns (Why aren't there good programs to help me with X? When will a word-processing program make it easier to do Y for writers?). However, some excellent, more broadly based teacher-preparation advice emerges from articles that address inservice training, especially in two recent collections.

The first collection, a special issue of *English in Texas* (Burns, 1987), contains short articles that explain how to use certain kinds of software in the composition classroom. The second collection, *Computers in English and Language Arts: The Challenge of Teacher Education* (Selfe, Rodrigues, & Oates, 1989), covers teacher education for computers and composition from elementary school through college years. The first section of this NCTE publication looks at model teacher-education programs, and the second focuses on specific ingredients in most teacher-education programs: setting up a program, creating activities with a word processor, prewriting with computers, networking, using databases, and evaluating training programs. We can extrapolate from the existing model programs several key issues that will be crucial for training teachers in the 1990s:

- Teachers and administrators must *choose* to develop computer/writing links in their classrooms and schools.

- The computer must be a focus for *writing*, not for drill or preprogrammed exercises.

- The best teacher-education programs are based on observations and research conducted in classrooms, that is, on the successful practices of teachers.

But even though the contributors to these collections address some key elements of inservice training, they assume that teaching composition is best managed by training English teachers to deal with the computer in a relatively traditional classroom or lab setting. We must go beyond conventional thinking regarding teaching and computers if we are to prepare our students and ourselves for the challenges of the 1990s, both in setting up the electronic writing context and in broadening that writing to enhance critical thinking across the curriculum.

We cannot rethink our teacher-education programs to address the computer's potential in teaching critical thinking without questioning the model of the traditional classroom. Yet, local concerns often deflect our attention from the larger issue of what constitutes the best (and also the most fundamental) teacher-education program for writing teachers in an electronic setting. Typically, teachers and teacher trainers have had to deal with the immediate problem of using the technology that is currently available. In many public and postsecondary schools, the proliferation of computers has outpaced any organized or clearly articulated plans for integrating the technology into the curriculum. Teachers, thus, have had to fall back on their own resources to integrate computer hardware and software imaginatively into what they already do. Moreover, just as teachers feel that they have achieved one level of integration, they are faced with new technology—video projection devices, hypertext software, long-distance and local-area networks, desktop publishing—and they must again rely on their own creativity and time to incorporate electronic writing into classroom activities.

More important, many teachers and most administrators assume that the computer is simply a transcription tool, one that does not necessarily change the teaching and learning environment critically and significantly except in matters of logistics. (Indeed, at many institutions, students are not permitted into a word-processing lab until they have a draft in hand.) As I argue below, this focus on the computer as a transcription device, although often unarticulated, represents a fundamental assumption about computers that must be changed if we are to help teachers make full use of the computer's potential in writing instruction.

The Computer as a Transcription Tool

For those writers and teachers who see the computer as simply a high-tech transcription device, any proposal that places the computer apart from other transcription tools will seem misguided. This device, some writers and teachers contend, simply allows writers to capture words, in the same ways that quills, pens, pencils, and typewriters capture words, and even in ways similar to stenographers or dictating machines. The tool, the argument continues, need not become the object of particular attention, or else we probably ought to train teachers how to have students use pencils most productively. Surely, some educators argue, teachers can exercise their common sense about whatever tools students use to transcribe their ideas onto paper. Many teachers feel that the computer is simply an expensive gadget that should well go the way of overhead projectors—nice to have around when needed but not to be used every day because computers take so much time to work with.

This view of the computer ultimately limits its usefulness to teachers and writers in academic settings. If the computer is seen as no more than an alternative transcription tool, then it be integrated in only limited ways within teaching and writing contexts. To see how the computer can change our notion of teaching writing, we need to take a radical leap of faith. We need to re-envision all of our comfortable, accepted notions of what we can effectively do when we teach writing. Please join me in a dream vision of a "writing class" of the 1990s.

The Computer as Writing/Teaching Medium

In 1995, some of us will pick up our rosters for the sections of "first-year composition" we are teaching that term. Ten students are registered in each section. (Total teaching load for the term is twenty students if the teacher is assigned two sections.) We might glance quickly at each roster to see which courses students are taking in conjunction with composition, for no longer is composition a course students take by itself. For example, the teacher might find that several students are taking philosophy courses, two students are taking history courses, three students are taking business courses, and the rest of the students are scattered through biology, animal science, engineering, and mathematics courses. We glance at the names of the teachers of these courses and realize that we know almost all of them from having worked in the cross-curricular writing project for several years now.

We head to our offices and check our electronic mail. We find the writing assignments from a number of our colleagues who will share students and students' writing instruction with us this semester. We may send notes quickly to the remaining instructors asking them to send us their plans for the term. Some of us may also ask each instructor to give students our e-mail addresses, our office addresses, and our office hours for this week so that students can come by to meet their instructors.

By the end of a typical day, only three students have dropped by their instructor's office to chat in person, but the others have all checked in by e-mail to make appointments for later in the week. We may ask each student to write a number of short "electronic journal" entries—some entries exclusively for the student's instructor and some to share with the students' peer critique groups that most instructors will set up during the first day.

From the end of the first day until the end of the term, we could spend as many hours with our twenty students as we did with the fifty students we used to meet in regular "classes" in the 1980s. But we read far more of their work in progress, and we spend much more of our time together talking and writing about their individual needs as students and writers.

We can do this because almost all of the students' writing is available to us through the computer. Students can work on computers in their dorms, in labs around campus, in the library, in the cafeteria. Many students carry portable computers to classrooms that do not have computers or terminals. As they think about their classes, students write. And as they think about their writing, they share their questions, concerns, victories, and roadblocks with their instructors by way of e-mail. Some of us may read journal entries addressed to us, journal entries addressed to peer critique groups, prewriting, drafts, revision commentary from peers and cooperating teachers, and final drafts on the screen in our offices. We may see each student at least once a week (even for a two-minute excuse such as "I just don't have time to talk about my paper right now") to remind students about the personality behind the computer commentary. Because we know exactly what problems each student is encountering, we can suggest specific remedies or problem-solving strategies, many of which will be electronic—searching databases, checking with electronic peer groups for advice, soliciting advice on electronic bulletin boards, and so on.

But Is This Teaching?

The dream vision above represents just one model of teaching by way of the computer, and I can envision several others—in classrooms filled with computers, for instance, or teaching over long-distance networks. But these visions all require far more individualized and group work on computers than we now generally have time for with students, and far more on-line intervention in the writing process as we watch papers taking shape over successive drafts.

No, I concede that this is not teaching according to the classroom model most of us are accustomed to, but teachers who have fostered individualized critical thinking through a variety of inquiry methods have often met with similar criticism. Using a computer as a writing/teaching medium is the least teacher-centered form of teaching I can imagine. But it is certainly teaching in the tutorial mode, and it finally fulfills the promise of the computer in the 1960s to revolutionize teaching to match the needs of the learner.

Can't We Just Continue What We're Doing Now?

Right now the teacher-education curriculum is reasonably effective, given certain assumptions about what writing teachers should do. We train English teachers (new graduate teaching assistants teaching first-year composition at the university, prospective secondary-school teachers completing their certification programs, and current teachers in the secondary schools) to stand in front of groups of twenty to twenty-five students and keep them reasonably attentive to activities that will help them write. We stress that teacher-centered activities, such as lecturing, are minimally effective, and that group activities should nudge students from being passive listeners to being active speakers, listeners, readers, and writers (Lloyd-Jones & Lunsford, 1989.) We show teachers a variety of tasks they can have groups and individual writers work on, and we ask the teachers to generate still others. We ask them to practice all the writing activities that they are learning about by having them work through several writing tasks of their own. And we mention that most of these activities can be done on a computer. When we are lucky enough to have a little extra time, we show the teachers the computer activities.

At my university, students in all teacher-certification programs are required to take one course that introduces them to PC's (how to format disks, how to connect to printers, how to review software, and even how to do some basic programming), but that course does not focus on instructional techniques, especially those for teaching writing.

Some universities are beginning to offer courses devoted to linking computers and composition instruction (see Barton & Ray, 1989). Unfortunately, my school offers this course at the graduate level, so it is inaccessible to undergraduates in teacher-certification programs. Still other schools offer special workshops for teachers interested in filling the gaps between computers and composition. But these courses and workshops reach only a small percentage of the English teachers in training and in place. If we add teachers in all disciplines who participate in writing-across-the-curriculum programs, then we are touching even fewer who need to know how to transform computers into a writing/thinking medium.

The traditional teacher-education curriculum guarantees that only the most innovative teachers—or perhaps the most bored— will ever move beyond seeing the computer as a transcription tool, the occasional locus of writing, rather than as the spark for critical thinking and writing and the medium for learning and teaching that it can become. Teacher education must refocus its energies to equip all teachers with the theory and practice of writing as learning (Emig, 1977; Nystrand, 1977; Irmscher, 1979; Griffin, 1982; Parker & Goodkin, 1987; and Spellmeyer, 1989; among others) and include in those practices not just our current writing-across-the-curriculum pedagogy but a full understanding of how an electronic writing medium enhances each learner's growth in writing and thinking. In short, as we see that computers fundamentally change writing, and as writing assumes a more dominant role in critical thinking in all disciplines, we must revise the teacher-education curriculum to reflect the importance of the computer for writers and thinkers.

What Do We Need to Do?

Thus, just as we need to radically re-envision our accepted notions of how to teach writing, we need to radically alter our teacher preparation.

On the theoretical level:

- We need to inculcate not just the notion of a writing process but the infinite variety of writing processes that a writer uses when faced with different writing tasks.

- We need to enrich our notions of intervening in writing without taking over the authority of the writer; my vision of the future crumbles if the writers are not absolutely committed to their own writing.

- We need to address reading and writing as critical thinking skills to see how better to integrate all the activities that enhance students' growth through school.

- We need to broaden our concepts of reading skills to include the special tasks related to reading text on computer screens. Teachers will need training in visual literacy to "see" a text as it appears on the screen (see Haas & Hayes, 1986; Haas, 1989; Selfe, 1989).

And we need to think through and begin the process of answering the following questions through research and scholarly projects.

- If we can understand some of what writers do in electronic settings, can we tap the potential of the computer as a research tool to test new theoretical constructs in writing? (See Collins & Gentner, 1987.) Shouldn't we train teachers to become researchers in their own "electronic" classrooms?

- If students are writing more about their classwork in all disciplines, how much will teachers need to know about critical thinking skills? (See Langer & Applebee, 1987.)

- What is the most appropriate role for the writing teacher (coach? arbiter? one of several critics?) who cooperates with a disciplinary teacher in the tutorial mode of teaching writing outlined above? How do we train teachers to adapt to different roles in different institutional settings?

- What is the appropriate role of the writing teacher in other models of teaching writing in electronic settings? How much training (and of what sorts) will teachers need to deal with students they never meet except through long-distance networks? Will cross-cultural issues become more central to our teaching concerns, and how do we prepare teachers for students from different linguistic and cultural backgrounds? (See Hull, 1984.)

- What must we teach teachers about discourse conventions that will help them move students more easily into various discourse communities, both academic and nonacademic?

- What kinds of writing activities best promote critical thinking in different content areas? How can a "writing teacher" cooperate with a content instructor to foster those critical thinking/writing activities? (See Siegel & Carey, 1989.)

- How will any of the academic writing activities impinge on writing that students will eventually do in nonacademic settings? Can we use electronic networks to introduce students to nonacademic peer groups while they are still in school? Should we prepare all teachers for this kind of teaching?

On the pedagogical level, we need still other elements added to a training curriculum to guarantee that the computer becomes a medium of writing instruction:

- Teachers must write on the computer to discover for themselves which word-processing techniques can affect different elements of the writing process and which ones clearly make paper preparation easier.

- Teachers must use e-mail to communicate to their peers and supervisors so that they learn the advantages and disadvantages of these kinds of electronic communications.

- Teachers must participate in electronic peer-critique groups to see how this commentary affects the teacher as another critic via e-mail or in person.

Several other questions follow from the above:

- How can we most effectively train teachers to look beyond local concerns to ask questions about computers and writing that reflect more basic issues of critical writing and thinking?

- How can we accommodate those teachers and students who are not yet able to use the computer as any kind of writing tool, i.e., for transcription or composing? (See Selfe, 1985; Hull, 1988.)

- How do the differing levels of formality affect writers who use only e-mail to address peers and writing coaches but write formal "papers" to address other academic audiences? How can teachers prepare themselves to deal with the paralinguistic elements of electronic writing?

- Should writers in peer-critique groups have the option to do any of their work in face-to-face sessions? What are the implications then for long-distance networks for peer critiquing?

- What special skills will teachers need to motivate writers to take advantage of an "electronic writing coach," a role unfamiliar to many teachers and most students?

- How do we best train teachers to teach collaboration with peer groups of writers who never meet one another face-to-face?

On the practical level, the most pressing questions do not focus on training issues because we can develop models and settings to train teachers. But the practical questions that we must answer are perhaps the most daunting:

- How can we convince administrators to pay for the time such writing instruction will take?

- How can we convince parents that writing instruction is most effective when it does not isolate elements of grammar for direct instruction?

- How can we assure that teachers across the curriculum agree with our positions on the necessity of linking writing with thinking in every academic endeavor from math to physical education?

If we expect to answer these questions, we must begin to work now on the practical issues, but we cannot ignore the theoretical and pedagogical ones. Administrators and parents will be convinced of the efficacy of the computer as a reading/writing/thinking medium only as teachers in all disciplines insist that it be used that way. If we continue to accept the computer only to place it in labs or classrooms that still depend on traditional models, we will be trapped into using the computer as a traditional transcription tool rather than as a tutorial medium with rich potential for individualized development of reading, writing, and thinking skills. Our colleagues in other departments will accept our premises about writing and critical thinking only after we work more closely with them and their students to build on the first efforts of the writing-across-the-curriculum movement. As a profession, teachers need to lobby for the time and financial support to work with students and colleagues on writing that students care about and on methods that teach students to write critically. And we will not reach these goals until teachers in all disciplines understand their roles as writing teachers in the electronic settings of the 1990s.

References

Arms, V. (1983). Creating and recreating. *College Composition and Communication, 24,* 355–58.

Barton, E., & Ray, R. (1989). Developing connections: Computers and literacy. *Computers and Composition, 6*(3), 35–46.

Bean, J. (1983). Computerized word-processing as an aid to revision. *College Composition and Communication, 34,* 146–148.

Bullock, R. (1984, April). The lure of the cursor, the fear of the byte: Affective responses to word processors [Special issue]. *Computers and Composition.*

Burns, H. (Ed.). (1987, Fall). [Special issue]. *English in Texas, 19*(1).

Collins, A., & Gentner, D. (1980). A framework for a cognitive theory of writing. In L. W. Gregg & E. R. Steinberg (Eds.), *Cognitive processes in writing* (pp. 51–72). Hillsdale, NJ: Lawrence Erlbaum.

Commission on the English Curriculum. (1979). *Essentials of English: A document for reflection and dialogue.* Urbana, IL: National Council of Teachers of English.

Emig, J. (1977). Writing as a mode of learning. *College Composition and Communication, 28,* 122–128.

Golub, J., and the Committee on Classroom Practices. (1986). *Activities to promote critical thinking.* Urbana, IL: National Council of Teachers of English.

Griffin, C. W. (Ed.). (1982). *Teaching Writing in All Disciplines.* San Francisco: Josey-Bass.

Haas, C. (1989). "Seeing it on the screen isn't really seeing it": Computer writers' reading problems. In G. Hawisher & C. Selfe (Eds.), *Critical perspectives on computers and composition instruction* (pp. 16–29). New York: Teachers College Press.

Haas, C., & Hayes, J.R. (1986). What did I just say? Reading problems in writing with the machine. *Research in the Teaching of English, 20*(1), 22–35.

Holdstein, D. (1989). Training college teachers for computers and writing. In G. Hawisher & C. Selfe (Eds.), *Critical perspectives on computers and composition instruction* (pp. 126–139). New York: Teachers College Press.

Hull, G. A. (1988). Literacy, technology, and the underprepared: Notes toward a framework for action. *The Quarterly of the National Writing Project and the Center for the Study of Writing, 10*(3), 1–3, 16.

Irmscher, W. (1979). Writing as a way of learning and developing. *College Composition and Communication, 30,* 240–241.

Langer, J.A., & Applebee, A.N. (1987). *How writing shapes thinking: A study of teaching and learning.* Urbana, IL: National Council of Teachers of English.

Lloyd-Jones, R., & Lunsford, A. (Eds.). (1989). *The coalition conference: Democracy through language.* Urbana, IL: National Council of Teachers of English.

Neilsen, A. R. (1989). Critical thinking and reading: Empowering learners to think and act. (Report No. 2 in Monographs on teaching critical thinking series). Urbana, IL: ERIC/RCS and the National Council of Teachers of English.

Nystrand, M. (Ed.). (1977). *Language as a way of knowing: A book of readings.* Toronto: Ontario Institute for Studies in Education.

Parker, R. P., & Goodkin, V. (1987). *The consequences of writing: Enhancing learning in the disciplines.* Upper Montclair, NJ: Boynton/Cook.

Rodrigues, D., & Rodrigues, R. (1986). *Writing with a word processor.* Urbana, IL: National Council of Teachers of English.

Selfe, C. (1985). The electronic pen: Computers and the composing process. In J.L. Collins & E.A. Sommers (Eds.), *Writing on-line: Using computers in the teaching of writing* (pp. 55–66). Upper Montclair, NJ: Boynton/Cook.

Selfe, C. (1989). Redefining literacy: The multilayered grammars of computers. In G. Hawisher & C. Selfe (Eds.), *Critical perspectives on computers and composition instruction* (pp. 3–15). New York: Teachers College Press.

Selfe, C., Rodrigues, D., & Oates, W. (1989). *Computers in English and language arts: The challenge of teacher education.* Urbana, IL: National Council of Teachers of English.

Siegel, J., & Carey, R. F. (1989). Critical thinking: A semiotic perspective (Report No. 1 in Monographs on teaching critical thinking series). Urbana, IL: National Council of Teachers of English.

Spellmeyer, K. (1989). A common ground: The essay in the academy. *College English, 51,* 262–276.

Chapter 6

Computers and Instructional Strategies in the Teaching of Writing

Elizabeth Klem and Charles Moran
University of Massachusetts

Research strongly suggests that writing on-line is different from writing with pen and paper. If this is the case, our teaching needs to take account of the difference. How should we teach our students in this new text environment? Existing research has some answers for us. But we are now in a time of rapid technological change, and we are ourselves, moreover, in an amphibious stage, operating as we do partly in print, partly on-screen. Despite the rate of change, and despite the fact that we seem poised between two worlds, we need to discover instructional strategies that will help us cope with the students, and the text environment, we now have.

Overview of Topic and Importance of Area

As our writing students increasingly gain access to computers, they become, to some degree, different students. How can we teach these new writing students? What instructional strategies are best suited to student writers working in this new writing environment? What guidance can the research of the past decade offer us as we attempt to discover how best to teach writing in the 1990s? Should we argue for, and expend our scarce resources on, computer-equipped classrooms? And, if so, how should we best teach in these facilities? Should we argue for public-access, computer-equipped writing labs? And how should our computer classrooms, or computer-writing labs, be equipped? Should we make style-checkers and heuristic programs available in these facilities? Should we install networked writing classrooms, and, if so, what is the best use we can make, as teachers of writing, of these new environments? And, if we teach, as most of us do, in conventional, non-computer-equipped classrooms, how can we best take account in our teaching of the fact that some of our students are composing, outside of class, in the new medium?

As we have read through the research in our field, we have tried to keep before us a realistic vision of the writing teacher in the 1990s. We know that most teachers do not now teach in up-to-date computer environments, and national priorities are such that this situation is likely to continue. As authors of this chapter, we'd like nothing better than to engage in unfettered future-think—imagine that we will all have access to hypertext or multimedia environments—and on the basis of this presumed techno-paradise generate a research agenda that would lead us to the appropriate instructional strategies for such an environment. But we know that while computers are arriving on campuses at an increasing rate, most schools, colleges, and universities do not supply sufficient technological resources for teachers or access for all of their students. In our secondary schools we still see "computer writing labs" in which there are four Apple IIgs computers for twenty-five students—none of whom has an Apple available at home. In our colleges and universities, only those students who can afford computers have them—and postsecondary writing teachers in research universities, chiefly poorly paid teaching assistants or part-time lecturers, are even less likely than their students to have access to the new technology. It is the writing teacher, often a low-status, marginalized worker, who is being asked to cope with this confusing and difficult situation.

Because we have kept this "real" writing teacher in our minds as we thought through the materials of this chapter, we have not given our millenial impulse free rein. We do not, however, want to be seen as neo-Luddites. It is clear to us that the computer as a writing tool is here to stay. Writers who have composed on computers seldom turn back. In addition, the computer holds the promise—elusive as this promise may now seem—of benefits to writers who have been marginalized. To these writers, who have perhaps failed in traditional classrooms, the computer presents a chance for a new beginning. In addition, a networked computer environment may encourage previously unheard voices to enter the discussion and, thus, may be a force for democracy.

Overview of Research

In this section, we review the research now available to us; and, as we can, we make the inferential leap from research findings to their implications for the design of instructional strategies appropriate to the teaching of writing in the 1990s. We need to say that we include under the banner of "research" here both carefully controlled studies and the narratives of teachers who are doing pioneer work in bringing new technologies into their teaching. We do this because we give equal weight to both kinds of report. There is value, certainly, in the well-funded research study. There is also value in the "report from the field," particularly when this report comes from a teacher who has thought long and hard about the implications of the new teaching environment.

For ease of analysis and reading, we have divided the research in the field into five categories: research on writers as they compose on computers, on writers as they read screen-text, on the effects of heuristic programs, on the effects of style-analysis software, and on the effects of networked computer environments. As we describe the research, we will lay out the implications we see in this research for the development of instructional strategies for the 1990s.

Writers Writing the New Text

The most important research in this category suggests that the computer, used as a word-processing tool, alters the nature of text itself and therefore alters the ways in which we write and read this new text. Researchers observe that the word-processing screen presents the writer with a different and perhaps liberating context in which to write. Moving beyond Diaute's (1983) observation that word processing relieves constraints on the writer, Marcus (1984) finds that "seeing words dance around a screen . . . generates quite a different sense of the risk involved" (p. 122) in any writing done on a computer. He argues that users "no longer feel their words are 'carved in stone' " (p.122) and sees this freedom as the primary benefit of the new medium. He describes a screen-specific kind of freewriting—"invisible writing"—in which the writer can "turn off" the editor-in-the-head simply by turning down the contrast on the screen. The impact of the new flexibility is seen as a definite asset by Catano (1985), who finds that in computer-writing, composing and revising take place together as the writer shapes the "fluid text," thus affirming in a new way Berthoff's (1984) observation that "revision is not a stage of composition but a dimension"(p. 95).

If the computer-as-word-processing-tool has changed the text and changed its relationship to the writer, then we, as writing teachers, must pay attention. The notion of "draft," which has always been a bit artificial, may be more difficult to sustain in the world of "fluid text." The word *draft* carries with it the sense of "draw," of the pen or pencil making semipermanent lines on paper. The keyboard is tactile, but not graphic: the computer translates a keystroke into a graphic symbol composed of temporarily illuminated phosphor dots. When the students in our computer-equipped classrooms balk at submitting "drafts," are they being lazy? Or are they responding more directly than we do to an aspect of the new text environment?

If the draft *is* an aspect of pen-and-paper composing, then it would be unlikely that we would learn much about students' writing on computers from looking at their drafts—and this has indeed been the case. A significant body of research has been driven by the question "Do students revise more, or less, when using word-processing packages on computers than they do when using pencil-and-paper methods?" To discover the signs of revision, researchers have compared students' drafts in the two modes. Early research argued that student writers would revise more rapidly and easily in the new text environment than they had in the old one (Bean, 1983; Daiute, 1983; Sudol, 1985). Subsequent research suggested that student writers did less revising on-screen than they would have on paper (Collier, 1983; Daiute, 1986; Harris, 1985; Hawisher, 1987). This finding is supported by Lutz's (1987) study of the revising/editing behaviors of professional and experienced writers and by Case's (1985) survey of university faculty.

Often, however, the new text has been presented to students, and handled by the researchers, as if it were the old text. Pufahl (1984) and Curtis (1988) argue that the Harris (1985) and Collier (1983) studies presented the computer to the writers as a fancy typewriter and, thus, discouraged the large-scale revising that the researchers were trying to measure. LeBlanc (1988) notes that Daiute (1986) and Harris (1985) measured changes between the mid-process and the final *drafts* of texts, overlooking much of the early writing. Hawisher's study (1987) also compares fixed drafts and thus, does not discover, as she says, "point-of-utterance shaping and composing'(p. 158).

If we, as teachers, still need to see drafts for our own purposes—to track a student writer's progress, for example, or to measure the quantity and quality of a writer's work, or to make plagiarism more difficult—then we'll have to require drafts in computer environments with a force heretofore unnecessary. Moreover, because many, if not most, of the changes that writers make in their work will not be visible in the new-text drafts—partly because the changes will have been made on-screen and not recorded on the draft, and partly because the printed draft does not have the crossings-out and marginal scribbling of the handwritten draft—we may need to develop new ways of tracking a writer's progress. We may be able to track and analyze students' keystrokes in the ways suggested by Smith, Rooks, and Ferguson (1989) in their description of the WE (WRITING ENVIRONMENT); or we may want to ask students themselves to tell us, in writing, about the changes and choices they have made as they composed their text.

If we choose to adapt wholly to the new-text environment, we may want to discover instructional strategies that do not involve the submission of a series of drafts. Certainly, we'll want to develop ways of "teaching" composing, ways of enabling students to use the fluidity of the new text to their advantage. These might include emphasizing the block-move functions of a word-processing program, or developing open-ended, short quick-write or free-write writing tasks and factoring them, unedited, into the semester's work.

Writers Reading the New Text

Writers are also readers; they read their own text and, on the basis of this reading, compose, revise, and edit. If the computer and word-processing package presents a new text to the writer, this new "reading" will have implications for the ways in which we teach writers working in the new medium. Haas and Hayes (1986) and Haas (1989b) have found that students working on-screen report less "text-sense." They do not see their whole text as easily in this new medium; they report feeling "lost." To get a global sense of the text, students needed to print their work and see it on paper. Almost certainly related to the screen-reading problem is Haas's (1989a) recent finding that writers using word-processing programs on computers plan less than do writers working with pen and paper only, and that more of the planning writers do on-screen is "sequential planning," or word-and-sentence-level planning that occurs close to the point of utterance. With computers, writers also do less "conceptual planning," by which Haas means the making of plans that "guide the creation of the conceptual meaning and structure of the text" (p. 194). Haas's findings resonate with earlier research that suggests that the word-processing medium draws the writer's attention to the "planning" of smaller units of the text (Collier, 1983).

It may be that we, and our students, need to learn more or better strategies for reading screen-text. For example, word-processing programs offer a "page-down" function, one that moves the text down three lines less than one screen. When the writer positions the cursor at the beginning of the third line from the top of the screen, the cursor becomes a marker for the first word on the next "page," thereby making it possible for the screen-reader's eye to move from screen-page to screen-page without a dislocating search for the beginning of the new text. Perhaps word-processing programs should be considered reading programs as well and should provide text markers independent of the cursor that will facilitate screen-reading. Until they do, as teachers we can "teach" our students to read on-screen, using techniques now available and encouraging our students to discover their own.

We know that many professional writers, and journalists in particular, write and edit on screen all day, seldom turning to paper. These writers do seem to be able to "see" their work adequately on-screen. We wonder if the difficulty that student writers now report with screen-text springs from the fact that they work with print-text most of the time and, therefore, have not yet developed the strategies they need to work comfortably with screen-text.

Moreover, student writers compose on-screen, but their work will be read, in almost every instance, in print. We need to be aware that the difference in medium may present rhetorical as well as conceptual complexity that calls for changes in our instructional strategies. As the text approaches publication, does the writer begin to "become" the reader and to read like a print-reader? And is this reader-based perspective more difficult to assume when the writer writes on-screen?

Perhaps until most text is read on-screen, some alternation between screen and paper will have to be managed (Bureau, 1989). It may be that we should teach students to compose on-screen but, as they approach print publication, teach them to bring their screens closer and closer to the 8.5 × 11 double-spaced, black-on-white format in which their work will be read. They can manage this either by printing their text or by using the page-view or printer-display functions of some word-processing programs. When large-screen monitors become less expensive and more widespread, we'll be able to encourage students who need to "see" their pages to move to these monitors at the appropriate point in their composing process.

The Computer as an Aid to Invention

The computer has long been seen as a tool that might facilitate and augment a writer's strategies for invention (Burns & Culp, 1980). There is a widespread sense that invention programs have unrealized potential (Burns, 1984; Rodrigues & Rodrigues, 1984; Spitzer, 1989). Research in this area is chiefly descriptive and anecdotal, as in Schwartz's account (1984) of her work with SEEN. Writers working with invention programs demonstrably produce "ideas," but does this rich mixture somehow find its way to a draft? And are invention strategies best presented via computer? Strickland (1987) has compared the results of invention strategies presented through computers with the results of the same strategies presented in conventional classrooms. He has found no difference either in the quality of writing or in the quantity of ideas generated. Yet he wonders, citing Diane Langston (1986), whether his results are the consequence of "an application of an old paradigm (paper-based invention heuristics) to the new technology (computers)" (p. 18). It seems to us that computer-assisted invention has exposed a problem inherent in the "old paradigm": the separation of writing into stages or steps in a process, and in particular, the separation of "invention" and "writing." Most invention programs now readily available—programs such as MINDWRITER or PRE-WRITE—are stand-alone programs. With these programs, the writer produces a pre-text which then, in some world beyond the program, becomes a draft.

If we accept these stand-alone invention programs, we may want to think of other ways of using them. Perhaps they'd be useful *after* the student has written? Or in mid-process, when the student's own strategies have reached their limit?

An alternative to such programs is a complex and expensive writing environment, with multiple windows that permit the writer to move easily from text to heuristic to text and back again in a seamless, recursive set of moves. Given fiscal reality, only a few sites will be equipped to handle such an environment in the near future, and these sites will be the locus of research in the design of writing environments (see Ross in this collection).

What we'll not want to do, current research suggests, is to stock our labs or networks with a range of invention programs and ask our student writers to choose what works for them (Rodrigues & Rodriques, 1984). This strategy places an enormous burden on both teachers and students. Teachers must know each program thoroughly—an investment of time and energy required, as we previously noted, of those who are already overworked and underpaid. The students, according to this model, must learn several programs as well and, having given each a fair trial, must be able to decide which will be most useful at particular points in their composing. Is student writing-time best spent learning how to operate and use a range of invention software? Or could the students' time be better spent writing and re-writing? We are reminded of Moffett's (1968) argument against textbooks, in which he consigns to the fires eternal all "indirect" methods of writing instruction (p. 204).

The Computer as Proofreader

Most powerful word-processing programs have become mini-writing environments, including in their range the ability to check the spelling of words in the writer's text against a list of "good" words. Designers of spell-checking programs find themselves on the horns of a dilemma: if the program checks your text against a massive word list, it will miss many wrong-word errors; if the program checks your text against a short word list, it will flag many perfectly good words. Existing programs do not "read" the text, and it is not likely that programs that parse will be widely available in the next decade. Writing students will therefore need to "learn" to use spell-checking programs. This learning will include learning to proofread after the spell-checking for wrong-word errors and learning to resist the tendency to remove all flagged words and to restrict one's vocabulary to that of the spell-checking program (see Ross in this collection).

We have not found any research on student writers' use of spell-checkers, but we have found a large body of research on text-analysis programs—a fact that surprises us because the programs seem pedagogically retrograde: both limited in application and focused upon the clean, well-proofread print-text. The attraction of these programs may be explained by considering that word-processing originated in industry as a computer tool for typing in, correcting, and formatting a document (Bridwell, Nancarrow, & Ross, 1984). The programs may appeal to us because our history makes us focus on errors we make in our use of the King's English. Or perhaps they play into our generation's New Critical training, which produces in us a natural affinity for a machine that can decontextualize discourse and quantify its surface features.

Research in this particular corner of our field divides neatly into two camps: some see the style-checking program as a teacher's and writer's aid, and others see the style-checking program as inaccurate and therefore confusing to the student writer. Kiefer and Smith (1983) suggest that "textual analysis with computers intrigues college writers and speeds learning of editing skills by offering immediate, reliable, and consistent attention to surface features of their prose" (p. 201). In a later piece, Kiefer, Reid, and Smith (1989) sound a more cautious note: the teacher must be careful, they warn, to make sure that the analysis is suited to the writing's genre, to its rhetorical context, and to the needs of the individual writer who is using the program.

Dobrin (1986) believes text-analysis programs are expensive distractions. He points out that the value of the information given by the programs depends on the way in which the user interprets and evaluates the information. He argues that "people who can evaluate the output correctly are the people who don't need the programs in the first place" (p. 23). Collins (1989) matched teachers' perceptions of error with the possible errors flagged by text-analysis programs. His findings are disturbing: excluding the spell-checking function of these programs, the "accuracy rates for finding the same errors as teachers would be 6% for MILLIKEN, 5% for SENSIBLE, and 2% for CONDUIT" (p. 34). Not only, as Dobrin had suggested earlier, can these programs become a second authority in the classroom, but they will generally disagree with the teacher, creating a confusing situation for the student writer.

Some teacher/researchers have gone to extraordinary lengths to make use of text-analysis programs in their writing courses (Smye, 1988). Others have developed what seem to us to be curious arguments for the potential value of quantitative, statistical information on one's own, and on others', writing (Garvey & Lindstrom, 1989). At this moment, however, text-analysis programs seem more likely to confuse than to help most student writers. It seems therefore unlikely that these programs will be widely used in our writing classes, unless we want to prepare our writers for the style-checking programs they may face in their places of employment.

The Networked Writing Classroom

Networks are just now becoming affordable and manageable, so there is little research that bears on the instructional strategies we should adopt in a networked teaching/writing environment. Nor is there evidence that the benefits of a networked writing classroom will outweigh the costs of such an installation, given the level of technical expertise and support that network management requires. Clearly the networked writing room is a wonderful place for research and an exciting place to teach, but an institution considering the installation of networked writing classrooms would need to understand that such a facility requires considerable institutional investment—not only equipment and technical support, but the staff-development time necessary to learn how to use the network in the service of the teachers' pedagogical goals.

Those who focus on the benefits to be gained from a networked writing classroom generally stress the interactive learning that this arrangement can provide. A networked writing classroom enhances the social, collaborative atmosphere that exists even in classes with stand-alone workstations (Gerrard, 1989; Sudol, 1985; Weiss, 1989). With the arrival of relatively inexpensive networking hardware and software, and with the design of "chat" or "CB" software that permits almost-real-time on-line discussions, we can now engage our students in on-line writing sessions that are dialectical and social. Batson (1989) argues that with a "CB"— Citizen's Band—system, "students and teacher can free-write together, throwing their ideas into a common 'pot'" (p. 251). The network's potential for collective, collaborative work carries with it a potential shift in the locus of power and control. As teachers open up the network to their students, they inevitably turn over some of their authority to these same students. This loss of control can be troubling to the teacher, yet both Batson (1989) and Kremers (1988) recommend that the teacher welcome, not resist, this redistribution of power.

Networks make possible electronic mail (e-mail), which has recently received some attention, partly for its potential as a heuristic device—a new kind of discovery channel for the exchanging of ideas—but also as the new kind of communication form it seems to be. Forman (1987) has examined the use of e-mail in a small corporation and finds it useful for all phases of the writing process—from the initial discussion of ideas through the final distribution of reports. Kinkead (1987) looks at e-mail in a classroom setting and finds it "intrinsically motivating," adding that it "provides a new way of communicating," perhaps more akin to a phone conversation than a letter (p. 341). She has found that, for peer work, "students seem to be able to take more risks in this type of conference than in the face-to-face model" (p. 339) because the written form of their comments encourages students to explain themselves more thoroughly and to become distanced readers.

New Directions for Research

Research gives us the information we need to develop instructional strategies that we may then use to achieve our instructional goals. The research agenda that we see for work in computers and composition during the next decade will blend naturalistic, ethnographic research with the ability of the computer, as a research tool, to count and to remember. The goals of such research will be to discover how writers write in the new medium, how teachers teach in the new medium, and how the computer has entered, and inevitably altered, the system that includes the writer, the text, and the teacher of writing. The trick in this research will be to find research questions that transcend software and hardware boundaries and that, therefore, continue to be useful as the technology evolves.

We list below a range of research questions that we need to begin to explore if we are to find the guidance we need in developing instructional strategies for our writing classrooms in the 1990s and beyond. We note that the focus of most of the research questions that follow is on *students* as they write on computers. This is because our students are not us. They are a different generation, one with a different relationship than ours to computers and to print-text. We may not be able to extrapolate usefully from our own writing/reading experience to theirs. At the least, we must observe our students, ask them questions, and listen to their answers. They will be, perforce, our co-researchers in this venture.

We begin with questions that will fill gaps we have discovered in our review of existing research:

- How do students navigate the "fluid text"? How do they compose in the new medium? And do differing composing procedures produce results that differ in kind? In quality?

- How do students go about reading text on-screen? Are there ways of reading screen-text that seem better than others?

- How do professional writers who work entirely with screen-text adapt to the new medium? Learn to see the text whole? Engage in large-scale planning?

- When students work with invention programs, does the use of a particular heuristic seem to be limited to the context of the program? Or are the questions/prompts to some degree internalized by the student writer? Transferred to other writing tasks, whether on-screen or off?

- How do student writers manage selection and movement of the "useful" material generated with the invention program into their drafts?

- Are there students who benefit from the use of style-checking software? If so, who are they? And what do they perceive these benefits to be? Do their perceptions square with their teachers' perceptions?

- To what extent does the presence of text-analysis software on a system disempower student writers? Or empower them? Do the program's norms become an Orwellian authority? Or do these norms become something like a video game—rules that the writer accepts for the time being but does not generalize.

- Does the norm set by the style-checking program change the students' perceptions of the teacher's role? Of the teacher's authority?

- Does peer interaction on a network differ in its content and character from spoken peer interaction in a conventional classroom?

- What effect does the use of "chat" using a real-time or synchronous conversation program have on the writing of a group of student writers? Can such an environment function as a heuristic?

- In real-time conversations on networks, who writes? Who is silent? Who feels empowered? Who disempowered? What conventions evolve among the participants in such conversations?

- How does the teacher adapt to the change in authority in a networked computer environment?

We conclude with what we think are the most important questions: those that have to do with students', and teachers', equitable access to the new technology.

- Does a student who spends some time writing on a computer, but more time writing with pencil and paper, derive important benefits from working on the computer? Is there transfer of learned skills from one text-environment to the other? Or is the student confused by the need to work both with print-text and with screen-text and perhaps, therefore, disadvantaged?

- Does a student who spends a semester in a computer-writing classroom, and who has little or no access to computers thereafter, gain or lose by the experience? What transfer is made between the computer environment and non-computer environments?

- What is the writing experience of students likely to be after they have left their school/college? To what extent, and in what ways, is computer-writing likely to be useful outside of the academy?

- Does the writing teacher who does not have access to a personal computer at home utilize the school's computers differently from the teacher who does have a personal computer at home?

- Do teachers who have access to personal computers teach their writing students differently, even in conventional classrooms?

- What is the typical "cost" to the teacher, in terms of time spent learning the system, of teaching in a computerized writing environment? And what are the perceived benefits?

If writing is really changing, and there seems to be general agreement that it is changing, then developing and testing new instructional strategies is work that writing teachers need to undertake. Yet teachers, schools, and students are, in that order, least likely to have access to new technology. As we wrote this chapter, this fact held in check our pedagogical imagination. Access, it seems to us, is the issue that drives all before it. Who has access, and to what? As teachers and researchers, we will have to come to grips with this mixed situation, where some students have full access, and some do not—and where those who have access work with different kinds of hardware and software. Discovering how best to teach in this changing and confused environment is our principal instructional challenge for the 1990s.

References

Batson, T. (1989). Teaching in networked classrooms. In C. L. Selfe, D. Rodrigues, & W. R. Oates (Eds.), *Computers in English and the language arts* (pp. 247–255). Urbana, IL: National Council of Teachers of English.

Bean, J. C. (1983). Computerized word-processing as an aid to revision. *College Composition and Communication, 34*, 146–148.

Berthoff, A. (1984). Response to Richard Gebhardt. *College Composition and Communication, 35*, 95.

Bridwell, L. S., Nancarrow, P. R., & Ross, D. (1984). The writing process and the writing machine: Current research on word processors relevant to the teaching of composition. In R. Beach & L. S. Bridwell (Eds.), *New directions in composition research* (pp. 381–398). New York: Guilford Press.

Bureau, W. E. (1989). Computers: Catalysts for change at Springfield High School. In C. L. Selfe, D. Rodrigues, & W. R. Oates (Eds.), *Computers in English and the language arts* (pp. 97–110). Urbana, IL: National Council of Teachers of English.

Burns, H. L. (1984). Challenge for computer-assisted rhetoric. *Computers and the Humanities, 18*, 173–81.

Burns, H. L., & Culp, G. H. (1980). Stimulating invention in English composition through computer-assisted instruction. *Educational Technology, 20*, 5–10.

Case, D. (1985). Processing professional words: Personal computers and the writing habits of university professors. *College Composition and Communication, 36*, 317–322.

Catano, J. V. (1985). Computer-based writing: Navigating the fluid text. *College Composition and Communication, 36*, 309–315.

Collier, R. M. (1983). The word processor and revision strategies. *College Composition and Communication, 34*, 149–155.

Collins, J. L. (1989). Computerized text analysis and the teaching of writing. In G. E. Hawisher & C. L. Selfe (Eds.), *Critical perspectives on computers and composition instruction* (pp. 30–43). New York: Teachers College Press.

Curtis, M. S. (1988). Windows on composing: Teaching revision on word processors. *College Composition and Communication, 39*, 337–344.

Daiute, C. A. (1983). The computer as stylus and audience. *College Composition and Communication, 34*, 134–145.

Daiute, C. A. (1986). Physical and cognitive factors in revising: Insights from studies with computers. *Research in the Teaching of English, 20*, 141–159.

Dobrin, D. (1986). Style analyzers once more. *Computers and Composition, 3*(3), 22–32.

Forman, J. (1987). Computer-mediated group writing in the workplace. *Computers and Composition, 5*(1), 19–30.

Garvey, J. J., & Lindstrom, D. H. (1989). Pros' Prose meets WRITER'S WORKBENCH: Analysis of typical models for first-year writing courses. *Computers and Composition, 6*(2), 81–109.

Gerrard, L. (1989). Computers and basic writers: A critical view. In G. E. Hawisher & C. L. Selfe (Eds.), *Critical perspectives on computers and composition instruction* (pp. 94–108). New York: Teachers College Press.

Haas, C. (1989a). How the writing medium shapes the writing process: Effects of word processing on planning. *Research in the Teaching of English, 23*, 181–207.

Haas, C. (1989b). "Seeing it on the screen isn't really seeing it": Computer writers' reading problems. In G. E. Hawisher & C. L. Selfe (Eds.), *Critical perspectives on computers and composition instruction* (pp. 16–29). New York: Teachers College Press.

Haas, C., & Hayes, J. R. (1986). What did I just say? Reading problems in writing with the machine. *Research in the Teaching of English, 20*, 22–35.

Harris, J. (1985). Student writers and word processing: A preliminary evaluation. *College Composition and Communication, 36*, 323–330.

Hawisher, G. E. (1987). The effects of word processing on the revision strategies of college freshmen. *Research in the Teaching of English, 21*, 145–159.

Kiefer, K. E., Reid, S. D., & Smith, C. R. (1989). Style analysis programs: Teachers using the tools. In C. L. Selfe, D. Rodrigues, & W. R. Oates (Eds.), *Computers in English and the language arts* (pp. 213–225). Urbana, IL: National Council of Teachers of English.

Kiefer, K. E., & Smith, C. R. (1983). Textual analysis with computers: Tests of Bell Laboratories' computer software. *Research in the Teaching of English, 17*, 201–214.

Kinkead, J. (1987). Computer conversations: E-mail and writing instruction. *College Composition and Communication, 38*, 337-341.

Kremers, M. (1988). Adam Sherman Hill meets ENFI: An inquiry and a retrospective. *Computers and Composition, 5*(3), 69–77.

Langston, M. D. (1986, March). *New paradigms for computer aids to invention.* Paper presented at the annual convention of the Conference on College Composition and Communication, New Orleans.

LeBlanc, P. (1988). How to get the words just right. *Computers and Composition, 5*(3), 29–42.

Lutz, J. A. (1987). A study of professional and experienced writers revising and editing at the computer and with pen and paper. *Research in the Teaching of English, 21*, 398–421.

Marcus, S. (1984). Real-time gadgets with feedback: Special effects in computer-assisted instruction. In W. Wresch (Ed.), *The computer in composition instruction: A writer's tool* (pp. 120–130). Urbana, IL: National Council of Teachers of English.

Moffett, J. (1968). *Teaching the universe of discourse.* New York: Houghton Mifflin.

Pufahl, J. (1984). Response to Richard M. Collier. *College Composition and Communication, 35,* 91–93.

Rodrigues, R. J., & Rodrigues, D. W. (1984). Computer-based invention: Its place and potential. *College Composition and Communication, 35,* 78–87.

Schwartz, H. (1984). Teaching writing with computer aids. *College English, 46*(3), 239–247.

Smith, J., Rooks, M. C., & Ferguson, G. J. (1989). *A cognitive grammar for writing. Version 1.0. TextLab Report.* Chapel Hill, NC: University of North Carolina.

Smye, R. (1988). Style and usage software. *Computers and Composition, 6*(1), 47–61.

Spitzer, M. (1989). Incorporating prewriting software into the writing program. In C. L. Selfe, D. W. Rodrigues, & W. R. Oates (Eds.), *Computers in English and the language arts* (pp. 205–212). Urbana, IL: National Council of Teachers of English.

Strickland, J. (1987). Computers, invention, and the power to change student writing. *Computers and Composition, 4*(2), 7–26.

Sudol, R. A. (1985). Applied word processing: Notes on authority, responsibility, and revision in a workshop model. *College Composition and Communication, 36,* 331–335.

Weiss, T. (1989). A process of composing with computers. *Computers and Composition, 6*(2), 45–59.

Chapter 7

Evaluating Computer-Supported Writing

Andrea W. Herrmann
University of Arkansas at Little Rock

As electronic technology for writing changes, the process and products of composition are also changing. A new literacy is emerging that includes more visual forms of writing and more on-line, interactive texts. Teachers of writing must make adjustments to appropriately evaluate students' performance as writers. Do our assessment procedures reflect how well students are learning the technology, how effectively they are acquiring the latest literacy skills, and how able they are to work and communicate within the changing context of the writing classroom? Specifically, what aspects of students' technological expertise are we evaluating and how do we evaluate it? Are we developing new standards for assessing written products that also reflect the increasingly social, collaborative, and interactive nature of writing within our computer-supported classrooms?

Professionals who teach writing in computer classrooms recognize that the content of writing courses has changed since precomputer days. We teachers continue to teach writing, but because we believe the computer is an important composing tool, we also provide instruction: this means helping students learn to use a word-processing program. Many of us also use other software in the writing classroom: spell-checking programs, thesauruses, text-analyzing programs, hypertext programs, and desktop publishing. Thus, as the use of computers continues to make inroads in educational settings, we have become teachers of technology as well as of writing.

As this chapter argues, word processing and other computer programs for writing are changing the process of writing, the type of writing produced, and our conception of written communication. Perhaps more unsettling, these matters are subject to continual change because of technological advances. Computer-assisted writing, thus, changes the nature of the composition classroom, including the social context within which writing is taught and learned, the teacher's expectations, and the students' performances. The use of computers, therefore, requires new ways of evaluating writers and writing.

How writing is best evaluated has become a thorny question among composition specialists. This is true partially because teachers have embraced the complexities of teaching writing as a process and have rejected the traditional role of teacher as simple evaluator of written products. As writing teachers change their pedagogical strategies, they reexamine traditional notions of writing evaluation, too. No longer content to leave the assessment of writing abilities in the hands of agencies administering one-time writing tests, teachers increasingly prefer to evaluate multiple drafts and pieces of student writing created over time. The confusing issue of assessment becomes even more complex with the introduction of electronic technology, because the tool, the writing context, and the nature of the writing change.

This chapter first looks at some of the critical issues involved in evaluating writers and writing in computers and composition classrooms. An overview of computers and writing research follows. Then the argument is made that classroom evaluation should be responsive to evidence that a new literacy is emerging and that computers are changing the nature of classroom contexts. Teachers need to assess students' technological competence in handling their computer tools and to create new criteria for evaluating students' written products. Finally, the chapter poses questions related to teaching and assessing electronic writing that our profession should strive to answer in the 1990s.

Classroom Teachers' Concerns with Evaluation

Most reports concerning the issue of evaluation center on analyses of students' written products: on the one hand, there are the large-scale tests, often limited to ascertaining whether a student has attained a minimum level of competence in writing; on the other hand, there are classroom teachers' concerns over evaluation. These concerns reach beyond minimum competency issues and are our focus here.

Through their assessments of student writers, teachers attempt to discern whether students are learning what they have been taught. Classroom evaluations help teachers decide when and how to change their instructional strategies. The failure of large-scale tests of writing to address the needs of teachers has spurred composition specialists to focus increasingly on the relationship between teacher evaluation and writing instruction. (For research on classroom-based evaluation of writing, see Brossel & Ash, 1984; Evans, 1985; Fagan, Cooper, & Jensen, 1975; Ruth & Murphy, 1984; Stibbs, 1981; and Ziv, 1984.) Of particular note is the seminal research by Nancy Sommers (1982) concerning the nature and importance of teachers' written comments on students' papers.

There is a growing number of composition specialists investigating the social context of teaching and learning to write within natural settings, including the classroom (see, for example, Calkins, 1983; Graves, 1975; Perl & Wilson, 1986; Heath, 1983). Understanding students as writers within communities is important to teachers no longer satisfied with simply assigning and grading writing, but intent on helping students successfully negotiate the entire writing process. Such research, along with insights from composition teachers and theorists, has contributed to changes in how writing teachers evaluate students' writing.

Instead of relying on tests of writing or final drafts, many teachers now evaluate students during the act of writing by observing and interacting with them in workshop settings, reading/assessing their multiple drafts and semester-long portfolios, and employing various other devices that allow close-up views of individual students' writing processes and progress.

Unfortunately, while writing teachers and researchers in the field of composition have become increasingly involved with the question of writing assessment, computers and composition specialists have virtually ignored this area of research. Of course, the assessment of writing in electronic classrooms encompasses many traditional areas of concern such as a student's skill in narrating a story effectively or in persuading the reader to a particular perspective on an issue. Whether students are writing with traditional tools or electronically, teachers hope to assess their growth as writers. But there are *new* issues, too.

For obvious reasons, research into the evaluation of student writers in traditional classrooms is not directed at students' skills—or their lack of them—in using their writing tools. Nor has research in the larger field of writing investigated students' ability to create texts with visual impact or to properly format, lay out, or design them. Although such areas have been previously viewed as outside the writer's domain, this chapter argues that these and related matters are becoming increasingly important teaching/learning issues within computer-supported classrooms and, thus, involve the assessment of writing. To date, however, such matters have not enjoyed a high order of priority in our research.

Computers and Writing Research

Although there are numerous reports of teaching/learning situations by teachers based on their classroom observations, there are surprisingly few studies based on systematically gathered data that examine in depth the process of learning to write with computers, including descriptions of the social action within classrooms. Few studies assess how, or how well, students acquire the skills and subskills necessary for using computers, observe the teachers' strategies, or examine how the process of writing with computers may differ from writing with traditional tools.

Studies that do assess these matters point to changes in writing and the teaching of writing. Understanding such changes is important if teachers of composition hope to make their evaluations responsive to students' changing behaviors.

The Process of Composing Is Changing

Certainly, some studies suggest that writing with computers is changing the process of teaching, learning, reading, and writing.

One study, a two-year ethnography (Herrmann, 1985a, 1985b, 1986), showed that all eight high school students in the study felt anxiety about learning to use computers for writing. Three of these students, those with reading and writing problems, had protracted difficulty learning to use computer technology in support of their writing, despite daily instruction over a school year. The social dynamics in this computer environment demanded new skills, both technological and interpersonal, of students and teacher. Instruction changed from segmented, sequenced, and linear to holistic, simultaneous, and interactive. Writing changed from private and individual to public and collaborative. While all students did not benefit equally from the opportunities to collaborate, those who cultivated collaborative relationships with one or more sympathetic classmates made noticeable gains as writers during the year.

Another ethnography (Dickinson, 1986), conducted in a first/second-grade classroom where the teacher encouraged students to share ideas, found that collaborative writing was more common when the students used a computer than it was when they wrote with paper and pencil. Furthermore, "collaborative work at the computer created a new social organization that affected interactional patterns" among the children (p. 357). Collaborative talk spanned a range of concerns from planning, spelling, and punctuation to matters of style.

Other studies also suggest that computers foster a collaborative writing environment (Daiute, 1986a; Heap, 1989; Papert, 1980; Selfe & Wahlstrom, 1986). Collaborative interactions are even more likely to occur in classrooms with computer networks. As Janet Eldred (1989) points out, computer networks increase the "connectivity" (p. 316) of the composition classroom, making possible a social context for writing by linking terminals, individuals, groups, and minds.

Neither the learning of computer skills nor the development of collaborative writing, however, occurs automatically. Both appear to depend upon appropriate instructional strategies. Whether or not the pedagogy fosters in students the abilities necessary for success in a computer-rich writing environment is best ascertained by periodic evaluations.

A large-scale study of writing (Bernhardt, Edwards, & Wojahn, 1989) that compared first-year composition students in twenty-four computer-using and non-computer-using sections indirectly suggests the need for technological instruction and evaluation of students' skill in using computer technology. This study found, among other things, that students in the computer sections consistently withdrew from the course more often, had worse attendence, were tardy more often, and failed to complete assignments more often. Although some students clearly benefited from using the computers, the study suggests differences in the ways that the computer-using students adapted to the technology. One possible explanation came from the students themselves, who typically advised teachers and lab assistants that there was a need for increased assistance in learning to use the computer commands and software.

Not only do students need to be taught how to competently manipulate the hardware and software, but research also suggests that computers make new literacy demands, particularly in terms of writing plans and reading strategies. Understanding the nature of these new literacy demands means that teachers will eventually be capable of designing assessments that take into consideration what computer-using writers actually do.

Studies by Haas & Hayes (1986) reveal differences in reading from computer monitors as compared to reading from hard copy. The researchers found, based on their interviews, that writers in the study had problems getting a sense of the whole text when reading from computer screens. Furthermore, writers in the study had difficulty in moving quickly to specific areas in the text and in detecting errors. Students complained, for example, that writing was "hard to see" (p. 24) and that finding the "center of gravity" (p. 24) in an electronic text was difficult compared to paper copy, where pages can be spread out. Although it is commonly assumed that the comprehensibility of a text depends solely on the quality of writing, rather than on features such as graphic design, the researchers conclude that "visual/spatial factors are importantly involved in the reading process" (p. 34). Visual/spatial factors include display variables such as the size of the computer screen and whether the level of resolution is high or low.

In a separate study of subjects with high levels of computer competence, Haas (1989) examined the effects on writers' planning processes using pen and paper, word processing, and both conditions. The results of her study point to important differences between planning done with pen and paper and planning done on the computer. When writers used word processing alone, there was significantly less planning before writing and significantly less high-level planning overall than when writers used pen and paper. At the same time, there was significantly more local-level planning when word processing only was used. These findings suggest that the choice of writing technology influences a writer's composing process and may exacerbate, rather than facilitate, certain difficult aspects of the writer's task (see also Klem & Moran in this collection). If, as this research suggests, technology may make aspects of writing harder, shouldn't the composition teacher's assessment practices be sensitive to such changes?

Some research, it should be pointed out, does not underscore the nature of change within electronic classrooms. Gail Hawisher's (1989) review of computers and writing research, particularly the findings from ten case studies, suggests that writers transfer existing strategies to their computer use. For example, students who did not revise extensively before word processing did not revise extensively using computers. Although it is highly likely that writers tend, at least initially, to use their existing strategies when learning to write with computers, it should be noted that five of the case studies took place over short periods of time—ranging from only a few days to ten weeks—and that three other studies did not report the time frame. Undoubtedly, writers require longer periods of time if they are to change their usual writing processes and adapt to the new tool, a factor that makes the findings from some of these case studies problematical.

In sum, a growing body of research suggests that using the new technologies in classrooms is changing the writing process, although we are only beginning to understand what this means in terms of how best to teach and evaluate student writers. Nevertheless, the aforementioned studies suggest that there is value in conducting in-depth assessments of students' reading/writing processes as they use computer technology. Such studies can reveal, among other things, how students use the technology, the problems they encounter, and the ways in which teachers might adapt their pedagogy to students' needs. When teaching, learning, and writing processes change, it seems reasonable to assume that what we evaluate and how we evaluate it should be reexamined in the light of such changes.

The Nature of Written Products Is Changing

Given what our profession knows about computer use after a full decade of observations in English classrooms, we are beginning to realize that assessment in electronic classrooms should be concerned not only with changes taking place in students' writing processes, but also with changes taking place in written products. The nature of texts produced electronically—whether for on-line or hard copy readers—can depart dramatically from traditional conceptions of writing. As the use of computers for composition increases and teachers and students explore the growing range of options, the need for our profession to understand how to evaluate such writing will be increasingly important. A good deal of experimental research has evaluated students' pre- and post-test writings in an attempt to discover whether using computers, per se, makes for better writing than that produced with traditional implements (see, for example, Daiute, 1986b; Hawisher, 1987). Most researchers have found that the mere act of using a computer does not affect the quality of writing (Bridwell-Bowles, 1989; Hawisher, 1989). Increasingly, researchers in the field of computers and composition are sensitive to the constellation of factors likely to influence a writer's growth and are questioning the wisdom of narrow cause-and-effect questions concerning writing improvement (Bridwell-Bowles, 1989; Bridwell-Bowles, Sirc, & Brooke, 1985; Herrmann, 1990).

However, it is important to recognize that the assessment of texts written using computers has relied upon evaluation instruments designed for nonelectronic pieces of writing, such as holistic scoring techniques and other analytical instruments such as Diederich's scale (1974). No studies, to my knowledge, investigate the issue of writing assessment by establishing, for example, new guidelines or assessment vehicles designed specifically for electronic texts. I am unaware of studies that assess students' written products using criteria that reflect the changing process the students went through, the changing environments in which the texts were produced, or the different nature of the more visually oriented texts that students can produce on computers.

Yet, if we accept Steve Bernhardt's (1986) notion that visually informative prose is pervasive and we need to teach it, then we should also accept the need to evaluate students' ability to create it. Bernhardt delineates eight dimensions of rhetorical control wherein visually informative texts and non-visually informative texts differ: the visual gestalt, development, partitioning, emphasis, subordinate relations, coordinate relations, linking/transitional/intersentential relations, and sentence patterns. He believes that "classroom practice which ignores the increasingly visual, localized qualities of information exchange can only become increasingly irrelevant" (p. 77). Thus, we need to teach students techniques to help them gain mastery over this more visual rhetoric.

In desktop publishing, which permits the assembly of various data files into a page-layout program, relationships between form and content take on new meaning as writers integrate ideas and words with graphics and other features involved in producing publications with great visual impact. According to Ruszkiewicz (1988), "the graphics revolution could lead to the reconceptualization of composing as a thinking act that enables more human beings to exercise more faculties, skill and imagination than was ever possible before" (pp. 14–15).

Patricia Sullivan also notes, in a chapter in this collection, that writers using desktop publishing and state-of-the-art word-processing programs (such as MICROSOFT WORD and WORDPERFECT) exercise control over both verbal and visual aspects in their texts. She points out that word processing is rapidly becoming "word publishing." The "challenges we face as we seize control of the page," Sullivan says, mean that the writer must now think carefully about "how the look of the page will affect the meaning of the text." The computer, thus, encourages writers to broaden their domain of expertise to the visual rhetoric of the page.

For these and other reasons, it seems clear that composition and technical writing courses will increasingly include desktop publishing (DTP). Wahlstrom (1989) indicates that DTP is part of a major transformation in information handling taking place in society today. She states that what the computer only hinted at, DTP now makes clear: fundamental alterations in the word/print relationship resulting from digital communication technologies. Like it or not, DTP and the changes it brings are part of the writer's world, and so they must be part of the world of the writing teacher and the writing program administrator as well (p. 163). Writing teachers must rethink their pedagogical priorities to include instruction in the technological and rhetorical skills that desktop publishing makes possible and makes necessary.

The "shift from text-based to graphics-based word-processing software" (Ruszkiewicz, 1988, p. 9) brings to the fore once again the question of what we teach and how we evaluate what we teach. What skills must students have in order to effectively integrate visual and verbal features of texts? What instructional problems arise? Does writers' involvement with graphics, for example, dominate their traditional concerns over crafting ideas in words? Does the complexity of learning to use the technology overwhelm the writer? Once we decide what and how to teach, we will need to decide on the criteria teachers should use in evaluating students' success—or their lack of it—in using this new medium.

While the nature of printed texts takes on new dimensions, our assessment practices will also need to take into consideration the fact that writing is also changing its form from fixed, paper-copy inscription to malleable and fluid streams of electronic information, according to Balestri (1988). This is particularly true of hypertext environments. Such applications alter the nature of text, according to the following passage by Moulthrop and Kaplan (1989), which includes their paraphrase of Ted Nelson:

> Instead of a rigidly delimited stream of characters (a bound volume), the text may be constituted as a collection of passages arranged arbitrarily in electronic memory and provided with an indexing system that allows its elements to be assembled into a variety of sequences (a random-access database). The textual database, when coupled with a program allowing users to explore and create links between passages, gives birth to hypertext, a system of writing that supports "non-sequential" (or poly-sequential) discourse. (p. 7)

The use of applications such as hypertext and networked computers suggests that written texts will be increasingly read on-line, rather than from hard copy, and that students will play new roles as writers and readers. For example, writing within this environment can be highly collaborative, with students expanding or modifying an existing electronic text. Furthermore, writing within a hypertext environment may mean that the organization, rather than reflecting a linear development of ideas, becomes an arbitrary collage of sequences intended to be read on-line, with each reader discovering the most appropriate sequence based upon his or her prior knowledge. Classroom evaluations in a hypertext writing environment must consider these and other factors. Grading, for example, can no longer be based on traditional judgments of coherence because the skill of writing segments of text that fit appropriately into multiple sequences of other segments demands a new sense of text and new literacy skills (see also essays by McDaid, Smith, and Moulthrop in this collection).

A New Literacy Emerges

It would appear that a new literacy is emerging out of our electronic revolution. In "Redefining Literacy: The Multilayered Grammars of Computers," Cynthia L. Selfe (1989) examines the different sets of conventions that individuals must learn, namely the conventions of the page and the conventions of the screen, if they hope to function literately within a computer-supported communications environment. Selfe points out that the grammar of written texts—things such as arrangement, structure, form, and appearance—are changing as a result of our new technologies. The fact that students within electronic environments now use color, flashing notes and headings, boldface type and so forth to "represent a visual revelation of logical structures" (p.13) is one of Selfe's compelling examples of this new literacy.

She maintains that

> our profession will have to work diligently in the next few years to identify and explore the changing nature of literacy within a computer-supported writing environment, and to consider the implications of these changes on our teaching. (pp. 13–14)

Not only must teachers develop pedagogical strategies, but they must also find ways of measuring what students have learned that are sensitive to the changing literacy requirements brought about by our new forms of communication.

Evaluation Must Respond to New Communicative Contexts

Although it is becoming increasingly evident that composition specialists need to assist students in learning new skills within new environments, this situation creates ambivalent feelings for many writing teachers. Writing teachers identify with the world of humanistic concerns: values, ideas, and the search for truth. Most of us do not see ourselves as teachers of mechanical skills. Consequently, we may tend to teach students to use computers halfheartedly or not at all, believing that students should pick up these skills themselves.

Of course, a number of writing teachers have reported integrating word-processing instruction into their courses (see, for example, Collins & Sommers, 1985; Daiute, 1985; Gerrard, 1987; Hawisher & Selfe, 1989; Selfe, Rodrigues, & Oates, 1989; Herrmann, 1985b, 1985c, 1988; Holdstein, 1987; Rodrigues, 1985; Rodrigues & Rodrigues, 1986; Sudol, 1985; Wresch, 1984). But even those who teach students how to use computers in their classrooms do not always, or even frequently, publish research studies or teachers' reports of classroom practices that discuss classroom testing or systematic assessment of students' evolving technological skills. Our profession's reasons for not assessing students in this way may be complex.

Teachers may be hesitant to create instruments that measure— or judge—students' mastery of the technology for two reasons. First, although many of us teach students the fundamentals of using the hardware and software at the beginning of the semester—that is, word-processing commands and procedures such as insertions, deletions, block moves, hanging paragraphs, search and replace, file management, formatting, printing, and the like—

and although we may continue to provide technological instruction throughout the course, we want the emphasis to remain on writing. The desire to keep the focus on writing means that, although we take seriously the teaching of the technology, we are reluctant to acknowledge its importance by measuring students' skills in acquiring it.

Second, because we hope to teach all students, even the anxious ones, it seems unfair, once we've convinced them that computers aren't so scary after all, to subject them to punishing tests of skill. Should we lower the grade, for example, of students who exhibit technological ineptness in a writing course? Writing teachers resist the idea of evaluating students' technological competence because of these ambivalent attitudes.

Yet, if we accept Billie Wahlstrom's (1989) challenge "to train writers to write well using the technology they will find in their work" (p. 164), we must acknowledge the importance of teaching students to use electronic writing tools. And if we value the teaching of certain skills, we should want to know whether or not students are learning them.

Assuming that the information revolution continues, we can expect the problems of integrating computer technology into the writing curriculum to intensify. The question we must ask ourselves is, given the far-reaching changes taking place in written texts, given our increasing understanding of the social nature of writing, and given the opportunities to collaborate in electronic environments, don't we need to consider seriously the need for changing classroom evaluation procedures in order to accommodate the new writing processes and the new written products students create in our computer-supported classrooms?

One convincing argument for assessment is the fact that programs for desktop publishing and hypertext are not learned quickly. People in the workplace take months to learn to use DTP effectively. We can no longer assume that students should pick up such technological know-how as best they can. As technology in the writing classroom becomes increasingly complex, writing teachers must assume responsibility for integrating technological instruction with writing. And as instructional practices change, evaluation practices, which should be a reflection of what we are trying to teach, must change, too.

Evaluations can no longer focus solely on written products using traditional criteria. Teachers need diagnostic information telling them whether students are mastering what is being taught, and students deserve grades that reflect the entirety of the teaching/learning situation, including changes in students' writing processes and written products as a result of using computer technology. Such testing might also encourage students to continue exploring the potential of the technology rather than learning only a few essential procedures, an approach that shortchanges students in acquiring important expertise. There are numerous possible ways in which teachers might deal with the matter of evaluation; hence, readers should consider the following discussion suggestive rather than comprehensive.

One evaluation approach for technologically complex writing classrooms might be to periodically assign ungraded process-based tasks throughout the semester aimed at assessing students' mastery of the technology. These assignments would start with simple skills and move to increasingly complex ones. For example, an early assignment in writing/desktop publishing might be to create a flyer to announce an event, including the selection of typeface and design; a more advanced assignment would consist of laying out newsletters, including headlines and graphics with wraparound text. Periodic assessments of technological skill serve a multiple purpose: (1) They provide an impetus with a deadline for students to acquire the technological skill; (2) they underscore the importance of learning the technology; and (3) they provide teachers with diagnostic information, making it possible to provide students with individual instruction as needed.

Another evaluation approach might be the end-of-the-semester portfolio—and, of course, the portfolio could consist of electronic files and/or hard copy. Although a successful product does not necessarily reveal the writer's process, it will probably continue to be our best barometer of the students' ability. Furthermore, portfolios provide students with the opportunity to receive feedback—concerning the content and form of their writing as well as the visual component of their work—from teachers and peers during the semester, without penalty. Students would have the entire semester to acquire competence with the technology and to make progress in their writing before receiving a grade.

As part of the portfolio, students might be asked to include self-evaluations that describe their process in creating each project. Such an approach is especially desirable when projects have been carried out collaboratively, so that the teacher becomes aware of what each student's contribution has been. These self-reports would develop students' metacognitive insights concerning what they did and why they did it. At the same time, these qualitative assessments would provide the teacher with a window into the students' activities. Who was the intended audience? What was the writer's purpose? Was this a collaborative writing task and, if so, who did what? What type of feedback did the writer receive from peers, teachers, and others? How long did the student work on the project? What parts of a project are boilerplated and why? What parts are original? What, if any, false starts did the student make before completing the task? What role did revision play?

The portfolios of students' writing could be evaluated from three major perspectives: (1) as an example of the student's writing, e.g., how effective is the writing given the audience, purpose, and content of the text? (2) as an indication of the student's expertise using the technology, e.g., how competently crafted is the total visual effect? The graphics? The layout? The fonts? The use of white space? and (3) as a reflection of the student's ability to integrate the writing with the technology to create a successful written product, e.g., how effective are the visual factors, given the audience, purpose, and content of the text? Does form follow function? Do the graphics improve or detract from the communication?

Questions for the 1990s

As we enter the 1990s, composition teachers, theorists, and researchers need to develop an increased awareness of the role that evaluation should play in our computer-supported classrooms. The following questions are intended to stimulate thinking along these lines.

- What kinds of changes in teaching are we and should we be making? How responsive is our teaching to the new demands caused by the technology? And how well do our evaluation processes reflect the changing content of our courses and our expectations concerning students' performances as writers?

- Do our assessments reflect the students' mastery of the technology? If so, what specific aspects of students' technological expertise are we evaluating and how are we evaluating it? If we are not doing this, why not?

- How are reading and writing in the classroom changing? How should such changes modify teachers' assessment of writers?

- How are students' texts which integrate writing, graphics, and design features perceived by readers?

- During the process of composing, are students receiving more oral feedback from teachers and peers in computer-supported classrooms than in traditional ones? What is the nature of the oral responses given to writers and their writing?

- When feedback is face-to-face, it includes the possibility of writer-reader dialogue. Does the meaning of the text get negotiated between the student and the reader/evaluator? If so, how? Do the oral responses support the writer's original intentions? Or do they interfere with them?

- Does oral feedback focus primarily on global concerns (e.g., content, organization, thesis), on sentence-level matters (e.g., grammar, punctuation, and spelling), or on some combination of the two? What influence does oral feedback have on students' revision strategies? On their written products?

- Are we developing new standards for evaluating students' computer-written products that take into account their increasingly different nature from those produced in traditional classrooms? For example, are texts intended as electronic communications evaluated differently from hard-copy ones? Do classroom evaluations encompass the student's effective use of visual features, such as typeface, white space, graphics, and the like? Exactly what are the different criteria being used?

- Do our evaluation procedures reflect the increasingly social, collaborative, and interactive nature of writing within our computer-supported classrooms? If so, how?

- How do electronic conferences shape and alter the writing medium and how must our assessments of student writers change as a result?

- How is writing done in hypertext environments being evaluated? What are the particular problems that arise in evaluating these?

- What role, if any, does testing play in electronic writing classrooms?

In short, are we making sufficient room in the writing curriculum for teaching electronic technology and assessing our students' control over that technology? Are the criteria used in our evaluation processes a reflection of the written, printed, or interactive texts that our students create? Once we decide what to evaluate and how to evaluate it, then we must assess our evaluation procedures to find out how effective they really are. As writers using the latest computer equipment produce texts that deviate from traditional notions of writing, teachers' assessments are likely to change. Investigations into this area should be fruitful.

References

Balestri, D. P. (1988). Softcopy and hard: Word processing and writing process. *Academic Computing, 2*(5), 14–17, 41–45.

Bernhardt, S. A. (1986). Seeing the text. *College Composition and Communication, 37,* 66–78.

Bernhardt, S.A., Edwards, P., & Wojahn, P. (1989). Teaching college composition with computers. *Written Communication, 8*, 109–133.

Bridwell-Bowles, L. S. (1989). Designing research on computer-assisted writing. *Computers and Composition, 7*(1), 81–91.

Bridwell-Bowles, L. S., Sirc, G., & Brooke, R. (1985). Revising and computing: Case studies of student writers. In S. Freedman (Ed.), *The acquisition of written language: Revision and response* (pp. 172–194). Norwood, NJ: Ablex.

Brossell, G., & Ash, B. H. (1984). An experiment with the wording of essay topics. *College Composition and Communication, 35*, 423–425.

Calkins, L. (1983). *Lessons from a child: On the teaching and learning of writing.* Exeter, NH: Heinemann.

Collins, J. L., & Sommers, E. A. (Eds.). (1985). *Writing on-line: Using computers in the teaching of writing.* Upper Montclair, NJ: Boynton/ Cook.

Daiute, C. (1985). *Writing and computers.* Reading, MA: Addison-Wesley.

Daiute, C. (1986a). Do 1 and 1 make 2? Patterns of influence by collaborative authors. *Written Communication, 3*, 382–408.

Daiute, C. (1986b). Physical and cognitive factors in revising: Insights from studies with computers. *Research in the Teaching of English, 20*, 141–159.

Dickinson, D. K. (1986). Cooperation, collaboration, and a computer: Integrating a computer into a first-second grade writing program. *Research in the Teaching of English, 20*, 357–378.

Diederich, P. B. (1974). *Measuring growth in English.* Urbana, IL: National Council of Teachers of English.

Eldred, J. M. (1989). Computers, composition pedagogy, and the social view. In G. E. Hawisher & C. L. Selfe (Eds.), *Critical perspectives on computers and composition* (pp. 201–218). New York: Teachers College Press.

Evans, J. A. (Ed.). (1985). *Directions and misdirections in English evaluation.* Ottawa, Ontario: The Canadian Council of Teachers of English.

Fagan, W. T., Cooper, C. R., & Jensen, J. M. (1975). *Measures for research and evaluation in the English language arts*. Urbana, IL: National Council of Teachers of English.

Gerrard, L. (Ed.). (1987). *Writing at century's end: Essays on computer-assisted composition*. New York: Random.

Graves, D. H. (1975). An examination of the writing processes of seven year old children. *Research in the Teaching of English, 9*, 227–241.

Haas, C. (1989). How the writing medium shapes the writing process: Effects of word processing on planning. *Research in the Teaching of English, 23*, 181-207.

Haas, C., & Hayes, J. R. (1986). What did I just say? Reading problems in writing with the machine. *Research in the Teaching of English, 20*, 22–35.

Hawisher, G. E. (1987). The effects of word processing on the revision strategies of college students. *Research in the Teachng of English, 21*, 145–159.

Hawisher, G. E. (1989). Research and recommendations for computers and composition. In G.E. Hawisher & C.L. Selfe (Eds.), *Critical perspectives on computers and composition instruction* (pp. 44–69). New York: Teachers College Press.

Hawisher, G. E., & Selfe, C. L. (Eds.). (1989). *Critical perspectives on computers and composition instruction*. New York: Teachers College Press.

Heap, J. L. (1989). Sociality and cognition in collaborative computer writing. In D. Bloome (Ed.), *Classrooms and literacy* (pp. 135–157). Norwood, NJ: Ablex.

Heath, S. B. (1983). *Ways with words: Language, life and work in communities and classrooms*. London: Cambridge University Press.

Herrmann, A. (1985a, March). *Collaboration in a high school computers and writing class: An ethnographic study*. Paper presented at the annual convention of the Conference on College Composition and Communication, Minneapolis. (ERIC Document Reproduction Service No. ED 258 256)

Herrmann, A. (1985b). Using the computer as a writing tool: Ethnography of a high school writing class. *Dissertation Abstracts International, 47*, 02A. (University Microfilms No. 86-02-051)

Herrmann, A. (1985c, November). *Teaching strategies for introducing word processing into the writing class.* Paper presented at the annual convention of the National Council of Teachers of English, Philadelphia. (ERIC Document Reproduction Service No. ED 276 037)

Herrmann, A. (1986). An ethnographic study of a high school writing class using computers: Marginal, technically proficient, and productive learners. In L. Gerrard (Ed.), *Writing at century's end: Essays on computer-assisted composition* (pp. 79–91). New York: Random House.

Herrmann, A. (1988). Teaching teachers to use computers. *English Education, 20,* 215-229.

Herrmann, A. (1990). Computers and writing research: Shifting our "governing gaze." In D. H. Holdstein & C. L. Selfe (Eds.), *Issues in computers and writing* (pp. 124–134). New York: Modern Language Association.

Holdstein, D. (1987). *On composition and computers.* New York: Modern Language Association.

Moulthrop, S., & Kaplan, N. (1989). *Something to imagine: Literature, composition, and interactive fiction.* Unpublished manuscript.

Papert, S. (1980). *Mindstorms: Children, computers, and powerful ideas* (1st ed.). New York: Basic Books.

Perl, S., & Wilson, N. (1986). *Through teachers' eyes: Portraits of writing teachers at work.* Portsmouth, NH: Heinemann.

Rodrigues, D. (1985). Computers and basic writers. *College Composition and Communication, 36,* 336–339.

Rodrigues, D., & Rodrigues, R. J. (1986). *Teaching writing with a word processor, grades 7–13.* Urbana, IL: ERIC/National Council of Teachers of English.

Ruszkiewicz, J. (1988). Word and image: The next revolution. *Computers and Composition, 5*(2), 9–15.

Ruth, L., & Murphy S. (1984). Designing topics for writing assessment: Problems of meaning. *College Composition and Communication, 4,* 410–425.

Selfe, C. L. (1989). Redefining literacy: The multilayered grammars of computers. In G.E. Hawisher & C.L. Selfe (Eds.), *Critical perspectives on computers and composition instruction* (pp. 3–15). New York: Teachers College Press.

Selfe, C. L., Rodrigues, D., & Oates, W. R. (Eds.). (1989). *Computers in English and the language arts: The challenge of teacher education.* Urbana, IL: National Council of Teachers of English.

Selfe, C. L., & Wahlstrom, B. J. (1986). An emerging rhetoric of collaboration: Computers, collaboration, and the composing process. *Collegiate Microcomputer, 4,* 289–295.

Sommers, N. (1982). Responding to student writing. *College Composition and Communication, 33,* 149–156.

Stibbs, A. (1981). *Assessing children's language: Guidelines for teachers.* London: National Association of Teachers of English.

Sudol, R. A. (1985). Applied word processing: Notes on authority, responsibility, and revision in a workshop model. *College Composition and Communication, 36,* 331–335.

Wahlstrom, B. J. (1989). Desktop publishing: Perspectives, potentials, and politics. In G. E. Hawisher & C. L. Selfe (Eds.), *Critical perspectives on computers and composition instruction* (pp. 162–186). New York: Teachers College Press.

Wresch, W. (Ed.). (1984). *The computer in composition instruction: A writer's tool.* Urbana, IL: National Council of Teachers of English.

Ziv, N. D. (1984). The effect of teacher comments on the writing of four college freshmen. In R. Beach & L. S. Bridwell (Eds.), *New directions in composition research* (pp. 362–380). New York: Guilford Press.

Part Three

The Promise of Hypertext: Changing Instructional Media

Introduction

> The presence of these personal computers . . . will change
> human lives in many ways. They will change work and play,
> but the most important change will not come through what
> the computers can do for us, but through their effect on how
> people learn.
>
> —Seymour Papert,
> "Society May Balk, but the
> Future Will Demand a Computer
> for Each Child"

Certainly Papert's (1981/1986) claim regarding the influence of electronic technology on the ways in which people learn has implications for those of us working in computers and composition studies. We would like to extend the argument further, however, and propose that the creation of hypertexts as new instructional forms may produce one of the more profound changes in learning associated with this new electronic age.

Hypertexts and hypermedia environments are radical departures from our linear notions of texts. Books essentially are repositories for the storage of sequential information. Although recent literary theory would argue with the assumption that readers progress from word to word, line to line, page to page until they have "finished" the text, this conception of book reading is a common one. Information in books is stored according to unchanging spatial representations. In any given book, the same information is presented in the same order on the same page every time the book is opened and used, hence the value of an index or a table of contents.

Hypertext environments have no such characteristics. Pure hypertexts need have no beginnings (at least none that are privileged by the label *beginning*), no static representation of information in a set order (every reader of a hypertext can create his or her "path" through a document and can change the representation of information each time a text is used), and no set ending. Hence, readers of hypertexts have the potential to become reader-writers who construct meaning by accessing "cards" and "stacks" of information and assembling them in different ways and orders—all according to their own interests and associations. Hypertexts require readers to navigate their own journey through a body of information, without a traditional index or table of contents to shape their perception or dictate their progress. Of course, the dangers of such uncharted journeys may be equal to the promises.

Part 3 presents us with a series of sequential articles that explore different aspects of hypertexts. In chapter 8, Henrietta Nickels Shirk introduces hypertexts and demonstrates how these new instructional texts may well change composition studies. She argues that metaphorical thinking is essential to constructing and understanding hypertextual structures—that students and software designers need more effective metaphors to navigate pathways through virtual spaces, through spaces that exist only in electronic form. In chapter 9, John McDaid asserts that hypertext must be viewed as a stage in the evolution of other media environments and that only from this perspective can we begin to understand how such a new medium might shape composition instruction. Turning to other issues of hypertext, Catherine Smith presents us with chapter 10, itself a text that mirrors hypertext designs by inviting readers to approach the chapter as they choose, perhaps beginning with the appendix rather than with the introduction. Although a written text cannot properly evoke the feel of virtual space, Smith's chapter asks us to play with some characteristics of hypertexts as she stresses the importance of the user/reader and the designer/writer in hypermedia environments. In chapter 11, Stuart Moulthrop discusses the relationship of hypertext to current political divisions in English studies. He argues throughout that the new medium more accurately reflects current literary theory with its emphasis on a changing network of textual relationships than it does the New Critics' notion of fixed meaning residing within an authored work.

These chapters illustrate that hypertext, an instructional medium still very much in its infancy, promises profound changes in the ways we think, learn, and teach. The authors of this section agree that the invention of hypertext may influence our intellectual lives as profoundly as the emergence of alphabetic writing in about 1000 B.C. and the printed book in the fifteenth century A.D.

Reference

Papert, S. (1986). Society will balk, but the future may demand a computer for each child. In G. Haas (Ed.), *Curriculum planning*. (4th ed.). Boston: Allyn and Bacon. (Original work published 1981).

Chapter 8

Hypertext and Composition Studies

Henrietta Nickels Shirk
Northeastern University

The software technology of hypertext is rapidly changing the old linear patterns of textual comprehension into nonlinear, individualized pathfinding through information. The potential to link a variety of media forms (text, graphics, animation, sound, and video) provides exciting sources of creativity for the designers of hypertext, while posing new challenges for writers' composing processes. Writers must understand current metaphorical and cognitive theories as they relate to the organization of linked information and the abilities of audiences to comprehend self-structured communication via the computer screen. Hypertext possesses the potential to change composition studies profoundly by requiring the creation of computer-based spaces enlivened by structural metaphors to aid the process of reader cognition, and by fostering a team-of-experts approach to composing processes. Among other questions about hypertext that scholars and researchers will want to address in the 1990s are the following: Exactly how do writers define their new roles in relation to the emerging technology of hypertext? In what ways is hypertext itself changing metaphorical comprehension and human cognition?

Hypertext is a rapidly expanding phenomenon of current computer information technology. Recent observers of hypertext are unanimous in predicting a proliferation of hypertext software within the next few years. The *Mass High Tech* newspaper forecast, for example, "a 128 percent annual revenue growth rate for hypertext on-line documentation, accompanied by a 113 percent growth in hypertext and hypermedia applications software" ("Hyper Is Hip," 1989, p. 6). But what does this exciting growth of a new software and its products mean for those interested in computers and composition studies? The many answers to this question lie first in understanding what is meant by the term *hypertext*; then in looking at what some major theorists say about hypertext; and finally, using this information to pose informed questions to set the stage for further meaningful research about hypertext and its relation to the study and practice of composition.

Definition of Hypertext

Hypertext is a phenomenon for which definitions are crucial. Generally, hypertext is a nonlinear approach to presenting information via a computer, which allows one to navigate cross-references simply and quickly in an order determined by the computer user. The Document Design Center describes it as follows:

> Unlike a book, where the material progresses from one page to the next in linear fashion, a hypertext document (or hyperdocument) is a collection of computer files. Users are free to trace a variety of paths through the material, choosing which files they will view and in what order. The files may include text, graphics, animation, sound, and even other programs, such as word processors, spreadsheet programs, or relational database managers. (American Institutes for Research, 1989, p. 1)

Recently, the terms *hypermedia* and *multimedia* have been applied to note the expansion of hypertext into a variety of nontextual media in addition to text, which can all be linked together for the purpose of communication. However, at the moment, *hypertext* remains the generic term.

The variations among the many views of hypertext point to the conceptual differences with which practitioners have applied this technology to solving real-world problems. More specific definitions of hypertext tend to fall into two general categories—the authoring-tool approach and the database approach. As Bill Atkinson, the creator of Apple Computer's hypertext product, HYPERCARD, states,

You can use it [HYPERCARD] to create stacks of information to share with other people or to read stacks of information made by other people. So it's both an authoring tool and sort of a cassette player for information. (Goodman, 1988, "A Conversation with Bill Atkinson," p. xxi)

The two views of hypertext collectively have the potential for changing the very rhetorical foundations of composition studies in ways about which one can only currently speculate.

Hypertext provides an effective alternative to the usual paper-based approach for organizing and accessing information. At its most basic level, hypertext is a database management system that allows the user to connect screens of information ("nodes" or "index cards") using associative links. To understand how this approach to organizing information developed, one must look briefly at the history of hypertext.

History of Hypertext Development

There are three individuals who are usually associated with the early development of hypertext concepts. Vannevar Bush (1945), director of scientific research and development for the Roosevelt administration during World War II, is generally believed to have provided the earliest conceptual framework for hypertext. Bush envisioned a hypertext machine which he called the "Memex," to manage the large volume of scientific information which was available at that time. His idea included the establishing of associative links and the ability to browse through the information by creating one's own "trails" through it. Bush's ideas were developed further by Douglas Engelbart at the Stanford Research Center in the early 1960s. Not only did Englebart's system serve as a large storage receptacle, it also functioned as a communications network and as a shared workspace where researchers could plan and design projects. Theodor Nelson took these ideas a step further beginning in the late 1960s and early 1970s with a project he called "Xanadu." As an on-line network designed to hold all of the world's literary treasures, "Xanadu" (still in development) also provides an interactive writing and conferencing environment. Nelson coined the term *hypertext*, and he believes that all of the information in the world can eventually be accessed via hypertext. Although we are still far from this vision of information access, there are now (because of the ubiquitous presence of the microcomputer) thousands of hypertext applications and over fifty hypertext authoring products currently in the marketplace. Bill Atkinson's development of HYPERCARD for Apple Computer in 1987 assisted in making hypertextual communications available to a broad audience.

From the perspective of composition studies, it is interesting to note that the technology of hypertext was developed by non-writers—typically by scientists, technicians, and programmers who were not writers by profession. Because of the interactive nature of hypertext and the ways in which it allows users to shape their own texts, it poses special challenges for the writers. Unlike the typewriter, which is a technological "stylus" that the writer can view without knowledge of its inner workings, hypertext is a writing tool that the writer must thoroughly understand in order to apply effectively.

It is, therefore, the definition of hypertext as an authoring tool that possesses the greatest interest for the field of composition studies, and it is here that major issues begin to surface. While the mere viewing of a hypertext document for the purpose of retrieving information is a passive act, most hypertext applications can also be used interactively—that is, each user can share in the creation and evolution of a document. The literature about hypertext applications abounds with descriptions of how it functions and of how its products can be used for practical applications. Articles by Dear (1988) and Loeb (1988) explore examples of various hypertext creation techniques. Other articles by Begeman and Conklin (1988) and Frisse (1988), and the excellent introductory survey of hypertext authoring tools by Conklin (1987) all discuss hypertext applications in real-world environments. For example, hypertextual communication is used to provide linkages within electronic mail systems, journals of ideas and exchange, bulletin boards, information management systems, and computer-assisted instruction. As practical and easy-to-learn tools for browsing, hypertextual systems have also proven effective in providing an easy method for accessing large databases of information, such as computerized information for museum attendees and on-line presentation of numerous reference and maintenance manuals. All of these authors, however, refer in various ways to the key issue for authors of hypertext—how to structure information that will be used interactively via the computer.

Structuring Information for Hypertext

As on-line documents, hypertext applications are intended to transcend the limitations of printed text by mimicking the brain's ability to access information quickly and intuitively through associative references (Fiderio, 1988). But the creators of hypertexts must know the principles of good screen format and design, techniques for creating effective links among nodes (pieces or chunks) of information, and at least the rudiments of computer-user interface design guidelines. Some of the issues about the functioning of the human brain and about the appropriate ways for information to be presented via the computer are currently being debated among theoreticians and practitioners. There are no ready-made answers for authors of hypertext applications. At best, the hypertext author can work toward contributing to this growing body of knowledge. Those in the field of composition studies can also contribute by sharing information about composing processes and the visual organization of material (although this may differ from the printed page as one considers the medium of the computer screen).

From the composing perspective, hypertext authors must be alert to two new ways of thinking about the presentation of information. First, there is the need to reduce one's material to a series of discrete units or nodes that are presented via a single computer screen, rather than through a preplanned sequential organization of pages. The way information within a hypertext document is divided into units and linked together will influence the ways in which the user (reader) will access such information. Biases, interpretations, and transitions are constrained differently in hypertextual authoring than they are in traditional linear text. As one critic of hypertext has observed, it "forces the author to express ideas in a fine-grained, separated manner, and this obscures the larger idea being developed" (Begeman & Conklin, 1988, p.

260). For those accustomed to writing in traditional linear, paper-based text, it is sometimes unnatural to break one's thoughts into discrete units related to a myriad of other discrete units, rather than to the logical, linear organization of printed pages. The freedom of choice inherent in hypertext communication places different responsibilities on the author for clarity and precision in communication. Knowing that a reader of hypertext will not necessarily elect to read the next sequential computer screen means that the designer of hypertext must view the information communicated through this medium from a multidimensional perspective, with the reader arriving at a particular point of communication from any one of a myriad of paths.

Second, there is the need for hypertext authors to develop underlying structures—mental models or metaphors—for their information. The many ways of navigating through hypertextual material also make it easy to get disoriented and lost—a common complaint among many hypertext users. Hypertext authors must develop carefully planned structures and networks of links which allow flexible accommodation of multiple users' needs. Such structuring, in part, can be accomplished by the creation of metaphors that assist the user in conceptualizing and finding information important to individual needs. Users can employ such metaphors as tools in creating their own contexts within vast bodies of information and thereby reduce the sense of fragmentation that hypertext communication (because of its inherent design assumptions) tends to create. Finally, as hypertext authors establish networks of links within information structures, they must think of themselves as multiple pathfinders, always attempting to anticipate possible routes to a given node of information. This authorial requirement diverges greatly from the traditional approach to communication via the medium of linear text.

Although these new ways of thinking about presenting information have been focused by discussions occasioned by the emergence of hypertext, they actually relate to broad areas of study and trends that have long been of concern to students of composition studies who have been interested in metaphorical theory and cognitive science as these fields relate to the creation of texts. Designers of hypertext must be aware of the need to create structures (or metaphors) for the virtual realities they build (see

Smith in this collection). Metaphorical theory as it relates to human cognitive processes is a fertile area of study for hypertext authors. Finally, composition practitioners have thus far been proponents of the uses of hypertext for collaborative writing (Havholm & Stewart, 1989; Delisle & Schwartz, 1989). All of these areas have much to contribute to the study and evolution of hypertext. Future development and application of hypertextual techniques will undoubtedly be eclectic, drawing on many of the same fields (such as studies of metaphor, human cognition, and collaborative learning) that have richly informed past and present theories of composition.

Of these three areas of concern to composition studies, examinations of the nature of metaphor are at present untapped by most hypertext authors. The study of metaphorical expression possesses the potential for meaningful sources of conceptual information and inspiration for hypertext authors. In the excitement of bringing hypertext information into the realm of practical problem solving, the roots of this new mode for communication in composition theory are often forgotten. But composition theory is one of the primary conceptual foundations of hypertext upon which any of its future successes must be built. Especially useful for understanding hypertext are literary essayists like Roland Bartel (1983), who are convinced that the study of metaphor should not be limited to the metaphors of poetry, but rather expanded to include ordinary experience. The metaphors software designers use in connection with hypertext can be simultaneously verbal, visual, and auditory.

Hypertext is a powerful tool that enables authors who use this software technology to create multiple metaphorical realities for diverse audiences. It involves creating links or paths through potentially vast bodies of information. To accomplish this task successfully, one must know more than how to write—or at least be willing to redefine the process of writing in new ways. Rather than the traditional view of writers placing words on paper or even on computer screens in terms of a single organizational structure, hypertext turns "composing" into a combination of delivery methods and organizational models. In fact, the number of these methods and models is limited only by the author's individual creativity.

Literature Review: A Look at Metaphorical Theory, Human Cognition, and Collaborative Writing

The study of hypertext encourages the melding of conceptual information from several different perspectives. The most influential of these areas in terms of studying hypertext discourse models are the aspects of composition theory that relate to the study of metaphorical expression, cognitive science, and the use of computers for collaborative communication and learning.

Unfortunately, composition theorists have only begun to directly address the new technology of hypertext. The newness of hypertext is evidenced by the fact that the first conference on hypertext was held in 1987 at the University of North Carolina at Chapel Hill. The twenty-eight papers presented at this conference have been published in a set of proceedings (Association for Computing Machinery, 1987). While such papers provide an interesting historical account of the growing number of hypertext applications, few of them address the underlying philosophical issues surrounding hypertext. For this perspective, one must begin by looking at the practical roots of hypertext as a software application.

Although not scholarly in the traditional sense, explanations of hypertext techniques and applications abound in the procedural literature accompanying hypertext products. These cover not only instructions for using hypertext, but also instructions for creating it. The two areas are not mutually exclusive, because successes and problems in implementing hypertext suggest ways that it can be (or could have been) more effectively created. These suggestions provide a practical foundation for viewing the more conceptual aspects of hypertext within the framework of composition studies.

Among hypertext reader instructions, Apple Computer's directions to the users of its hypertext product, HYPERCARD, provide typical commentary. While explaining the meanings of "card" (one screenful of information), "stack" (a collection of cards on a common theme), and "tool" (one of which is the little human hand one uses to navigate about the screen), Apple (1987b) advises, "Browsing is HYPERCARD's term for roaming around cards and stacks" (p. 3), and "to browse" is to wander through HYPERCARD stacks (p. 207). The notion of roaming, browsing, and wandering through information via the computer is troubling to those accustomed to the visual cues provided by paper-based information. These visual cues provide conventional landmarks such as page numbers and headers, tables of contents and indices to assist in the process of locating information. From a hypertextual computer screen, the reader can go almost anywhere, but also nowhere, if all the options are not readily apparent.

From a hypertext user's (reader's) perspective, getting lost in hyperspace is a psychologically threatening possibility. Shneiderman and Kearsley (1989) have commented on the fact that "getting lost in a hypertext database is a common and serious problem. There are two aspects to this problem: not being able to find desired information, and getting disoriented" (p. 49). These authors suggest that single-word links that do not provide much context for searching, poorly designed databases, databases designed for purposes different from those of the current user, and disorientation because of lack of current location information relative to the overall structure of the database all contribute to the perception of being lost in hyperspace. A contributing aspect of this problem may also result from the fact that conventions are still being discovered, negotiated, and established for the new medium of hypertext.

Aside from the technological aspects of chunking information into manageable pieces and creating links among them, the most challenging of the techiques for creating hypertext is the notion that producers of hypertext must establish an underlying metaphor for presenting information. The practical literature on hypertext is filled with numerous (although sketchy) admonitions for creating hypertext metaphors. One of the earliest sets of guidelines, issued by Apple Computer (1987a) to designers of software products, gave advice on using Apple's desktop interface:

> Use concrete metaphors and make them plain, so that users have a set of expectations to apply to computer environments. Whenever appropriate, use audio and visual effects that support the metaphor. (p. 3)

And more recently, Apple (1989) has advised HYPERCARD stack designers:

> Real world metaphors can help convey the user's navigation options. [They] furnish additional information about how the subject matter is laid out and how it can be traversed. Your subject matter will often influence your choice of metaphor. . . . Stack structure can also influence metaphor choice. (pp. 38–40)

Apple then goes on to provide several examples of linear and tree stack structures. Linear structures can be modeled by metaphors such as cassette players or film projectors, while tree structures can be modeled by metaphors such as organization charts, maps, or books.

Other explicators of HYPERCARD (Daniels & Mara, 1988) suggest that one should first brainstorm to obtain a list of real-world scenarios (professions, industries, places, things, events) that employ some or all of the same terminology used in describing the information and/or intelligence for the hypertext product; then choose the particular scenario that most closely reflects the features and functions of the proposed hypertext product; and finally "immerse yourself in the metaphor" (p. 131). Metaphor immersion is not a mental skill that comes naturally for most writers (designers and architects) of information, unless one happens to be a poet—and even poets struggle with finding appropriate metaphors.

Metaphorical Theory

Although these meager guidelines for the construction of metaphors from the literature on hypertext are not intended to be scholarly work, they do relate to an age-old body of rhetorical study and knowledge. A potentially fruitful, but underdeveloped, source of information to assist hypertext design is the study of metaphorical theory. Researchers who have perceived the important link between language and perception may provide some meaningful direction for developing and evaluating hypertext metaphors. The study of metaphor is vast and intertwined with the related fields of poetics, linguistics, and cognitive psychology. Philosophical approaches to understanding metaphor actually go back to Aristotle, and metaphors have a long tradition in literature and literary criticism, and in discussions about the composing process. For the purposes of studying and creating hypertext, more recent commentators on metaphor may have significant contributions. A few of these are mentioned here.

In *Metaphor and Reality* (1962), philosopher Philip Wheelwright opened much of the recent discussion on the nature of metaphor by suggesting that "the test of essential metaphor is not any rule of grammatical form, but rather the quality of semantic transformation that is brought about" (p. 71). This metamorphosis, Wheelwright maintains, may be described as

> semantic motion; the idea of which is implicit in the very word "metaphor," since the motion (*phora*) that the word connotes is a semantic motion—the double imaginative act of outreaching and combining that essentially marks the metaphoric process. (pp. 71–72)

Although Wheelwright's examples are primarily from the fields of anthropology, mythology, and poetry, his perspective on metaphorical thought is an important precursor for the more cognitive approaches that have followed. By linking the dynamic quality of metaphors with the ways in which the human mind seeks greater understanding of its environment, Wheelwright's concept of semantic motion not only merges several disciplines but also points toward a cognitive approach to metaphor—both of which are essential to effective hypertext development.

The cross-disciplinary aspect of studying metaphorical thought is aptly described by Ricoeur in *The Rule of Metaphor: Multi-Disciplinary Studies of the Creation of Meaning in Language* (1975). Ricoeur looks at metaphor from the different perspectives of rhetoric, semantics, and hermeneutics. His theme is that "metaphor is the rhetorical process by which discourse unleashes the power that certain fictions have to redescribe reality" (p. 7). In *A Cognitive Theory of Metaphor* (1985), MacCormac links the creation of metaphor with the cognitive process of acquiring knowledge. His interdisciplinary analysis of metaphor as "a cognitive interaction" (p. 6) grounds it firmly in an interaction between philosophy and psychology, including linguistics. Both of these books, along with

Wheelwright's earlier work, provide a scholarly foundation for the study of metaphor and for the study of creating metaphorical structures in which to communicate hypertextually.

In their less academic coverage of metaphor, Lakoff and Johnson, in *Metaphors We Live By* (1980), aptly demonstrate that metaphor is not mere poetical or rhetorical embellishment but a part of everyday speech that affects the ways in which humans perceive, think, and act. Reality itself, they suggest, is defined by metaphor. Likewise, Marvin Minsky in *The Society of Mind* (1985) observes that there are two ways of defining a metaphor. An easy functional definition is that "a metaphor is that which allows us to replace one kind of thought with another" (p. 299). But a structural definition of a metaphor is more difficult and results only in an endless variety of processes and strategies. He agrees with Lakoff and Johnson that there is no boundary between metaphorical and ordinary thought. As Minsky states, "No two things or mental states ever are identical, so every psychological process must employ one means or another to induce the illusion of sameness. Every thought is to some degree a metaphor" (p. 299). Minsky's views of metaphor are particularly appropriate for those creating hypertext discourse models because they demonstrate how crucial this technique is for understanding any subject matter. The endless variety of processes and strategies inherent in metaphor is also inherent in the assumptions behind hypertext. Likewise, an ineptly applied metaphor, or (worse) no metaphor at all, within a hypertext communication results in confusion.

However, rather than exploring these metaphorical foundations of hypertext to their advantage, some of the current writers on computers and writing have focused instead on the applications of hypertext in the classroom and industry. These practitioners have been quick to see the practical application of hypertext for composition students and for those who must write in business environments. Most of these researchers have been interested in hypertext as a powerful mechanism for supporting the process of writing and for contributing to collaborative writing and learning.

Writing, Thinking, and Collaboration

One of the most interesting applications of hypertext concepts is the use of hypertext to support the processes of writing, complex mental activities that use many different kinds of thinking. Smith, Weiss, and Ferguson (1987) have reported on WE (WRITING ENVIRONMENT), currently under development at the University of North Carolina at Chapel Hill. WE is a hypertext writing environment that can be used to create both electronic and printed documents, and it is intended for professional writers who work within a computer network of workstations. Based on a cognitive model of writing, WE supports each of the major phases of writing by providing a series of structural modes that support information units as "nodes," which in turn can be moved from one place to another as a text is developed. Relationships can be defined among these nodes in the form of directed hypertextual links. This system provides a network mode (for the exploratory phases of document development), a tree mode (for building an integrated hierarchical structure for the document), an editor mode (for standard text editing), and a text mode (for constructing a representation of the continuous document). These authors believe that, "as a tool for professionals, hypertext . . . will become a supporting utility over which more constrained applications will be developed rather than the primary application system itself" (pp. 12–13). In many respects, they suggest, hypertext is a state of mind. It is especially effective in supporting the exploration phase of writing, because exploratory thinking usually occurs early in the development of a set of ideas. Such thinking is an integral part of the overall cognitive process of all writing activities. They foresee a time when large distributed databases of hypertextual documents will exist for the support of thinking and writing.

A recent paper from conference proceedings provides further evidence for interest in the use of hypertext to support writing. Havholm and Stewart (1989) report success in using Owl International's hypertext system, GUIDE, to teach the concepts of intertextuality as it applies to specific seventeenth-century texts in a literature course. Because students created their own hypertext documents for the literary texts they studied, and shared them among themselves, they were forced to commit themselves to their own interpretations of the texts they considered and to test and question the theory of intertextuality. According to this theory, meanings arise not from a text in isolation but from the connection of texts, and all texts have their beginnings in the language, sign systems, and cultural codes available in previous texts. GUIDE allowed students to create in the literary texts or pictures they studied links to other related works. Not only were these students forced to become deeply acquainted with seventeenth-century culture, but they also began to specialize in collecting information in various topic areas, which they then shared with each other through a hypertextual library. Havholm and Stewart believe that the use of hypertext in their course encouraged the students to engage in critical thinking by fostering individual "pathfinding" among an original text and its related sources and by providing these individual "pathfinders" the ability to collectively use a shared database. These techniques enabled students to unlock themselves from paper-based interpretations and to create their own textual analysis and interpretations.

Other reports about the effectiveness of hypertext as a collaborative writing tool have been made by writing practitioners in industry. For example, an article by Delisle and Schwartz (1989) focuses on the practical application of this technology in the workplace. These authors find strong evidence for the effectiveness of hypertext as a tool for writers. It supports virtually all the activities in the writing process—from gathering and organizing information to document preparation. And it can be used to prepare both conventional paper documents and on-line hyperdocuments. Using the hypertext system NEPTUNE, developed at Tektronix, they have experimented with teams of authors working on large technical documents. In this system, each author creates a separate context for making changes to portions of the document. When an author checks out a portion of the document to work on it, that portion is automatically set to "read-only" for the other authors. After the modifications are completed, the author uses NEPTUNE's merge operation to install the new version in the master context, and the locks on the portion are then released.

Likewise, Yoder, Akscyn, and McCracken (1989) find that the shared database capability of KMS, the hypertext product they use, supports their collaborative work. They believe that every collaborative act is an act of communication, and they demonstrate how hypertext enables them to create a database of knowledge, including articles, plans, reports, and memos, from which they can work collaboratively. According to these authors, people require convenient access to each other's work in order to interact efficiently. They use the model of a construction site to demonstrate how collaboration takes the form of developing a large structure (the shared database) that is a composite of many smaller structures. Typically, a group of writers and others sharing a KMS database builds a hierarchical global index that provides access to the common areas (such as a group bulletin board) and shared projects (such as proposals in development). In addition, members of the group can add shortcuts through the database by placing direct links to their own work from the work of their colleagues.

While in the past work in industrial settings has been typically accomplished through oral and paper-based traditions, using a hypertextual computer system now allows for the linking of related information and events, as well as for rapid access by those requiring specific information. As in academic environments, hypertext can allow for greater flexibility, productivity, and creativity than is otherwise possible in a non-hypertextual and non-computerized environment.

One of the tasks for the future will be to assimilate the meaningful and related aspects of composition theory into an underlying conceptual structure that will assist in the creation of more effective hypertext discourse models than are currently available. In John Sculley's (1988) words, composition theorists and educators must prepare "students to take their place in a world that has not yet come into existence" (p. vii). The world of the future will undoubtedly include hypertextual communication. The exact shape of this communication is yet to be determined, through the efforts of further research.

A Research Agenda: Future Questions Regarding Hypertext

The existing literature surrounding hypertext suggests several potential areas for future research. These concerns constellate around three major areas: defining and creating hypertext metaphors, applying and analyzing the effectiveness of hypertext discourse models in the human learning experience, and setting some meaningful plans for future hypertext development.

Each of the following questions is accompanied by some suggestions for approaching the attainment of its possible solution(s). This commentary is intended to expand on the questions and to inspire further thought, rather than to limit them. It is not intended to provide answers, but rather to pose questions for a future research agenda.

Concerns about Metaphors

- What is a metaphor (philosophically, linguistically, cognitively, and practically speaking), and how does one distinguish an effective hypertext metaphor from an ineffective one?

The metaphorical basis of hypertext needs to be explored further. We must find a more accurate definition of a hypertext metaphor than those which presently exist in literary and cognitive realms. However, such a unique definition should incorporate and synthesize well-informed data from literary, philosophical, linguistic, and cognitive perspectives. It should go beyond these existing fields of study into conceptual areas that will define the new hypertext discourse models.

In *Understanding Media: The Extensions of Man* (1964), Marshall McLuhan observed that

> each new technology creates an environment that is itself regarded as corrupt and degrading. Yet the new one turns its predecessor into an art form. . . . Today technologies and their consequent environments succeed each other so rapidly that one environment makes us aware of the next. Technologies begin to perform the function of art in making us aware of the psychic and social consequences of technology. (p. ix)

From the perspective of McLuhan's theory, the computer has turned the non-technological desktop into the art form of a computerized metaphor. But the ubiquitous metaphor of the desktop (and its related images of files and documents) is destined to be supplanted by new metaphors. The technology for presenting information via hypertext will itself give birth to new mental models and constructs of human discourse—virtual realities not yet imagined.

There is much research still to be accomplished in the definition of the metaphors that structure hypertext discourse models. McLuhan's perception of the ever-changing characteristics of technological media may provide the beginnings of a foundation upon which new metaphors will be established.

- What are the most effective techniques for creating meaningful metaphors (virtual realities) that comprise the basic underlying structures of hypertext communication?

Immersing ourselves in metaphors may be part of creating effective hypertext discourse models, but it is a very late step in a difficult creative process that begins with finding the appropriate metaphor to convey information effectively. At present, we know the least about this crucial first step.

Marvin Minsky in *The Society of Mind* (1985) uses the term *uniframe* to define "a description designed to represent whichever common aspects of a group of things can be used to distinguish them from other things" (p. 331). Hypertext discourse is the linking of the common aspects of uniframes. Minsky suggests that

> good metaphors are useful because they transport uniframes intact, from one world into another. Such cross-realm correspondences can enable us to transport entire families of problems into other realms, in which we can apply to them some already well-developed skills. However, such correspondences are hard to find since most reformulations merely transform the uniframes of one realm into disorderly accumulations in the other realm. (p. 299)

Hypertext provides the tool for transporting uniframes from the actual world into the virtual world of the computer, but its underlying metaphors of discourse risk becoming merely disorderly accumulations without a proper understanding of the ways in which metaphors are created and function. Minsky's helpful but preliminary observations and warning may be useful as we begin to discover new techniques for creating and designing hypertext metaphors.

Concerns about Cognition

- What are the cognitive aspects of hypertext discourse models, and how do they influence knowledge acquisition—i.e., will the tool of hypertext ultimately influence how one learns?

Those involved in the creation of hypertext need to observe and understand current developments in the field of cognitive psychology and its related interest in artificial intelligence. Answers to questions about how the human brain functions and how we learn are still being sought and debated. Some psychologists believe that the tools used to solve problems and gain information influence the cognitive processes of the tool user (Vygotsky, 1986). According to this theory, a tool such as the computer (or hypertext) becomes a way of shaping the mental models and problem-solving skills of the individual applying it. As an attempt at mimicking the nonlinear aspects of human thought, hypertext also possesses the potential for influencing the ways in which we think.

Recently, some psychologists have suggested that the computational model of the computer is the model which should be applied to the human mind. In *The Computer and the Mind* (1988), Philip Johnson-Laird concludes that

> mental processes are the computations of the brain. . . . There is a remote possibility that the computations of a human mind might be captured within a medium other than a brain. A facsimile of a human personality could be preserved within a computer program. . . . The concept of interacting with a dynamic representation of an individual's intellect and personality is sufficiently novel to be disturbing. It raises moral, metaphysical and scientific issues of its own. (pp. 391–392)

Hypertext begins to make such computational models of the human mind possible.

Glimpses of the future to be provided by hypertext discourse presently raise many more questions than answers:

- How involved do we want the computer to be in the learning process?

- Will there be degrees of computer involvement in human activities?

- What kinds of subjects and learning situations best lend themselves to hypertext presentations?

- What roles will artificial intelligence and expert systems play in hypertext and in a society which uses hypertext as a primary communication medium?

- Is there the potential for modifying the distribution of knowledge (and therefore social and political) power in our society through the use of the vast hypertextual bodies of information that will become available to those who have access to this technology?

- How will the new hypertextually created diverse discourse communities be integrated into already existing discourse communities and into each other?

The list of questions could continue, but they begin to group themselves around two major issues—concern for the individual and concern for the group.

- What will be the impact of the continuing individualized and collaborative learning and knowledge made possible by the application of hypertext on education in general and on composition studies specifically?

The technology of hypertext provides a dualistic approach to learning and the acquisiton of knowledge. On the one hand, hypertext is a powerful tool for individualized learning; on the other hand, hypertext is also a powerful tool for collaborative efforts. This dichotomy need not be mutually exclusive, as both aspects receive further research and definition.

Although Anthony Smith is speaking about the influence of the computer on the newspaper industry in *Goodbye, Gutenberg* (1980), he points to a concern that could be equally leveled at hypertext. While the invention of the printing press made consistent information widely available to the masses, he says,

> the new media coming into existence in our own time have the
> tendency to individualize information, to make the acquisition
> of knowledge a matter of private choice. . . . The new
> computer-based technologies, now rapidly developing in
> most industrialized countries, offer the individual the chance
> to escape from general audiences into tiny groups selecting
> information according to atomized and itemized choices. . . .
> Today a fascinating cultural reversal is underway: the
> individual is being offered, to an ever greater extent, individual
> access to a totality of information. (pp. 321–322)

The processes by which individual access to information is
mediated are crucial to hypertext, and they need to be examined,
criticized, and related to the collaborative processes also provided
by hypertext.

Hypertext developers envision that many different authors
might work on the same document collaboratively. The dynamic
quality of hypertext documents results not only from the fact that
readers can create their own links through the material, but also
from the fact that readers can change and annotate the contents of
the material as they read.

The advantages of hypertext for establishing large databases of
collaborative knowledge are obvious. However, what is not so
obvious are the kinds of technical questions that have been raised
by Shneiderman and Kearsley (1989):

> Collaboration raises many difficult technical issues. Is
> there a version for each author? If there is only a single
> version, what happens if one author deletes portions that
> contain links to another author's documents? Does there
> need to be a way for authors to identify their contributions, or
> are all contributions treated anonymously? (p. 50)

While Shneiderman and Kearsley go on to suggest that one possible answer is to create a virtual copy of the document for each
author based on that author's changes, they recognize the attendant technological problem of reconstituting a series of such
virtual documents. Such logistical and technical issues must be
resolved before hypertext can be broadly applied as a tool for
collaborative work.

The individual and collaborative issues relating to hypertext
raise the further questions of authorship and ownership of information, especially when that information is not only in the form of

text but also presented in other kinds of media. We do not know where the technologies associated with hypertext will take us, nor who should take us there.

Concerns about Future Development Directions

- What is the proper role for various media (graphics, animation, sound) in hypertext documents—i.e., how will composition, hypermedia, and multimedia be redefined?

Metaphors need not be only verbal; they may be visual as well. And, as the technology develops, they may very well be expressed in terms of all five senses. In fact, many commentators observing the current directions of information presentation suggest (as does Anthony Smith, 1980) that "words have lost their hard edges in the age of the audio-visual. A world of facts is dissolving into a factless world overloaded with information, dominated by images" (p. 325).

Should there be standards for hypertext design? In the not-so-long-ago early days of desktop publishing, experts in the field were dismayed by the resulting proliferation of poor design techniques as novices began to apply the many publication design tools that technology made available to them. Without a firm grounding in the basics of document design, the resulting products were typically lacking in professional quality and therefore communicated ineffectively. Likewise, hypertext and hypermedia applications face the same potential disasters as they are applied by those unschooled in their techniques. For those accustomed to communicating primarily with words, the expansion of hypertext into hypermedia will require the development of graphic skills.

Current observers of hypermedia development have pointed out that hypermedia instruction is not merely a vision of the future—universities and colleges are currently developing and implementing hypermedia courses in a wide variety of fields. As Raker (1989) observes about hypermedia,

> Current programs and applications are merely preliminary
> steps in the development of an innovative and meaningful
> technology that will change the way we organize information

and present instruction. Research will be undertaken to
determine how this technology best facilitates learning. (p.
19)

As a new technology of information, hypertext will undoubtedly have a profound influence on the evolving patterns of thought
and social organization of our society. Assuming that standards
(or at least guidelines) for effective hypertext presentation of
information are necessary, the question of their proper sources
becomes important:

- Who are the appropriate creators for hypertext discourse
  models—what kind of aptitude, training, and educational
  backgrounds should be required for such individuals?

Hypertext communication requires an understanding of how to
structure information in terms of human cognition and how to use
a variety of visual and audio techniques beyond text. The skills
required for effective hypertextual communication undoubtedly
reside in more than one individual. Hypertext application development requires the work of writers, animators, musicians,
video producers, graphic artists, and database designers. It is
perhaps best considered as a unified team effort, with each expert
contributing to the whole. However, this means that each con-
tributor must understand and appreciate the contributions of the
other experts. Writers will no longer create in solitary environments; they will become contributing members of hypertext development teams. All such contributors need to contemplate the
philosophical and theoretical foundations of hypertext and work
toward developing a rhetoric for hypertext.

However, there is a glaring absence of commentary from
composition experts in the theoretical literature about hypertext.
Communication theorists need to become involved in the evolution of hypertext. They must not leave all the theoretical definitions of hypertext discourse models to the technological experts
who are creating hypertext tools. Most of the articles on hypertext
currently being published by composition theorists are descriptions
of how a specific hypertext tool has helped them solve particular
classroom problems or expand on the techniques they normally
use for teaching. If those concerned about communication do not

participate in the development of new theories for the new technologies available in the field, others will accomplish this task without them.

Concluding Thoughts

Research on the theoretical and practical applications of hypertext is in its infancy, and therefore merits some cautionary admonitions. Marvin Minsky's advice about computer technology should be considered:

> You have to form the habit of not wanting to have been right for very long. If I still believe something after five years, I doubt it. Anything you hear about computers ... should be ignored, because we're in the Dark Ages. We're in the thousand years between no technology and all technology. You can read what your contemporaries think, but you should remember they are ignorant savages. (Brand, p. 104)

Those of us "ignorant savages" participating in the hypertext revolution should not ignore each other. We need each other's expertise in a team environment, but we must also examine our own and other's expertise from the perspective that we are all part of an emerging information technology. It is only as open-minded creators of the future of hypertext that we will collectively possess the potential to significantly change the ways in which individuals and society perceive and assimilate information. The emerging hypertext discourse models for human communication will ultimately require both individual and group creativity.

Such discourse models may also require us to revise our notions of creativity and the act of writing. Hypertext enables all of us to become both creators of paths through information and pathfinders through information structured by others. As we have seen, the challenges connected with hypertext communication are not so much technological as philosophical and conceptual. Further knowledge of the functioning of metaphor, cognitive processes, and the nature of collaboration is required. The uses of artificial intelligence and expert systems in hypertextual communication are only now being explored. As the printing press accomplished a knowledge revolution in the time since Gutenberg, hypertext may also create a fundamental change in the fabric of our society. It will unquestionably influence future communication processes within education, research, and business. But it will most profoundly change the theoretical foundations of composition studies as the notion of the writer as communicator is augmented by that of the writer as architect of information. As creators of multiple pathways through information, today's writers will undoubtedly abandon linear written communication as they begin to further develop the multidimensional realm of hypertextual communication.

References

American Institutes for Research. (1988, October). What is hypertext? *Simply Stated: The Newsletter of the Document Design Center*, p. 1.

Apple Computer, Inc. (1987a). *Human interface guidelines: The Apple desktop interface*. Reading, MA: Addision-Wesley.

Apple Computer, Inc. (1987b). *HyperCard user's guide*. Cupertino, CA: Apple Computer.

Apple Computer, Inc. (1989). *HyperCard stack design guidelines*. Reading, MA: Addison-Wesley.

Association for Computing Machinery. (1987). *Hypertext '87 proceedings*. Chapel Hill, NC: University of North Carolina.

Bartel, R. (1983). *Metaphors and symbols: Forays into language*. Urbana, IL: National Council of Teachers of English.

Begeman, M. L., & Conklin, J. (1988, October). The right tool for the job. *Byte*, pp. 255–266.

Brand, S. (1987). *The media lab: Inventing the future at MIT*. New York: Viking Penguin.

Bush, V. (1945, July). As we may think. *Atlantic Monthly*, pp. 101–108.

Conklin, J. (1987). Hypertext: An introduction and survey. In I. Greif (Ed.), *Computer-supported cooperative work: A book of readings* (pp. 423–475). San Mateo, CA: Morgan Kaufmann Publishers, Inc.

Daniels, J., & Mara, M. J. (1988). *Applied HyperCard: Developing and marketing superior stackware.* New York: Simon & Schuster.

Dear, B. L. (1988, August). HyperCard: What is it? *Byte*, Special Edition, pp. 71–75.

Delisle, N. M., & Schwartz, M. D. (1989). Collaborative writing with hypertext. *IEEE Transactions on Professional Communication, 32*(3), 183–188.

Eldred, J. M. (1989). Computers, composition pedagogy, and the social view. In G. E. Hawisher & C. L. Selfe (Eds.), *Critical perspectives on computers and composition instruction* (pp. 201–218). New York: Teachers College Press.

Fiderio, J. (1988, October). A grand vision. *Byte*, pp. 237–244.

Frisse, M. (1988, October). From text to hypertext. *Byte*, pp. 247–253.

Goodman, D. (1988). *The complete HyperCard handbook* (2nd ed.) New York: Bantam.

Havholm, P., & Stewart, L. (1989). Thinking with hypertext. In *Proceedings of the National Educational Computing Conference* (NECC'89) (pp. 356–361). Eugene, OR: International Council on Computers for Education.

Hyper is hip. (1989, August 14–27). *Mass high tech: New England's high technology newspaper*, p. 6.

Johnson-Laird, P. N. (1988). *The computer and the mind: An introduction to cognitive science.* Cambridge, MA: Harvard University Press.

Lakoff, G., & Johnson, M. (1980). *Metaphors we live by.* Chicago: University of Chicago Press.

Loeb, L. H. (1988, August). HyperCard: How does it work? *Byte*, Special Edition, pp. 75–80.

MacCormac, E. R. (1985). *A cognitive theory of metaphor.* Cambridge, MA: The Massachussetts Institute of Technology Press.

McDaid, John. (1989). Breaking frames: Toward an ecology of hypermedia. *Proposal Abstracts from the Fifth Computers and Writing Conference*, May 12–14, 1989, University of Minnesota, pp. 58–60. Washington, DC: Gallaudet University.

McLuhan, M. (1964). *Understanding media: The extensions of man* (2nd ed.). New York: The New American Library.

Minsky, M. (1986). *The society of mind.* New York: Simon & Schuster.

Raker, E. J. (1989, August/September). Hypermedia: New technology tool for educators. *The Computing Teacher*, pp. 18–19.

Ricoeur, P. (1975). *The rule of metaphor: Multi-disciplinary studies of the creation of meaning in language* (R. Czerny, with K. McLaughlin and J. Costello, Trans.). Toronto: University of Toronto Press.

Sculley, J. (1988). Foreword to S. Ambron and K. Hooper (Eds.), *Interactive multimedia: Visions of multimedia for developers, educators, and information providers.* Redmond, WA: Microsoft Press.

Shneiderman, B., & Kearsley, G. (1989). *Hypertext hands-on!: An introduction to a new way of organizing and accessing information.* Reading, MA: Addison-Wesley.

Smith, A. (1980) *Goodbye, Gutenberg: The newspaper revolution of the 1980's.* New York: Oxford University Press.

Smith, J. B., Weiss, S. F., & Ferguson, G. J. (1987, October). *A hypertext writing environment and its cognitive basis.* A TextLab Report #TR87-033. Chapel Hill, NC: University of North Carolina.

Vygotsky, L. (1986). *Thought and language* (A. Kozulin, Trans. and Ed.). Cambridge, MA: The Massachussetts Institute of Technology Press.

Wheelwright, P. (1962). *Metaphor and reality.* Bloomington, IN: Indiana University Press.

Yoder, E., Akscyn, R., & McCracken, D. (1989). Collaboration in KMS, a shared hypermedia system. In K. Bice & C. Lewis (Eds.), *Wings for the mind: Conference proceedings of the human factors in computing systems* (special issue of the SIGCHI Bulletin, pp. 37–42). New York: The Association for Computing Machinery.

Chapter 9

Toward an Ecology of Hypermedia

John McDaid
New York Institute of Technology

Hypermedia, or nonlinear, computer-based writing can have effects as profound and far-reaching as the older communication technologies of spoken language and print. Where there was linearity and hierarchy, we now have the potential for associative connection and plurality. To best appreciate this shift, we need to look at hypermedia within its ecological context, as a stage in the evolution of media environments. With this understanding, we can begin to examine the native biases of the medium to see how well they fit our goals as theorists and teachers of composition. We may begin to ask questions about the role hypermedia can play in the teaching of writing. How do media shape texts? How do writing and reading in different media shape the mind of the writer? What will be the effects of a technology that has the potential to subvert the linearity inherent in previous media?

Shortly after the invention of time travel, a group of researchers at MIT's HyperMedia Lab secured an Annenberg-Sony grant to investigate the effects of this new medium by paying a visit to the long-deceased guru of media change, Marshall McLuhan. Donning their tie-dyed tee-shirts and love beads, they ventured back to Toronto in the 1960s, where they cornered McLuhan in a coffee shop on Younge Street.

"Hypothetically, of course," inquired the cagey researchers, "what would be the effect of a medium which would, oh, say, allow people to travel in time?"

McLuhan replied instantly: "The answer, of course, is You."

—John McDaid,
Hypermedia and Composition:
Issues for the 2090s

In addition to going in for a cheap laugh, this apocryphal future fiction is meant to introduce the sort of mental jujitsu essential to an ecological appraisal of hypermedia. What this essay will suggest is a way of looking at the evolution of media as a recursive phenomenon, occasioned and constrained by physical and social conditions. This approach should help us, as teachers of writing, to reenvision the role of composition and its pedagogy within the emerging paradigm of hypermedia.

What is meant by an ecological perspective on media? Take McLuhan's famous saying, "The medium is the message." A helpful translation is "Media are environments." The "world," the environment you are experiencing right now, is brought to your consciousness by the natural media of sense. We tend to call this direct physical presence of the world "unmediated," but only in a naive, day-to-day fashion. If pressed, we would admit that our perceptual thresholds—seeing a certain spectrum of electromagnetic radiation, hearing a certain range of vibration—are limits that condition our knowledge of the world in important ways. Media are not passive conduits of information, but active shapers and massagers of messages. To fully apprehend the character of the world they bring us, we must see them as an ecosystem: interacting, shaping, and re-presenting our experience. We are, of course, no longer supplied solely by natural media—in fact, the majority of our information about the world is technologically constituted to some degree. This fact makes investigations of media's shaping effects or ecology important. If we are to teach students to understand particular media well enough to craft messages in them, an understanding of ecology is essential.

This chapter, then, examines the symbolic ecology of hypermedia. First, some definitions will be attempted of the paradigmatic media and their characteristics. Next, each of the media, their characteristics, and their cultural impacts will be discussed. Finally, the chapter offers speculations about the shape of hypermedia discourse and suggests its consequences, specifically for the practice and teaching of composition. A series of questions that will confront us in the coming decade(s) concludes the essay.

The Media Ecosystem

> Electric technology does not need words any more than the digital computer needs numbers. Electricity points the way to an extension of the process of consciousness itself, on a world scale, and without any verbalization whatever. (p. 83)

> —Marshall McLuhan,
> *Understanding Media*

Media theorists traditionally identify three paradigmatic technologies in the history of communications: orality, literacy, and electronics. Each technology shapes the epistemologies, rhetorics, and social structures of the cultures that employ them (Ong, 1982; Eisenstein, 1979; Postman, 1985, 1988). The imputed effects of orality and literacy are fairly well understood (if still somewhat subject to debate); however, as theorists have looked at electronics, their focus has usually been on radio and television. And although these "electric" technologies have been with us in some form for over a hundred years, the truly "electronic"—that is to say, the digitally electronic—have existed less than fifty. What we have viewed as electronic media are in fact "faux" electronic media.

There is reason to suspect (or hope?) that the effects of the digital technologies may be of particular importance to those of us involved in computer-based composition. So while "faux" electronic broadcast media have hitherto borrowed heavily from the metaphors and methodologies of the oral world and the printed page, there has arisen what appears to be digital technology's emergent form, hypermedia.

What Is Hypermedia?

Hypermedia is Theodor Nelson's (1987) term for computer-mediated storage and retrieval of information in a nonsequential fashion. An extension of Nelson's earlier coinage, *hypertext* (for nonsequential writing), hypermedia refers to the linking and navigation of material stored in any medium: text, graphics, sound, music, video, and so forth (p. 0/2). In everyday usage, the words *hypertext* and *hypermedia* are interchangeable. A familiar example of hypermedia is the ubiquitous information kiosk one finds in airports and highway rest stops: a screen that presents a menu of choices, which one may access by touch. But the ability to move through textual information and images is only half the system; a true hypermedia environment also includes tools enabling the user to rearrange the material. A true Nelsonian hypertext does not say, "No user-serviceable parts inside."

That hypermedia is the ideal expression of digital technology was argued as early as 1945 by Vannevar Bush, who first projected a personalized information system he called the "memex," which allowed users to connect and reference mixed-media material instantly across disparate domains (Bush, 1987). It is this linking, this building of trails to construct hybrid documents of associational value rather than linear sequence that marks hypermedia's radical departure from the faux electronic technologies of radio and television.

Not until the 1960s, with the work of Englebart and Nelson (Rheingold, 1985), did hypermedia begin to take shape in computer labs. And it was not until the 1980s that hypermedia made its way to the microcomputer, in programs like GUIDE, STORYSPACE, and HYPERCARD. Such systems bring to the average personal computer user the possibility of active navigation through, and construction of, information-spaces containing any type of digital— or digitalizable—content whatsoever. Because the conversion to digital form and our dependence on computers are the defining characteristics of true electronic environments, I would like to follow Baudrillard (1983) in suggesting the term *digitality* (to parallel *orality* and *literacy*) as the shorthand descriptor for this emerging paradigm.

So What?

If McLuhan's epigraph about digitality providing a direct extension of consciousness is suggestive of the impact of electronics, composition theorists have ample justification for concern. Although McLuhan usually intends his words as a probe rather than a prediction, what can we make of the promise—or threat—of a medium that could dispense with words entirely? Is this a further erosion of mediated discourse predicted by Neil Postman (1985) in *Amusing Ourselves to Death?*

Or could it be that this technological form represents a "counter-blast" (McLuhan & Parker, 1969) against precisely such erosion? Could the faux electronic forms–for example, television—be analogous to the intermediate phases of literacy? Havelock (1976) and Ong (1982) describe a series of evolutionary stages between orality and literacy as a function of the spread of the encoding and decoding abilities. Early electronic media, especially within the context of consumer capitalism, retained print's one-way, one-to-many hierarchical nature. Only recently, with digital computers and the convergence of audiovisual technologies, has the capability of many-to-many communication and the potential for a "polylogical" Great Conversation emerged, a conversation in which marginalization vanishes and the desire to reduce complex issues to Right Answers gives way to resonances along a spectrum of interpretation. In this model, television can be thought of as the "scribal" phase of digitality, paralleling the scribal print culture "broadcast" from reader to copyist.

The Medium Is the Mirage

> And you may ask yourself—
> Well . . . how did I get here?
>
> > —D. Byrne and B. Eno,
> > "Once in a Lifetime,"
> > *Remain in Light*

If the media of communication can so deeply affect human consciousness by mediating transactions with reality, how can we ever get outside this system? What are the variables to which we need pay attention? Theorists categorize media according to the way they shape messages: the extent to which they are visual or auditory, their degree of abstraction, and the ease of the coding scheme, among others (Ong, 1977; Innis, 1951; Havelock, 1976). Out of this concern for formal features arises the division of media into oral, literate, and electronic, each of which will be investigated in detail below. In addition, McLuhan (1964) posits a state he refers to as the "unified sensorium" (p. 67), a prelinguistic but symbolic mental life that preceded orality, which he regards as an Edenic balance and harmonious integration of the senses. In this view, it is only by deviating from this Blakean consciousness, only by succumbing to linearity and reification, that the Word is created.

The Word and Its World

Orality describes the state of cultures whose predominate form of communication is the spoken word. Although there can be no hard evidence for such assertions, one must assume language to be of extreme antiquity, perhaps deeply implicated in the rise of organized human endeavor many tens of thousands of years ago. The characteristics of oral cultures are linked to the features of spoken language: its evanescence (Ong, 1982); its origin in the human lifeworld (Ong, 1982); and its involvement with hearing, a sense modality that is inclusive rather than detached (McLuhan, 1964) (Fig. 1). [The following tables, representing correlations between media and their social impacts, are derived from the work of Elizabeth Eisenstein, Eric Havelock, Marshall McLuhan, Walter J. Ong, and Neil Postman.]

Author	Text	Audience
physically present	audible	physically present
capable of response	evanescent	
contextually related	recursively shaped by context	forced to track text in time
culturally enabled		

Note: Orality gives rise to texts which are formulaic but flexible.

Figure 1: Characteristics of orality

Orality is the base upon which other communication technologies build. Phonetic literacy, which Havelock (1976, p. 25) traces back to 700 B.C., emerges against the ground of underlying oral culture—in fact, the cultural shape of orality creates the need for further technological extension. Although Jacques Ellul's (1964) strong determinist view that technology shapes culture to its own ends may not be warranted, there is evidence that sociotechnic factors in the Greek world militated against a solely oral culture. Orality's inability to innovate, its ineffectiveness as a durable and transportable code, and its inability to adequately homogenize an expansive empire served as the springboard for alphabetic literacy (McLuhan, 1964).

Two hypotheses are presented here: each medium arises by building recursively upon its predecessor, taking the previous technology as "content," and each medium arises at the intersection of enabling technology and recursively engendered environmental pressure (Fig. 2).

Media	Mind	Universe	Culture	Technology
metaphor	group	sacred	conservative	hunting
rhetoric		infinite	ear-based	farming
religion		eternal Now	human	trade

Note: Oral texts lead to a formulaic pattern of information management, and oral cultures inherit this predisposition.

Figure 2: Characteristics of oral cultures

The characteristics represented in Figure 2 may not seem problematic, and in fact, for some theatres of operation, oral language worked quite well. But the Greeks found themselves poorly served by the evanescence of speech, just as we today find ourselves at a juncture where the linguistic conceptions occasioned by day-to-day reality have broken down. Unlike prelinguistic symbols, which were inclusive potentials for meaning, oral language cuts up the world and then exteriorizes it, projecting it onto the world as the way things ARE. And language-level decisions about "the way things are" were formed at pretty low levels of sophistication—a range of experience that included only the inexplicable cycling of Nature and a few crude human technologies like fire, Folsom points, and, perhaps, the inclined plane. Conceptions formed in such media environments break down quickly when operated at relativistic velocity or on a submicroscopic scale. Language makes us good at billiards, bad at quantum tunneling. This way of thinking may become a non-trivial issue as we discover which of these skills, in the long run, is more important.

The Text Remains the Same

Literacy radically alters the sensory ratios of the cultures that employ it. The world of print is highly visual, abstract, and disincarnate. It separates the "word" from its origins in human experience, and makes possible the development of readerships not bound by space and time. Havelock (1976) has pointed out the epistemological implications of Greek alphabeticism. Previous syllabary notations relied on consonants. But consonants are real, discrete; they exist in isolation. Vowels, on the other hand, exist only as a flow; they are the most ephemeral of the sounds which "exist only when . . . going out of existence" (Ong, 1982, p. 32). The snaring of these most evanescent abstractions indicates a powerful ability to decompose and classify. As went vowels, so went the external world. Consider the philosophies that arose in the period immediately following the introduction of this powerful new technology. Ong (1982) has pointed out that Plato's world of ideas is a silent, impersonal, abstract space removed from the lifeworld . . . much like the world of disembodied reason stored in print (p. 32).

Orality enabled social organizations to build up to the point of information overload. And it may have been the nascent fascination with the recursive act of talking about talking (or, as they say in the trade, rhetoric) that led to the idea of bringing some sort of order to the speech act—attempting to set it down somehow, a recursion which yielded writing (Fig. 3).

Of the variety of representational systems developed in response to the information overload of memory-based orality, one

Author	Text	Audience
physically absent	visible	physically absent
incapable of response	permanent	contextually dislocated
culturally disabled	shaped at the point of of "utterance"	recursively con- structs text with multiple readings

Note: Written texts achieve innovation through analysis and hierachy, enabling absent readers to "reconstruct" meaning.

Figure 3: Characteristics of literacy

flavor was particularly successful: alphabetic script. McLuhan (1964) makes much of the fit this technique achieved with the growing desire to grasp and manipulate the universe: taking the flux of speech and chiseling out a relatively few meaningless and arbitrary symbols, which could then be combined to form the infinite complexity of texts—recursive indeed.

As effective a technology as the alphabet is, it has serious problems. As with all extensions of one sense, it pushes us further from synesthetic manifold of pretechnological sensory experience, further from the Unified Sensorium. McLuhan (1964) argues that the alphabet freed us from the "tribal trance of resonating word magic and the web of kinship" and through the power of letters as "agents of aggressive order and precision" gave us "empires and military bureaucracies" where individuals were alienated from their "imaginative, emotional and sense" lives (pp. 88–90).

Writing, McLuhan says, gives us an eye for an ear. Speech may have been more linear than prelinguistic symbolization, but at least speech vanished; its sequentiality was a result of our predicament as Beings-in-Time, rather than something deliberately designed in. (In computer jargon, a bug rather than a feature.) In contrast, writing is the embodiment of linearity, of tracking down, of hierarchizing. It is the formulaic "beginning-middle-endness" of writing that we invented it for. In many ways, this development was not such a good thing. Inevitably, the teeth that shape our spoken words have been exteriorized as the lead slugs packed into the maw of the printing press, and the heating up of text accelerates capitalism, democracy, Protestantism, and gives rise to the book-driven, specialist, curricular school (Fig. 4). All of this describes fairly well where we are, and brings us to the threshold of the next recursion.

The analytic world of print has begun to crumble under the weight of its information overload. Paper-based consciousness struggles to forge the connections necessary to comprehend eleven-dimensional superstring theory, non-zero-sum geopolitics, or the "etiquette" of the *Society of Mind* (Minsky, 1986). We have reached a limit, and the recursive process of writing about writing has yielded the next step: hypermedia.

Media	Mind	Universe	Culture	Technology
alphabet	individual	alienated	progressive	logic
machines		successive	eye-based	math
consumer		discrete	technical	science

Note: Written texts support hierarchical patterns of organization, both in information and culture.

Figure 4: Characteristics of literate cultures

Hypermedia: Web of Maya or Isis' Net?

Print is dead.
—Egon Spengler,
Ghostbusters

McLuhan's observation that "electric technology does not need words" is on the verge of becoming true. Electronic technologies have "reached ... a critical mass" (Postman, 1985, p. 28), and have superseded the spoken and printed word as the major vehicles of acculturation and communication. Hypermedia has grown out of (but is more than) intertextuality and reader-response theory (see

Moulthrop in this collection). In fact, by analogy to literacy, these represent pretechnological responses to the environmental pressure built up by the information overload of linear print. Hypermedia environments make possible texts that can be reorganized as one desires, and that can, in at least a rudimentary sense, be queried, finally putting to rest Plato's often-cited denunciation of texts as fixed, unresponsive objects. But just as the residually oral Plato scorns the new medium of print, the residually literate distrust the digital. As McLuhan (1964) noted,

> Such . . . is the austere continuity of book culture that it scorns to notice these liaisons dangéreuses among the media, especially the scandalous affairs of the book-page with electronic creatures from the other side of the linotype. (p. 193)

Hypermedia's nonlinear textual spaces allow multiple readings to actualize discrete, individual texts, explications of an underlying virtual order. More like the "real world," where meaning is made transactionally, hypertexts possess a multiplicity of possibilities, each of which is equally valid and none of which is the "correct" order or story. The reader comes to a hypertext not as a passive receiver of a predetermined order, but as an active constructor of the text. True, books can be read out of order, but the printed order is suggestive—and as Kaplan and Moulthrop (1989) even say—controlling:

> The fixed arrangement of pages always militates in favor of that "automatic" reading from first to last which branching narrative attempts to subvert. Thus the more intricate page-turning a text demands, the more conscious its reader is likely to become of the native sequence which [s]he is being made to violate. Instead of liberating the narrative imagination, the technical difficulty of poly-sequential books inoculates readers against too much heterodox thinking. (p. 9)

Thus an important distinction for the composition professional lies in the varieties of hypertextual experience. We and our students may profit more, at least initially, by investigating and composing hypertexts with aesthetic rather than purely functional objectives. I do not mean to exclude "expository" hypertexts; rather, exposition in hypertext becomes even more artistic—

the linking and building of webs is a highly complex, aesthetic process. What I do want to exclude is the recapitulation, in this new medium, of the established truths about how to convey information.

Two arguments underpin this decision. First, as McLuhan (1964) frequently pointed out, art is an anti-environment, and artists the "radar antennae" of humankind who

> exult in the novelties of perception afforded by innovation. . . . [They glory] in the invention of new identities, corporate and private, that for the political and educational establishments, as for domestic life, bring anarchy and despair. (p. 12)

The second—and more prosaic—reason is that because hypermedia is in its incunabula, the body of texts available as examples is small, and most of them (even many which call themselves "art") are simply reproductions, in the new medium, of existing works, much like incunabula texts of print (McLuhan, 1962).

Most existing hypertexts are what Michael Joyce (1988) has characterized as "exploratory" (p. 11). In such works, the hypertextual component is limited to navigational devices that facilitate exploration of an information space. The user remains in "audience" mode, and the jobs of reader and of author remain separate and different. Although these early hypertexts represent a step in the direction of digitality, they fall short of what Joyce calls "constructive hypertexts," texts which fully engage the reader. According to Joyce,

> Constructive hypertexts . . . require a capability to act: to create, to change, and to recover particular encounters within the developing body of knowledge. . . . These encounters, like those in exploratory hypertexts, are maintained as versions, i.e., trails, paths, webs, notebooks, etc.; but *they are versions of what they are becoming, a structure for what does not yet exist.* (p. 11) [Italics mine]

In other words, knowledge "in" constructive hypertexts exists not as a preconceived truth waiting impatiently to be discovered, but rather as a potential, lurking in a Heisenbergian way. Until we create it, link it, write it, recover it, "It" does not exist; the Truth is our truth. We create this knowledge contextually and share it electronically not by convincing someone that we are right, but by following their exploration of our links and exploring theirs in order to negotiate our shared and disparate spaces (Fig. 5).

A new medium is, at bottom, a new way of translating and organizing experience and a new way of sharing it. It is to be anticipated that these translations of experience—and their ramifications for culture—will be profoundly different from those of print (Fig. 6). In the same way that the sequential, linear printing press gave rise to sequential, linear systems, we have begun to see, in a variety of disciplines, the importance of recursion (our models of the writing process), of holistic thinking (Japanese management styles), and integrative rather than mass-market culture (micro-marketing, narrow-casting, electronic bulletin boards). The technologies underpinning the digital recursion offer insight: rather than the hierarchies of traditional computer programs, the new "object oriented languages" create a system of computational "entities," each with some degrees of autonomy, which "work together" to accomplish a task. Writing a program in this model is not as much like punching keys on a calculator as it is like being a preschool teacher.

Author	Text	Audience
implicated in text	multisensory	virtual presence
limited response	flexible, active	contextually prompted
paraculturally[a] enabled	recursively created in the "reading"	actualize idiosyncratic texts from the virtual

Note: Digital "texts" are created through interaction, and yield new opportunities on each reading. The terms "author" and "audience" lose meaning as the roles become more symmetric.

[a]The author of a hypertext can make certain aspects of their culture recoverable. This "paracultural" enablement is roughly analogous to the parasocial interaction supplied by broadcast media.

Figure 5: Characteristics of digitality

Media	Mind	Universe	Culture	Technology
icons	holistic	recursive	integrative	parallel processing[a]
tele-presence[b] sense-balanced		self-similar[c]	sense-balanced	object-oriented languages
AI/robots		relativistic	parahuman[d]	hypermedia

Note: Hypertexts suggest ways of organizing information and culture which are active, decentralized, and nonlinear.

[a]Computer systems with multiple processors simultaneously manipulating data.

[b]Remote operation of devices supported by realistic presentation of sensory information.

[c]Patterns of organization repeated at differing levels of detail.

[d]The human scale of oral cultures freed from their media constraints; the Global Village.

Figure 6: Characteristics of digital cultures

The Potential of Hypermedia Discourse

So what then is the ecological perspective on hypermedia composition? The circuitous route we've taken so far in defining this rough beast is an indication of how difficult it is to encode one technology within another. As Isadora Duncan's apocryphal explanation of dance goes, "If I could tell you what it meant, there would be no point in dancing it" (Carpenter, 1972, p. 33). Nor is this a facile sidestepping of the issue. Hypermedia is, literally, a process that must be experienced; it is a process in time. Imagine trying to explain in a completely oral culture your brand new idea for books. It is difficult to get anyone to understand because there is no language for that which does not exist in the oral world. You, with this idea of language bound up on paper, are obviously not right in the head.

Ted Nelson (1987) has suggested thinking of hypermedia as the general phenomenon of which linear texts are a special case. A linear text in this view is a hypertext of which only one possible track or series of links has been actualized, with a canonical link structure (top left to bottom right, turn page) that has become so inculcated as to have vanished in a Barthesian mythological sleight-of-hand. Teaching "writing," therefore, is like teaching a child how to draw only straight lines. It will probably enable them to draw straight lines eventually, but it does not open up the more interesting questions of curves, or spheres, or the constraints of dimensionality itself. Teaching writing as a hypertext-design discipline is analogous to presenting the straight line as a degenerate member of the class of two-dimensional curves—an interesting and powerful member of the family of dimensional rhetorics, but not the only member. Hypermedia decentralizes authority even among rhetorics.

Another spin is to view hypermedia composition in light of the theory of media evolution sketched out previously. Picture McLuhan's Unified Sensorium, the many-at-onceness of symbolization, as the starting point. As an artifact of our predicament as Beings-in-Time, we develop primitive media strongly flavored by single-channel linearity. (We can only hear linearly.) When these media shatter the Unified Sensorium, we climb through a spiral of orality and literacy to return (this time with full consciousness, as James Joyce might suggest) to a hyper- or multi-mode reunification of the senses.

The need for such reunification—and the danger of failure—is especially significant in light of Postman's (1988) most recent critique of mass media: "It is clear that our engineers, not our poets, are the unacknowledged legislators of our time" (p. xiii). Here we have an electronic medium that, in the hands of the poets, can be a precise and powerful technology that replaces passive viewing with active involvement, and that provides a means to achieve the connectivity and coherence leeched from modern culture by the primitive hybrid fusion of print and electronics. It seems we are in the midst of a "phase change" between technologies, when the characteristics of the defining medium become momentarily apparent (McLuhan, 1964, p. 27). Here is an opportunity and, for composition theorists, a responsibility.

We already know that writers need to be active shapers of knowledge, that we must constitute ourselves in polylogic rather than monologic roles, and that the writing classroom needs to be a transactional space. If we examine the fit of these goals with hypermedia—and print—we may well discover that what we've been trying to do all along has been to teach in a hypermedia mode, but that we have been constrained by our print-driven environment.

And lurking behind our self-interest and idealism is the still-turning wheel of evolution. Orality and print, arising out of the linear lifeworld, have profound limitations. Our "common sense," comprised of those cognitive constructs occasioned by experience with linear media, breaks down in the face of a universe that is mostly not human-sized, is unsettlingly discontinuous, and is decidedly nonlinear. Ernst Cassirer (1923) has described relativity as "the shattering of the highest law of motion taught us by experience" (p. 39). The order of events depends on the frame of reference—a difficult notion for the linearly im-printed.

The leading edge of the recursion is already here. Parallel processing, object-oriented languages, and hypermedia discourse are aspects of this digital paradigm, one of interactive fictions and simulated realities. Unhinged from the requirements imposed by archaic media, consciousness can bootstrap itself into conceptual frameworks literally unimaginable today, where relativity is not the shattering of any law at all, but is as intuitive as the inertia of a moving car.

What is at stake in this recursion is the transformation of consciousness. There are tremendous vested interests: the very institutions many of us work for specialize in training people to accept and become narcotized by linearity and its infrastructure. What Moulthrop (1989) has called the "military-entertainment complex" (p. 265) waits eagerly to turn hypermedia into just more HyperMTV. But we, as teachers of writing and as computer visionaries, are uniquely situated to take advantage of the possibilities of hypermedia. We already have the institutional mandate to develop discourse skills. As professionals, we must push for the recognition of hypermedia as possible and necessary in the classroom, and present ourselves as capable teachers and powerful theorists ready to accept the challenge of shaping this new technology.

Such an approach entails posing and answering some questions.

Questions for Hypermedia Research

- Does working with hypermedia in fact facilitate the teaching of composition? Or are we just wasting our time? Is there an attitudinal shift about composition measurably different from traditional approaches? From word processing? Does hypertext increase awareness of intertextuality? Is there a transfer of organizational/macro-level revision skill from hypertexts to written texts?

- What forms will hypermedia take when users and readers do not bring to it conventions of the printed page? How will these forms challenge current curricula? Is this a good thing? In media-rich, cross-disciplinary environments, what texts will be produced? This might involve a whole first-year core, team-taught by curricular specialists as well as media theory folk, visual designers, and composition specialists—an alternative "seminar" where everything is networked and linking, rather then "subjected" to compartmentalization. How would this affect curricular boundaries? How would teachers and students feel about it? Most challenging, could this be used to reshape doctoral programs into real communities of inquiry?

- How do we grade hypertexts? Do we? If not us, who? Is there any interrater reliability in hypermedia? What norms would emerge from a study of grading and what different grading methodologies would be appropriate (student grading, negotiation, hyper-portfolios, electronic democracy)? What new methodologies will emerge?

- Are the predicted social and cognitive impacts of digitality borne out in actual practice? How can we assess these from within a print worldview? What measures must we create?

We need to consider both cognitive factors and human-machine interaction studies of the relative effectiveness of various hypermedia design approaches. We also need long-term, thick anthropological fieldwork rather than empirical feature-counting. On the immediate agenda, of most utility may be participant-observer phenomenological analysis, guided by an awareness of the biases of media.

- If hypermedia seems to be having effects, how do we decide if they are good or bad? What can we do about them based on this judgment? Can we control the medium or must it control us? Can we come to an understanding of the embedded values of hypertext? How can we create forums for discourse about the issue of control? Can the composition organizations fit hypermedia within their mandate? Can networks and electronic conferences like Megabyte University play a role in consensus formation? How can we train teachers to cope with media environments? What changes can be effected at graduate schools of education?

- Can the shape of hypermedia discourse be accommodated within current classroom and academic practices? If not, how must things change? Can the specialist, book-driven university survive the implosion of knowledge latent in hypermedia? What happens when we try inserting hypermedia into current classes? What will we learn from watching the evolution of hypermedia pedagogy?

- How can inequalities of access, particularly thorny with expensive hypermedia workstations, be addressed? What forms of activism are appropriate and necessary? What do we want? Who gets it? Who controls it? Who pays, and how? What possibilities are there for funding? Will partnerships with computer companies be fruitful? While some companies have realized the importance of higher education as a greenhouse for ideas, how can we make others hear our messages? How do we convince the development community that there is a wide audience for the kind of software that truly hypermedia-literate students can be involved in creating? How can we get desktop hypermedia at a reasonable cost? What forms of internal activism will ensure that not solely the engineering schools, but the humanities, receive such technology?

- What is the potential for new collaborations, for hypertext groups and conferences? How can we convince administrators that hypermedia is significant?

Whole new forms of human communication do not arise in every generation. Only twice before have such changes been unleashed. In hypermedia lies immense possibilities to enact and shape a technology—and hence a culture—of empowerment and difference. Who is going to answer these crucial questions? Who is ready to seize this opportunity and bring on the digital recursion?

As McLuhan will have said, "The answer, of course, is You."

Acknowledgments

I thank Gail Hawisher for her helpful and patient editorial assistance. I am indebted to Michael Joyce, Nancy Kaplan, and Stuart Moulthrop for their support and insights. And a special thanks to Karen Marlow-McDaid for her help in shaping this text.

References

Baudrillard, J. (1983). *Simulations*. New York: Semiotext(e) Inc.

Brillstein, B., (Producer), & Reitman, I. (Director). (1984). *Ghostbusters* [Film]. Los Angeles: Columbia Pictures.

Bush, V. (1987). As we may think. In T. Nelson, *Literary Machines*. (Available from Ted Nelson, Project Xanadu, Palo Alto, CA). (Reprinted from *Atlantic Monthly*, July 1945).

Byrne, D., & Eno, B. (Composers). (1980). Once in a lifetime. Song on *Remain in Light* [LP Record]. New York: Sire.

Carpenter, E. (1972). *Oh, what a blow that phantom gave me!* New York: Holt, Rinehart and Winston.

Cassirer, E. (1923). *Structure and function and Einstein's theory of relativity.* New York: Open Court.

Eisenstein, E. (1979). *The printing press as an agent of change.* Cambridge: Cambridge University Press.

Ellul, J. (1964). *The technological society* (R. Merton, Trans.). New York: Vintage.

Havelock, E. (1976). *Origins of western literacy.* Toronto: The Ontario Institute for Studies in Education.

Innis, H. (1951). *The bias of communication.* Toronto: University of Toronto Press.

Joyce, M. (1988, November). Siren shapes: Exploratory and constructive hypertexts, *Academic Computing, 3*(4), 10–14, 37–42.

Kaplan, N., & Moulthrop, S. (1989). *Something to imagine.* Manuscript submitted for publication.

McLuhan, M. (1962). *The Gutenberg galaxy.* New York: New American Library.

McLuhan, M. (1964). *Understanding media.* New York: McGraw-Hill.

McLuhan, M. & Parker, H. (1969). *Counterblast.* New York: Harcourt, Brace & World.

Minsky, M. (1986). *The society of mind.* New York: Simon and Schuster.

Moulthrop, S. (1989). Hypertext and "the hyperreal." In *Hypertext '89 Proceedings* (pp. 259–267). New York: ACM.

Nelson, T. (1987). *Literary machines.* Available from Ted Nelson, Project Xanadu, Palo Alto, CA.

Ong, W. (1977). *Interfaces of the word.* Ithaca, New York: Cornell University Press.

Ong, W. (1982). *Orality and literacy.* New York: Methuen.

Postman, N. (1985). *Amusing ourselves to death.* New York: Viking.

Postman, N. (1988). *Conscientious objections.* New York: Knopf.

Rheingold, H. (1985). *Tools for thought.* New York: Simon and Schuster.

Chapter 10

Reconceiving Hypertext

Catherine F. Smith
Syracuse University

Current hypertext systems support only a thin layer of rational, goal-directed thinking assumed to be universal for all users. The prevailing model of hypertextual thinking is drawn from problem-solving approaches in cognitive psychology. A "thicker" theory of knowledge making that recognizes difference and particularity in mental life as it is socially, culturally, and historically constructed is needed to enrich hypertext theory, design, and use. Gendered thinking illustrates this need. A multidisciplinary feminist perspective reopens the key question: can we conceive hypertext systems and applications to facilitate the complex ways that people think, read, and write?

Hypertext is emerging as a new medium for thinking, reading, and writing in many disciplines, including composition. It promises to become a redefining technology, a tool that reshapes not only practices but also abstract understanding of the thinking, reading, and writing activities it supports. Before that happens, even as we welcome its happening, we benefit by critically reviewing the conceptions of hypertext that are now driving design and development. This essay argues that those conceptions are too narrow.

Hypothetically , three different practical visions of hypertext are possible: as system, as application, and as facilitation. The first two are now available. We have hypertext systems, for example Apple's HYPERCARD, as environments to work within. And we have hypertext applications. We can, for example, build interactive texts for our courses or rolodexes for our personal record keeping within HYPERCARD. But both the system and the application are still constrained by system design, by what system design predetermines users can and cannot do. As a profession, we should be working toward the third possibility, hypertext as facilitation. In

224

this vision, the user, not the system, determines what can happen. The user and the system cooperate in creating a medium of intellectual action. The medium facilitates.

But we can't get there from here unless we first recognize and address the gaps in the theories of knowledge making currently informing hypertext design. The gap addressed by this chapter is the neglect of social and cultural context. Missing in most hypertext theory is acknowledgment that thinking is to some extent socially, culturally, and historically constructed and that thinkers, as a result, may differ in how they form ideas. During the next decade, hypertext systems and applications must be responsive to that potentiality.

The organization of this chapter reflects the diversity of its readers and the dimensions of its argument. Part I speaks to readers inside and outside of composition studies who are knowledgeable about hypertext, critiquing and reworking its vision in feminist, cross-disciplinary terms. Part II steps back to provide a more general (though argument-related) background on the history of hypertext, its disciplinary origins, its current role in composition research, and its need for a new cross-discipline to ground future research and development. Part III is heuristic, reframing old questions about knowledge and suggesting points for departure in hypertext research. A "Narrative Definition" (see "Appendix") sketches hypertextual reading and writing in an educational setting.

Readers are invited to approach the chapter's sections in the order they prefer. Readers familiar with computers but new to hypertext may wish to skim first the narrative definition (see "Appendix"), then read part II, followed by parts I and III. Experienced readers may wish to read part I, skim or omit part II, and read part III.

Part I: Hypertext as It Is, and What It Lacks

The current conception of hypertext includes five key elements:

- *virtual worlds*, or the projection by the user of complex mental spaces, malleable intellectual gestalts

- *dynamism*, or continual reworking of the mental spaces, alteration of the gestalts

- *human engagement*, or a human thinker

- *machine situatedness*, or the computer system as the setting of activity

- *connectivity*, or system links

Together, these concepts—virtual gestalts, human interaction with a technological environment, and system connectivity—constitute a loose paradigm that informed early hypertext theory and development. Vannevar Bush in the 1940s, Douglas Engelbart in the 1950s to the present, Ted Nelson in the 1960s to the present, and hypertext research and development groups in universities and the computer industry (e.g., Apple's HYPERCARD developers) can all be generally located in reference to this early set of assumptions (Bush, 1945; Engelbart & English, 1968; Engelbart, Watson, & Norton, 1973; Nelson, 1965, 1986).

Development and description of hypertexts up to now have necessarily emphasized technical connectivity, or what happens inside the machine. (That's why, when you ask what hypertext is, you often are told how it works, rather than what it is or does.) But a second kind of connectivity is implied by hypertext (and recognized by Engelbart's early automation of cooperative work). Humans come to computer systems with prior (and present) experience in many kinds of interaction. For a user, electronic experience interconnects with surrounding experience outside the technology. A wish to explore this second kind of connectivity—the user's varied interactivity—and its implications for hypertext motivates the central argument in this chapter.

At present, theorists of system design are beginning to acknowledge this second kind of connectivity. Terry Winograd and Fernando Flores (1986) note, for example, that "a person who sits down at a word processor is not just creating a document, but is writing a letter or memo or a book. There is a complex social network in which these activities make sense" (p. 1). With Engelbart's attention to workplace communications in the 1970s, cooperative work applications are making evident the need for more research on what surrounds people's uses of computers and not only research on the devices themselves (*Proceedings*, 1986; Smith & Holland, 1989). However, in relation to hypertext, this kind of research is only beginning, as shown by the relatively small number of papers (five or so) on collaborative work submitted for the Hypertext '89 Conference (*Hypertext '89 papers*, 1989).

Virtuality

The fulcrum of the original paradigm underlying hypertext is virtuality, or Ted Nelson's "structure of seeming"— the *look* and *feel*, the projection of possibility that a system presents (1986).

Before interactive systems, including hypertext, virtuality was mainly a programmer's concept, a feeling for the "area of storage where the programmer builds data structures and composes programs" (Bolter, 1985, p. 85). This virtuality is logical space, modeled on machine logic.

Interactive systems, contrastingly, are intended for end-user control, not programmer control. They imply a different kind of virtuality, a space for intellectual action by a user. A faceted vision of possible uses of this virtual space has emerged during hypertext's short history. The major facets, so far, include

* intimate supplement to memory (Bush's "memex," 1940s)

* information space (Engelbart's augmented knowledge workshop, 1950s, 1960s, and 1970s)

* learning space (Papert's microworld, 1960s)

* literary space (Nelson's docuverse in hyperspace, 1960s and 1970s)

* experience space (virtual realities, cyberspace, 1980s and 1990s)

The notion of virtual space as an intimate supplement to a user's memory was introduced after World War II. At that time, Vannevar Bush imagined a scientist/problem solver motivated by a wish to apply scientific knowledge to postwar problems. This user, or problem solver, proceeded by manipulating source texts (in a microfilm-based workstation, the "memex"). He webbed personal intellectual associations, creating paths or "trails" through sources. Bush (1945) only generally characterized this territory of personal interaction with information as an "intimate supplement to memory" (p. 106).

Douglas Engelbart (Engelbart, Watson, & Norton, 1973) continues to imagine virtual spaces for users in business and industry. Influenced by Bush's ideas, Engelbart began in the 1950s and 1960s to develop computer-based workstations for "knowledge workers" in the workplace. Engelbart formally characterizes *information space* as the "place where knowledge workers (professional, managerial, technical) do their work" in an "augmented knowledge workshop" (p. 7). Information space, in Englebart's conception, is a virtual office or meeting room.

Seymour Papert's (1980) *microworld* of the LOGO user is a virtual classroom for young learners, a space for learning. "The microworld [is] an incubator . . . a growing place for powerful ideas or intellectual structures" (p. 25). Originally developed by Papert and associates for application by young children learning mathematics, LOGO is a learner's system for reinventing the logical world in which principles such as Newton's law of motion apply. Users then appropriate these principles for personal knowledge by inventing other worlds rooted in personal experience where the laws would or would not apply.

Ted Nelson's (1986) *docuverse*, or universe of documents, is a virtual library. It exists in hyperspace, or literary space potentially containing all texts and any reader's associations linking them.

Virtual reality, as defined by Pollock (1989), is anybody simulating their own, or someone else's, or a robot's, reality in cyberspace by wearing "computerized clothing" (helmets or gloves wired for processing sensory data, your own or another's) or by manipulating the performance of mechanical devices (robots) (pp. 1, 27).

Virtuality, or virtual space, in the future will apparently continue to evolve as a user's phenomenon. Apple's HYPERCARD, for example, is characterized as programming for the rest of us, and it gives us virtuality as popular culture. With HYPERCARD, even with its limits, we have entered the Age of HCEV—Here Comes Everybody's Virtuality.

Now that's getting interesting. Coming with it are Everybody's Differences, which is where gender enters the picture.

Your Place or Mine? Gendered Virtuality

Well-established, richly debated feminist theory questions phenomenological differences in women's and men's worldviews. That theory represents the sorts of discussion about thinking missing from hypertext theory. To suggest how feminist phenomenology might inform the idea of hypertext, we can consider the mid- and late-twentieth-century feminist perspectives of Virginia Woolf, a contemporary of Vannevar Bush, and of Mary Daly, a contemporary of Ted Nelson. In this section, Woolf's and Daly's perspectives on gendered thinking are appplied to Bush's and Nelson's conceptions of hypertext.

Woolf articulated differences in women's and men's conceptual environments in *Three Guineas* (1938):

> When we look at the same things, we see them differently. What is that congregation of buildings there, with a semi-monastic look, with chapels and halls and green playing fields? To you it is your old school, Eton or Harrow; your old university, Oxford or Cambridge. . . . But to us, who see it through the shadow of Arthur's Education Fund, it is a schoolroom table, an omnibus going to a class, a little woman with a red nose who is not well educated herself but has an invalid mother to support. (pp. 6–7)

The conditions shaping women's vision were the differences between women's and men's education and economic status in the first half of the twentieth century. Arthur's Education Fund is Woolf's metaphor for the family's and the state's provision for the education of sons, who go to schools and universities, but not for daughters, who learn at home or in trade institutes from ill-educated teachers. The effect of these social differences was difference in women's and men's views of the "same" society and culture they shared.

In *Three Guineas*, published in 1938 as Europe and England faced war, Woolf locates the origins of war in social organization. Through the literary device of answering letters soliciting contributions of money, or guineas, she explains why women might not necessarily support efforts to preserve a "world" society and culture. Woolf rejected a global "world" view of human experience, arguing that deep-rooted social differences are the fundamental sources of tyranny. Efforts to prevent or contain national outbreaks of tyranny were less essential, even in crisis conditions, than efforts to understand the causes, the homely, ordinary beginnings of tyranny in the organization of home life, in educational systems, and in professions. Radical, or root, thinkers who try to understand cause in this way are inevitably separate, or apart, from others who try to create change without this understanding. Apart, root thinkers are "Outsiders," members of Woolf's Society of Outsiders. They see things fundamentally differently from insiders, even thoughtful insiders like, perhaps, Vannevar Bush. Outsiders perceive different social problems and different solutions. Their intellectual world differs from insiders', too. An Outsider, perhaps untrained as a formal thinker or skewed by the victimization that she brings (perhaps unacknowledged) to intellectual work, might find that when she uses a memex or enters a virtual space designed as a supplement to memory, her associations, unlike Bush's rational inquirer's, are blocked, or they proliferate without a focus, or disappear altogether when a troublesome idea occurs, or they conform to nobody else's ideas. Denial, forgetting, displacement, idiosyncrasy—not only forward-moving, productive thought—may enter into Outsiders' experience of thinking with technology, related to the cognitive effects of their other experience.

In the second half of the twentieth century, Mary Daly in *Gyn/Ecology* (1978) more directly specifies the sorts of cognitive effects of gender for women that I have just sketched in Woolfian terms. Daly sees both deconstructive and constructive possibilities, for which she offers new metaphors. "Spooking" is her name for the deconstructive "pattern detection" that occurs in the mind of an Outsider, sensitized by social difference and cultural alienation. Daly optimistically articulates a constructive mental methodology for breaking out of old patterns and bringing new ones into existence. This is Daly's "spinning" that the poet Olga Broumas calls "the methodology/of a mind/stunned at the suddenly/possible shift of meaning" (Daly, p. 314). Daly concludes *Gyn/Ecology* with a projection of the "Spinster" mind peculiarly, powerfully reassociating and reconstituting its world:

> Spinsters spin and weave, mending and creating unity of consciousness. In doing so we spin through and beyond the realm of multiply split consciousness. In concealed workshops,

> Spinsters unsnarl, unknot, untie, unweave. We knit, interlace,
> entwine, whirl, and twirl. Absorbed in Spinning, in the ludic
> celebration, which is both work and play, Spinsters span the
> dichotomies of false consciousness and break its mindbinding
> combinations. (p. 386)

Daly's vision of the solution assumes a problematic "unity of consciousness," and it is ambivalent about technologies: "Significantly, when applied to a product of technology, *spin* sometimes has negative meanings . . . a car spinning its wheels or an airplane falling into a tailspin." (I think of disk-thrashing.) She continues, "The power of Spinning cannot be reduced to the technological. It is spirit spiraling, whirling" (p. 391).

Nevertheless, a virtual reading (a re-writing) of Daly (in view of Woolf and Nelson) is constructed here to suggest how a user's social situation might mediate the user's virtuality. When her work is applied to the original hypertext paradigm, Daly raises to prominence the cognition of social and cultural experience that a human thinker might bring to experience with electronic hypertext. Most important, Daly (like Woolf) realigns relations between two key elements of the original hypertext paradigm, virtuality and connectivity. If connectivity is primarily defined not as system connectivity, but rather as linkage between the user's experience outside and inside the machine, then virtuality becomes seemingly grounded in being. Context, the user's situation, is present in content, the user's ideas.

Architecture helps me explain why this is so. As feminist theory brings context into view, a design discipline such as architecture offers methods for viewing it.

Architecture and hypertext share the intellectual requirement of virtuality understood as a complex space, with real and imaginary components. Both are design disciplines, demanding that a thinker work the gestalts, pattern intellectual space. Knowing how architecture accounts for context can illuminate how hypertext design, so far, has neglected it (*Working Papers*, 1989).

For one architectural theorist, Christopher Alexander (1967),

> The ultimate object of design is form. . . . When we speak of
> design, the real object of discussion is not the form alone, but
> the ensemble comprising the form and its context. . . . The
> form is the solution to the problem; *the context defines the problem.*
> [italics added] (p. 15)

How do you begin to recognize a problem embedded in its context?

> The designer must first trace his design problem to its earliest functional origins and be able to find some sort of pattern in them. (p. 15)

> *Irregularities are the functional origins of form. . . . The incongruities in an ensemble are the primary data of experience.* [italics added] (p. 27)

Irregularities, incongruities, spooks, seeing things differently are the functional origins of form, including forms of ideas. Alexander's embedding of design in the work's context and his pinpointing of design origins in cognitive dissonance offer a theoretical basis for considering how perceivers in a shared society or culture might see different worlds, different problems with different origins, and different solutions. With Woolf and Daly, our profession can come to understand gender as a differentiating force in perception.

Anthropology can help trace a path of difference from perception to symbolic behavior. In the cross-disciplinary gloss on hypertext being constructed here, social anthropology and cultural anthropology offer methods for viewing symbolic processes as the conversion of one domain of experience into another, with social experience fueling the conversion.

Anthropologist Mary Douglas (1970) proposes that our systematic symbolizing thought is based on the system humans "know" best, the body. The physical experience of the body converts into emotional attitudes and symbolic behavior. Determining the nature of the conversion are social experiences. Douglas postulates two bodies, a physical body and a social body:

> The human body is common to us all. Only our social condition varies. The symbols based on the human body are used to express different social experiences. . . . There is a strong tendency to replicate the social situation in symbolic form by drawing richly on body symbols in every possible dimension. (Preface and pp. 65–81)

Douglas applies her observations to cosmology, finding evidence of the two bodies' effect on theory (particularly religious ideas) of the structure and origin of the universe. We can also apply her observations to virtuality. I find myself thinking about Mary Douglas and the two bodies, physical and social, when I read in *The New York Times* or *Scientific American* about virtual realities, or simulations intended to replicate actuality. "Artificial realities have three components," says *Scientific American*,

> imagery, behavior, and interaction. Realistic imagery helps the user to interpret information. . . . These images behave [realistically] . . . [and] the user interacts with an artificial reality in much the same way as he interacts with the three-dimensional world, by moving, pointing, . . . talking, and observing from many angles. (Foley, 1987, p. 128)

But the reading of Woolf, Daly, and Douglas given here claims that we do not all interact with the three-dimensional world in the "same" way. Have the designers of virtual realities encountered our differences? Do the systems those designers design know about difference?

Part II: Hypertext, Cognition, and Composition—Review of Research and Theory

Hypertext relies on new technology to enable an old activity. The activity is making connections among texts and among thoughts. Now melded with evolving computer capabilities, new functions of connecting are being implemented in systems grouped under the term *hypertext* (Nelson, 1965; Conklin, 1987).

Hypertext as a technology emerged in theory and implementation by particular individuals in engineering disciplines such as Vannevar Bush and Douglas Engelbart, who were interested in applying war-expanded scientific knowledge to the solution of social and practical problems (Bush, 1945; Engelbart & English, 1968). In another discipline, literary studies, others immediately recognized conceptual kinship and potentially great practical implications relating the proposed new technology to text processing (Nelson, 1965; Smith, 1970, 1975, 1978, 1982). However, hypertext has grown up not in its polyglot original matrix of engineering and literary theory but in a single discipline, computer science. Thus, the development of hypertext has been keyed to developments in a technical specialty. Primarily, hypertext is a younger sibling to artificial intelligence, the science of the human mind as an information processor.

Hypertext theorists have been concerned with cognition from the beginning. Two interests have predominated, based on two views of the potential usefulness of hypertext. These views may be characterized as "passive" versus "active" uses, or, essentially, browsing versus authoring. The terms *passive* and *active* distort, because all hypertext use is active and because the two main applications, browsing and authoring, are not mutually exclusive. Yet, distinctions between (relatively) static and dynamic forms of hypertext increasingly appear in the research literature to delineate stages in the evolution of systems and to raise finer-grained questions for further theory, design, and development (Halasz, 1989; *Hypertext '89 Papers*). In this chapter, the distinctions are helpful for clarifying which cognitive issues are being addressed and which are not, yet.

Passive hypertext, understood as browsing and reading, focuses on the cognition of reading "nonsequentially" and working with large databases of existing text. For example, in associative browsing one identifies objects of attention in text (nodes), creates relationships among them (links), and handles information overload (i.e., maintains coherence and comprehension) while "navigating" among nodes and links. This is a view of hypertext as world knowledge, retrieved and applied by the user.

Active hypertext, understood as creating and designing, focuses on the cognition of discovering, externalizing, and communicating internal knowledge, for example, constructing nodes as well as links; organizing and representing structures; and revising representations, structures, or content. This is a view of hypertext as personal knowledge, constructed by the user.

A Composition Focus

Both views of hypertext are interesting to composition teachers and scholars, but "active" hypertext is most relevant. Composition teacher/researchers have begun exploring the relevance

(Slatin, 1988). Some, as system designers, are applying research in writing processes, reading comprehension, and learning theory to the design and testing of computer writing environments with hypertext capabilities (Smith & Lansman, 1989; Neuwirth, Kaufer, Chimera, & Gillespie, 1989; Neuwirth & Kaufer, 1989; Kozma, 1989).

The cognitive activity supported by these computer writing environments is document production, the complex mental system by which people represent ideas in written texts. The component cognitive processes of this activity—identified as exploring, managing memory, using sources, planning, organizing, providing for readers' comprehension, drafting, and revising—are supported by writing environments. Experiments using one such system, WRITING ENVIRONMENT (WE), suggest that the computer's mediation encourages functional interdependencies among processes, products, goals, and constraints in writing processes. On the basis of these interdependencies, cognitive theories of writing can be revised. Componential views of writing processes give way to integrative views. "Cognitive modes," or combinatorial units of cognitive activity larger than their component processes and cutting across writing activities, are hypothesized (Smith & Lansman, 1989).

Such revisions, particularly the hypothesis of cognitive modes, are on the right track, pointing to interdependencies in the mind/machine interaction that begin to disclose the psychology of hypertext.

However, these revisions offer only a partial view of hypertextual writing and reading. Because they are not designed primarily for hypertext applications (they focus on document production), computer writing environments do not fully implement hypertext. More important, when they are designed according to problem-solving models of cognition, they largely preclude the possibility of full hypertext, according to arguments in this chapter. Problem solving is a specific kind of thinking—purposeful, individual-centered rationality. As a model of cognition, problem solving neglects affect and context. But idiosyncracies and surroundings do matter, and the interdependency of idiosyncracies and surroundings may be very important. Thus, an enriched, or even an adequate, conception of hypertext entails complexities in writers' identities, personalities, and situations that shape their cognition. Particular people produce texts, comprehend texts, and learn in particular times and places. Virtuality is situated. What's more, it isn't entirely rational.

Therefore, we will look further into composition research to account for affective and contextual dimensions of writers' cognition that might be applied to hypertext development. What we find is suggestive, but still insufficient.

Affect is treated in composition research either very specifically, e.g., for its manifestation in disabilities such as writing anxiety (Bloom, 1984), or very generally, e.g., for its integral role in the development of abstract reasoning and rhetorical awareness (Moffett, 1968). Context is treated from within multiple, widely ranging definitions—biological, psychological, social, cultural, linguistic (Phelps, 1984).

If the design and evaluation of better computer writing tools, such as hypertext, depends on advances in the psychology of writing (Kellogg, 1989), then these are important, if scattered, beginnings for such a psychology. A survey of composition research in the subarea of the cognition of writing illuminates the vitality a psychology of writing might have as a research domain and how it might contribute to understanding the psychology of hypertext use. However, advances are likely to be greatest if research is broadly cross-disciplinary, integrating work on symbolic processes now active in numerous disciplines (Phelps, 1984; Warnock, 1984).

A cross-discipline serving as the locus of research on composing activity is arguably the best intellectual ground for future development of hypertext. Composition may be a good candidate discipline. It is likely that hypertext research grounded in composition studies could recover its original matrix vision, loosening the grip of single specialized technical disciplines on its development. However, composition, even as a new discipline now defining itself, may carry traditional associations with linguistic symbolization and with textual artifacts that are too strong, that would discourage the needed view of ideation as something not limited to verbal representation and text production.

A better alternative may be to identify a new hypertextual cross-discipline. An excellent candidate would be the ludic Spinning we could call "knowledge work/play." This discipline would focus on "knowledge work" as identified by Engelbart, and "knowledge play" as it is now being identified by writers and critics of interactive fiction (Joyce, 1988; McDaid, 1989; Moulthrop, 1989a, 1989b). Richard Lanham (1988–89) identifies the human characteristic captured by binocular work/play:

> We can plot the motival structure which animates the object we see, or our viewing of it, or the creation of the object, on a spectrum which runs from the most intense competition for hierarchical ranking to the most spontaneous, gratuitous behavior which we perform just for the hell of it, because the performative muscles want to fire; careerism at the left, saintly simplicity at the right. (p. 277)

Part III: Questions for Hypertext in the 1990s

Knowledge work/play, or the new discipline evoked by hypertext, is capacious. It invites ecological views of mental life and the hypertext presence in it. A discipline of knowledge work/play needs a psychology, a sociology, a biology, a semiotic, a science of the artificial, an aesthetic, a philosophy, and so forth. In the late 1980s and in the beginning of the 1990s, this discipline began putting itself together, as evidenced by the emergence of grassroots users' groups, special conferences on hypertext, and special issues of computer journals. A selected list includes the Hypertext series of conferences (Hypertext '87, Hypertext '89, the European Conference on Hypertext '90); Hypermedia '88; and Hypertext II (held in England, 1989)—as well as special issues of *Communications of the ACM* and *Educational Technology* in 1988. These gatherings and collections web together numerous disciplines and professions—computer science, anthropology, medicine, law, and creative writing—as well as cross-disciplines: cognitive science, composition. Their "critical mass" of interrogatory, international, interspeciality plurality may eventually result in a corporate self-definition of a field of inquiry, something like knowledge work/ play. Participants in such ventures already attest to the impact of hypertext on their traditional methods and meanings. They seem minds stunned with possibility.

For the remainder of this chapter, then, we can speculate on some big questions that a discipline of knowledge work/play might address. Answers, even traditions of answer, already exist for each of the questions that follow. My aim, however, is heuristic. I hope to re-ask ancient questions at a sufficiently general or intuitive level to provoke fresh analysis and new synthesis, to invite novel as well as established approaches. As we enter the 1990s, it is useful to review inherited thought about knowledge making. For example, William James's metaphor of streams of consciousness, developed in the 1890s, informed much of modern psychology and may offer perspective on a postmodern hypertext.

Questions here are limited to two familiarly accepted, perpetually controversial oppositions in mental life—conscious/unconscious and individual/collective—and to one basic process, mediation, that seem to me basic for defining knowledge work/play. Within each open-ended question that follows, I propose starting points for hypertext reconsideration. However, the main purpose of the following questions is to get on the map some large issues that are implicit and largely unaddressed in hypertext conceptualization to date: the accessibility of knowledge, the individuality of knowledge, and the role of mediation in constructing knowledge. These issues are then reduced in an accompanying short list of research and methodology questions.

Is Knowledge Conscious?
(Do We Know What We're Thinking?)

William James, whose psychological theories helped found the science of psychology in the 1890s, may be helpful as we try to imagine a psychology of knowledge for the 1990s. James (1958) hypothesized,

> In each of us . . . some kind of consciousness is always going on. There is a stream of consciousness, a succession of states, or waves, of fields (or of whatever you please to call them), of knowledge, of feeling, of desire, of deliberation, etc., that constantly pass and repass, and that constitute our inner life.
> . . . We have thus fields of consciousness . . . and [they] are

> always complex. They contain sensations of our bodies and of the objects around us, memories of past experiences and thoughts of distant things, feelings of satisfaction and dissatisfaction, desires and aversions, and other emotional conditions, together with determinations of the will, in every variety of permutation and combination. (p. 28)

> In the successive mutations of our fields of consciousness, the process by which one dissolves into another is often very gradual, and all sorts of inner rearrangements of contents occur. Sometimes the focus remains but little changed while the margin alters rapidly. Sometimes the focus alters, and the margin stays. Sometimes, again, abrupt alterations of the whole field occur. (p. 30)

If knowledge develops in a stream of successive, mutable fields permeated by influences from the organism and its environment, then a field description of knowledge would include the nature and dynamics of "the inner life," or *affective processes*: forgetting and denying as well as remembering and recognizing associations, rejecting as well as acknowledging connections. Hence, for hypertext research, studies of tacit knowledge and of inner speech in composition theory would be a place to start toward broader views of the hypertext knowledge stream (Polanyi, 1962; Vygotsky, 1962; Moffett, 1968; Woolf, 1976).

Hypertext has the potential to augment human thinking processes. So far, however, the only processes designers have addressed are conscious and rational ones. The salient operation of current hypertext is to make links between intellectual objects, requiring the human thinker to create the links explicitly. Dynamic succession of (perhaps opposed) knowledge states, shifts of field and focus, conceptual blocks, implicit links not yet recognized by the thinker—none of these is addressed by designers in the current hypertext vision.

The validity of the question "Is knowledge conscious?" is acknowledged in creativity theory and writing process theory. In writing process research, for example, methods such as think-aloud protocols receive their sharpest critique for their limited ability to access the less verbalizable aspects of writers' thinking. Current hypertext has the same limitation and is open to the same critique.

Is Knowledge Individual?
(Whom Do We Have in Mind?)

When you think about human thinking, what do you visualize? Probably something like Rodin's "The Thinker." Typically, we theorize a sole human, thinking. Yet groups pervade human working and playing life. How does the common reality of working and playing with others condition individual mental life? Attention is beginning to be paid to this question from a constructionist perspective across a number of disciplines. A recent proposal for research integrating cognitive science and sociology/ anthropology directly states the problem:

> American cognitive science, true to its current coalition between cognitive psychology and artificial intelligence, assumes the seat of intelligent behavior to be in the heads of individual thinkers. Mind is *a priori* attributed to the individual, and the search for processes and structures that explain the phenomena of mind is likewise restricted to individual crania. The neglect of *collective thinking* marks a significant gap in our understanding of human cognition and . . . learn-ing. . . . The current challenge is to develop a perspective that apportions cognition both to individuals and to the group. [italics added] (Smith & Holland, 1989, pp. 3–4)

Development of hypertext engages this challenge. Semiotic studies of social, cultural, and historical mediation in intellectual and psychological development are starting points (Foucault, 1972).

Hypertext is a two-part equation, mind and machine. The individual mind interacts with artifacts or the communicated presence of other minds in the environment created by interaction with the machine. This inherent and complex collectivity is the least recognized aspect of hypertext.

Is Knowledge Direct? (How Do We Know?)

Wordplay helps, here: knowLEDGE is a holding place; knoWING is moving from one holding place to another, migrating, rappeling, taking flight. *Ledges* and *wings*, *nodes* and *links*— both pairs are metaphors for objects and events in thinking. They structure our view of thinking and enable us to talk about it. Nodes and links are taken from current technical descriptions of hypertext systems; they are the nuts and bolts (so to speak) of current technical talk about hypertext (Conklin, 1987). I made up ledges and wings here to demonstrate the possibility of talking about hypertext differently (inspired by Daly & Caputi, 1987). The point is not which metaphor is preferable. Rather, the point is the generality of *active processes,* including metaphor formation, and the role of *mediating devices,* including metaphors, in knowledge work/play.

To understand that human conceptualization may be structurally as well as representationally metaphoric and to examine bases of metaphor in physical and social experience, we can turn to studies that are starting points for looking at mediation in knowledge work/play (Lakoff & Johnson, 1980; Douglas, 1970). Other studies of the use of mental tools in human cognitive development and of the role of cultural meaning systems in providing mental tools are also starting points (Vygotsky, 1962, 1978).

Finally, studies of mediation through physical tools, particularly computers, should be included in describing knowledge work/play in the age of hypertext (Lanham, 1988–89; Smith, 1989; Smith & Lansman, 1989; Winograd & Flores, 1986).

Questions for Research and Methodology

These large questions—the accessibility, individuality, and mediated nature of knowledge—demand further reduction to specific topics for experimental inquiry. Following is a short list to begin the reduction and extend the search for methods:

- How does tacit knowledge enter the mind/machine interaction?

- What research methods best inform us about both sides of the mind/machine interaction?

  —empiric observation?

  —ethnographic description of particular hypertextual writing and reading events in context?

—system-recorded, statistically analyzed transcripts of actions performed in the computer while reading and writing?

—combinations of these methods?

• How can we define computer system functions analogous to and capable of supporting unconscious thinking? Stated another way, how can we loosen direct control by the system and conscious control by the user so that system and user become knowledge co-operators?

• What analytic frameworks do we need to understand group thinking, reading, and writing? Do individual process models apply to group work?

• Can we apply methods from multiple disciplines—from cognitive anthropology or from the sociology of work, for example, on how new tools or instruments alter the social organization of work or play—to understanding electronic writing and reading?

• What metaphors for thinking prevail in discourse about composition—in composition theory, teaching practice, textbooks, experience accounts of individual or group writing processes?

• What metaphors for thinking prevail in discourse about computing—in hypertext design theory, descriptions of computer systems for writing, user documentation for idea-processing software, experience accounts of individual or group electronic writing processes?

Conclusions: Hypertext as It Might Be

If hypertext is to facilitate thinking, it must handle complexity beyond the problem of getting lost in hyperspace, or information overload. *Thick facilitation* is based on understanding that thinking is "thick," or sociologically, psychologically, and biologically complex. Thick facilitation means enabling users to construct personal or group environments for work/play according to their evolving (a) situations, (b) goal-directed functions, (c) resistances, (d) epiphanies, and (e) operational sophistication (learning from the medium as they use it).

The key word here is *co-evolution*. Knowledge should co-evolve in the user and the system. Envision the user supporting ideas— or fighting them, or groping with them—by thinking instrumentally *and* collaboratively with the medium. As new knowledge emerges, the user reconfigures the system to go from there. The experience of thinking changes the electronic world. The user teaches the system. This virtuality is an electronic world embedded in an experiential one.

Ted Nelson (1986) ringingly proposes that

> the starting point in designing a computer system must be the creation of the conceptual and psychological environment— the seeming of the system . . . the virtuality. You begin there and decide how it *ought* to be, and then make that vision happen. (p. 3)

It's the right invitation. Accepting it, writing teachers can make hypertext an electronic "zone of proximal development" (Vygotsky, 1978). Electronically rendered, this zone consists of real people's ideas progressively disclosed in electronic work/play, and helped by other people and by the medium. Systems and applications ought to be designed around one main principle, that of augmenting and facilitating human thought processes.

System designers are beginning to focus on this principle. In parallel, writing teachers and writers need to design hypertextual pedagogies. Teaching will necessarily change as the medium of writing and reading moves away from printed pages and toward electronic environments. Writers and writing teachers can participate in shaping the hypertext medium.

Appendix

The following sketch is offered as an alternative to narrowly or technically defining hypertext. To give the new reader a feeling for hypertext, the sketch begins in familiar practice—word processing by a student writer—and suggests ways (based on actual or proposed system capabilities) that hypertextual reading and writing go beyond word processing.

Narrative Definition

A writer enters a cluster of computer workstations in her university dormitory one evening. In the cluster are individual machines networked to allow communications between stations and with other sites. In the system on the network are databases of textual, video, and audio materials along with software for using them. The student notices that work groups from her class fill the cluster, although she seems to be the only member of her group who is working in this particular cluster.

She brings two tasks to this environment, to read a text (an academic journal article) and to write a response. She is to respond individually in light of a consensus about the article's argument reached through discussion by her work group. She will do all her work on-line (without paper) because her class has experimentally agreed do its thinking, reading, writing, and communicating electronically.

She calls the article onto her screen from a common file created for her class. Assignments, audio- and videotapes, drafts of work-in-progress, and written commentary are stored in the common file for use by class members and associated others. The assigned reading has been prepared as a hypertext (either by the original writer, the course instructor, or a student) with direct links between passages of verbal text to other passages in the article or in other texts, or to commentary by multiple readers on the selected passage, or to sections of video- or audiotapes. The reader may also attach her branching thought to a selected passage, query another reader's response, or otherwise intervene constructively during her reading, if she wishes.

She does. As she reads, she frequently selects passages, jots her own notes about them on the screen, reads another's comment, jots her response to the comment, recalls a related reading for a class the previous year, calls up the part she remembers from the common file still available for that class and hooks it to her current reading, recalls the paper she wrote in that earlier class, brings that paper up (from her personal knowledge base, where all her academic work over four years is stored) and hooks it to the growing text of her current reading. She continues reading, disclosing or suppressing the attached material in windows on the screen as she chooses.

As she works silently at her machine, groups of other students around her talk noisily about what they are doing at theirs. Consensuses proliferate around her. She half-hears.

She pauses to check the on-line bulletin board to see who else in her work group is reading now, elsewhere. She finds a groupmate in another cluster across campus and sends him a message. They talk for awhile by sending messages back and forth. Her ideas change as they communicate; she records their conversation and notes the revision in her idea of the article's argument. After they close, she decides to check the on-line catalog of the university library for more recent sources on the subject. No luck. She may do a database search later, but not tonight.

She declares her reading finished for now. She stores a personal version of the article with its attachments in her personal knowledge base.

She starts composing. She calls up brainstorming aids and a structure editor from the system as she feels the need. She graphically maps ideas as they build. She occasionally calls up bits of text or other maps from her personal knowledge base as she works. She continues restructuring her idea map for this assignment. When she achieves one she likes, she asks the system to query her knowledge base for the key terms she has used to name chunks of the map. If it finds other instances of those terms in her knowledge base, the system will retrieve and analyze them, then bring her new possible relations of those key terms incorporating earlier uses in other contexts (that she has forgotten). It does. She considers the findings, accepts one, and changes her map accordingly. She declares a current version of the idea map ready, and stores it. She then plans an order of sections and paragraphs (an outline) for her verbal text, and stores it.

She begins producing a text. As she enters drafts, she analyzes the evolving written text dynamically against her idea map and document outline. She considers placing a piece of the map directly into the text as a graphic overview to preview an extended point. A mail query from her groupmate interrupts her. She sends him her map; he reads it and returns it, reorganized, with comments. She considers, accepts some of the reorganization, attaches his map with his name to her map, and continues writing. In the meantime, she has decided not to include a graphic overview in the text itself, but she continues to consult the maps to help her stay on track as she develops the extended point. She will eventually incorporate the key terms and their named relations from the map as section headings in the text. She decides, in other words, to bring the language structure (but not the visual structure) from the map into the text.

At some point, she declares her draft text ready for public response. She stores a "ready" copy in the common class file and in her personal knowledge base. She saves the system record of all her actions during this evening's work session in the common file's folder for ongoing research by members of the class.

Over the next few days, other students in her work group and the instructor collect "ready" versions, enter comments or suggestions, and return "response" versions to the common file. Writers collect the "response" versions, revise as they see fit, and store a "finished" version in the common file.

Discussions of these texts and their related system records take place later that week in this writer's class and in a collaborating class three thousand miles away at a partner university experimenting with networked composition courses. Several months later, the instructor draws on some of these texts while conferring with other writing researchers who are exploring group influences on individuals doing cooperative writing. These teacher/researchers are comparing two kinds of group interaction, network communications (system-recorded) and ordinary conversations (videotaped), as these modes simultaneously occur during work sessions in which individual students compose and revise a cooperatively conceived document. Research questions focus on how the two simultaneous forms of interaction differently affect individuals' writing and revising.

Acknowledgments

I especially thank Cynthia L. Selfe of Michigan Technological University and Gail E. Hawisher of the University of Illinois at Urbana-Champaign for welcome initial encouragement; the HYPERCARD group in the Syracuse University Writing Program (Jack Beaudoin, Lydia Doty, Henry Jankiewicz, John Lauden, Roberta Kirby-Werner, and Don Wagner) for spirited discussion and implementation; and John B. Smith of the University of North Carolina for generous collaboration in developing the ideas presented here.

References

Alexander, C. (1967). *Notes on the synthesis of form.* Cambridge, MA: Harvard University Press.

Bloom, L. Z. (1984). Research on writing blocks, writing anxiety, and writing apprehension. In M. G. Moran & R. F. Lunsford (Eds.), *Research in composition and rhetoric: A bibliographic sourcebook* (pp. 71–90). Westport, CT: Greenwood Press.

Bolter, D. J. (1985). *Turing's man: Western culture in the computer age.* Chapel Hill, NC: University of North Carolina Press.

Britton, B. K., & Glynn, S. M. (Eds.). (1989). *Computer writing environments: Theory, research, and design.* Hillsdale, NJ: Lawrence Erlbaum Associates.

Bush, V. (1945). As we may think. *Atlantic Monthly, 176* (1), 101-108.

Conklin, J. (1987). Hypertext: An introduction and survey. *IEEE Computer, 20*(9), 17–41.

Daly, M. (1978). *Gyn/Ecology: The metaethics of radical feminism.* Boston: Beacon Press.

Daly, M., & Caputi, J. (1987). *Webster's first new intergalactic wickedary of the English language.* Boston: Beacon Press.

Douglas, M. (1970). *Natural symbols: Explorations in cosmology.* New York: Pantheon Books.

Engelbart, D. C., & English, W. K. (1968). A research center for the augmentation of human intellect. *Proceedings of the 1968 Fall Joint Computer Conference* (pp. 395–410). Montvale, NJ: AFIPS Press.

Engelbart, D. C., Watson, R. C., & Norton, J. C. (1973). *The augmented knowledge workshop.* (Report No. 14724). Menlo Park, CA: Augmentation Research Center, Stanford Research Center.

Foley, J. D. (1987, October). Interfaces for advanced computing. *Scientific American, 257.*

Foucault, M. (1972). *The archaeology of knowledge.* New York: Pantheon Books.

Halasz, F. (1989). Reflections on Notecards: Seven issues for the next generation of hypermedia systems. In J. B. Smith, F. Halasz, & N. Yankelovich (Eds.), *Hypertext '87 Proceedings* (pp. 345–365). New York: Association for Computing Machinery.

Hypertext '89 papers. (1989, November). (Manuscripts submitted for the Hypertext '89 Conference, Pittsburgh, PA).

James, W. (1958). *Talks to teachers on psychology, and to students, on some of life's ideals.* New York: Norton. (Original lectures presented in 1892.)

Joyce, M. (1988, November). Siren shapes: Exploratory and constructive hypertexts. *Academic Computing, 9–12, 38–41.*

Kellogg, R. T. (1989). Idea processors: Computer aids for planning and composing text. In B. K. Britton & S. M. Glynn (Eds.), *Computer writing environments: Theory, research, and design* (pp. 57–87). Hillsdale, NJ: Lawrence Erlbaum Associates.

Kozma, R. B. (1989). *Hypertext and learning: The case of* LEARNING TOOL. Manuscript submitted for the Hypertext '89 Conference.

Lakoff, G., & Johnson, M. (1980). *Metaphors we live by.* Chicago: University of Chicago Press.

Lanham, R. (1988–89). The electronic word: Literary study and the digital revolution. *New Literary History: A Journal of Theory and Interpretation, 20,* 265–290.

McDaid, J. (1989, May). *Breaking frames: Toward an ecology of hypermedia.* Paper presented at the Fifth Conference on Computers and Composition, Minneapolis, Minnesota.

Moffett, J. (1968). *Teaching the universe of discourse.* Boston: Houghton Mifflin.

Moran, M. G., & Lunsford, R. F. (Eds.). (1984). *Research in composition and rhetoric: A bibliographic sourcebook.* Westport, CT: Greenwood Press.

Moulthrop, S. (1989a). Hypertext and "the hyperreal." In Norman Meyrowitz (Proceedings Chair), *Hypertext '89 Proceedings,* 259–267.

Moulthrop, S. (1989b, Fall). In the zones: Hypertext and the politics of interpretation. *Writing on the Edge: A Multi-Perspective on Writing, 1*(1), 18–27.

Meyrowitz, N. (Proceedings Chair). (1989). *Hypertext '89 Proceedings.* New York: Association for Computing Machinery Presses.

Nelson, T. (1965). The hypertext. *Proceedings International Documentation Federation.* Cited in J. B. Smith, F. Halasz, & N. Yankelovich (Eds.), *Hypertext '87 Proceedings* (p. vii). New York: Association for Computing Machinery Presses.

Nelson, T. (1986). *Literary machines* (6th ed.). San Antonio, TX: Project Xanadu.

Neuwirth, C., & Kaufer, D. (1989). The role of external representation in the writing process: Implications for the design of hypertext-based writing tools. In N. Meyrowitz (Proceedings Chair), *Hypertext '89 Proceedings* (pp. 319–341). New York: Association for Computing Machinery Presses.

Neuwirth, C., Kaufer, D., Chimera, R., & Gillespie, T. (1989). The NOTES program: A hypertext application for writing from source texts. In J. B. Smith, F. Halasz, & N. Yankelovich (Eds.), *Hypertext '87 Proceedings* (pp. 121–141). New York: Association for Computing Machinery Presses.

Papert, S. (1980). *Mindstorms: Children, computers, and powerful ideas.* New York: Basic Books.

Phelps, L. W. (1984). Cross-currents in an emerging psychology of composition. In M. G. Moran & R. F. Lunsford (Eds.), *Research in composition and rhetoric: A bibliographic sourcebook* (pp. 27–64). Westport, CT: Greenwood Press.

Polanyi, M. (1962). *Personal knowledge: Towards a post-critical philosophy.* Chicago: University of Chicago Press.

Pollock, A. (1989, April 10). What is artificial reality? Wear a computer and see. *The New York Times*, 1, 27.

Proceedings. (1986, December). First Conference on Computer-Supported Cooperative Work, Austin, Texas.

Rose, M. (1983). *Writer's block: The cognitive dimension.* Carbondale, IL: Southern Illinois Press/Conference on College Composition and Communication.

Slatin, J. M. (1988). Hypertext and the teaching of writing. In E. Barrett (Ed.), *Text, context, and hypertext* (pp. 111–132). Cambridge, MA: Massachussetts Institute of Technology Press.

Smith, J. B. (1970). A computer-assisted analysis of imagery in Joyce's *A Portrait of the Artist as a Young Man.* Doctoral dissertation, University of North Carolina, Chapel Hill.

Smith, J. B. (1975, Winter). Thematic structure and complexity. *Style*, *ix*(1), 32–54.

Smith, J. B. (1978, Fall). Computer criticism. *Style*, *xii*(4), 326–356.

Smith, J. B. (1980). *Imagery and the mind of Stephen Daedalus: A computer-assisted study of Joyce's* A Portrait of the Artist as a Young

Man. Lewisburg, PA: Bucknell University Press (Associated University Presses).

Smith, J. B. (1982, Winter). Toward a marxist poetics. *Style, xvi* (1), 1–21.

Smith, J. B. (1989). *Experimental studies in human-computer information systems.* Manuscript proposal.

Smith, J. B., Halasz, F., & Yankelovich, N. (Eds.). (1989). *Hypertext '87 Proceedings.* New York: Association for Computing Machinery Presses.

Smith, J. B., & Holland, D. (1989). *Collective cognition and work cultures.* Manuscript proposal.

Smith, J. B., & Lansman, M. (1989). A cognitive basis for a computer writing environment. In B. K. Britton & S. M. Glynn (Eds.), *Computer writing environments: Theory, research, design* (pp. 17–56). Hillsdale, NJ: Lawrence Erlbaum Associates.

Vygotsky, L. S. (1962). *Thought and language.* E. Hanfmann & G. Vakar (Eds. and Trans.). Cambridge, MA: Massachusetts Institute of Technology Press.

Vygotsky, L. S. (1978). *Mind in society: The development of higher psychological processes.* M. Cole, V. John-Steiner, S. Scribner, & E. Souberman (Eds.). Cambridge, MA: Harvard University Press.

Warnock, J. (1984). The writing process. In M. G. Moran & R. F. Lunsford (Eds.), *Research in composition and rhetoric: A bibliographic sourcebook* (pp. 3–26). Westport, CT: Greenwood Press.

Wertsch, J. V. (1985). *Vygotsky and the social formation of mind.* Cambridge, MA: Harvard University Press.

Winograd, T., & Flores, F. (1986). *Understanding computers and cognition: Toward a new foundation for design.* Norwood, NJ: Ablex.

Woolf, V. (1938). *Three guineas.* New York: Harcourt, Brace and Company.

Woolf, V. (1976). A sketch of the past. In J. Schulkind (Ed.), *Moments of being: Virginia Woolf's unpublished autobiographical writings.* New York: Harcourt Brace Jovanovich.

Working papers. (1989). Syracuse University Writing Program Hyper-Card Group.

Chapter 11

The Politics of Hypertext

Stuart Moulthrop
University of Texas at Austin

The continuing evolution of electronic writing systems—from word processing to hypertext to interactive multimedia—promises substantial change in the way we produce and receive texts. Because electronic text creates a "social space" that is expansive and pluralistic, it favors approaches to writing as a constructive, associative activity rather than as a subordinated encounter with authoritative "works." Literary theorists have projected the possibility of such a discourse, but always within the substantial limitations of print. Meanwhile, teachers of composition, more familiar both with the notion of writing as "process" and with the computer as a communication medium, have begun to translate these theories into alternative practices. Clearly, both teachers of writing and theorists of literature must contribute to the development of new technologies of writing. But these groups are currently divided by an academic order that regards the study of literature as central and the teaching of composition as secondary or marginal. Some of our most important questions for the nineties may therefore be political. What practical consequences will changes in the writing medium have for academic discourse? How will these changes affect the social structure of colleges and universities? Will the distinctions between "center" and "margins" tend to collapse? Can institutional arrangements be found that are free of invidious distinctions?

In five years computer-mediated writing will be the mainstream of academic discourse.

—John B. Smith,
Fifth Computers in Writing
Conference, 1989

Though one might question John Smith's timetable, it is hard to find fault with his premise. Scholars and teachers will almost certainly become more deeply invested and involved in electronic writing during the next decade. While we will no doubt go on producing books and monographs and assigning essays and research papers, we may also find ourselves reading and writing in networks, hypertext webs, and interactive multimedia environments. In a "multi-tiered" information universe where print coexists with electronic forms (Horowitz, 1986), it will become increasingly difficult to limit our activities to traditional print channels, especially as publishers and journals begin to adopt new technologies. Early versions of electronic writing systems were proposed by Vannevar Bush in the forties and Douglas Engelbart in the sixties, but the most influential vision of this medium has been Theodor H. Nelson's notion of "hypertext." Nelson (1987b) defines hypertext as "non-sequential writing" (p. 29), in which a body of discourse exists in computer memory as an accretive, open-ended matrix to which new components and linkages may continually be added. In the last half of the eighties, there was a major influx of interest in hypertext and multimedia linking systems ("hypermedia"), driven by the introduction of powerful applications for personal computers (e.g., Owl's GUIDE and Apple's HYPERCARD).[1] The implications of these developments for teachers and scholars are considerable. As Richard Lanham (1989) recently put it, we are on the brink of a "digital revolution" (p. 265) in academic discourse that may utterly transform the way we think of texts, leading us away from the codex book and toward more complex and dynamic forms of written language.

The consequences of this revolution will be social and practical as well as aesthetic and theoretical. I will suggest in this chapter that Lanham's "digital revolution" is a first step away from what Gilles Deleuze and Félix Guattari (1987) call "arborescent culture" (p. 8), in which the controlling model of discourse is the hierarchical or genealogical tree, where branches and offshoots are subordinated to a single taproot. The coming changes in textuality allow us to create a different kind of linguistic structure, one that corresponds more closely to Deleuze and Guattari's "rhizome," an organic growth that is all adventitious middle, not a deterministic chain of beginnings and ends. So far, the cultural establishment has been able to restrict such destabilizing ideas by confining them to the hothouse of literary theory, but the current direction of technological development suggests that this resistance is no longer feasible. Lanham's predicted revolution promises to create a new information ecology in which the hothouse walls will come down and strange new growths will spring up across the land. This outbreak is bound to affect scholars and teachers concerned with the writing process and its pedagogy. In the next ten years, we will probably have to confront serious challenges to our reception and conception of text. The resulting changes could drastically alter the institutional status of writing teachers, though, of course, this is hardly the first time a new educational technology has given rise to predictions of sweeping change. Hypertext and hypermedia give us a real opportunity for change. The most important questions before our professions, then, may be practical and political rather than theoretical.

From "The Work" to Hypertext

It is best to begin by drawing some links to the past. The changes that seem likely to arrive in the nineties are really accelerated repetitions of movements that have been running through the literary world since the fifties and sixties. Post-structuralist criticism has put "the text"—an indefinable, associative network of verbal relationships—in place of "the work," the bound and author-ized volume that was the object of earlier literary study. "While the work is held in the hand," Roland Barthes (1979) observed, "the text is held in language: it exists only as discourse" (p. 75). Figures like Barthes, Derrida, Foucault, and Fish have compellingly criticized the duplicitous authority of writing, its claim to evoke a presence in which it does not participate, its attempt to articulate a discourse which in fact it delimits or betrays. By way of an alternative, they ask us to consider language not as a hierarchy but as a network of relationships: the model for written discourse is no longer a linear chain of reference but a recursive, allusive web of correspondences.

Yet the printed page and the bound volume are precisely the wrong media for this new perspective on writing. They lead not to fluidity or multiplicity of expression but to the hegemony of a stable, exclusive, and singular strain of discourse (McLuhan,

1964). To receive *Writing Degree Zero* in a bound volume invokes the same overwhelming irony as reading the printed text of Plato's *Phaedrus*: any subversive warning about the limitations of writing or print is overridden by the far more potent message of the medium—its proclamation of permanent, indisputable, materialized authority. Print subjects the "text" of Socrates or Barthes to an operation (in every sense of the word) from which it emerges as a delimited, safely legitimated "work." On seeing these critiques of textuality overcome by the medium they have begun to question, we might well think of Wordsworth's complaint:

> Oh! why hath not the Mind
> Some element to stamp her image on
> In nature somewhat nearer to her own?
> Why, gifted with such powers to send abroad
> Her spirit, must it lodge in shrines so frail?
> ("The Prelude," V. ll. 45–49)

Technology now provides an answer to Wordsworth's demands—electronic writing systems, which do come "somewhat nearer" to the complex electrodynamics of consciousness. As Deleuze and Guattari (1987) observe, "Many people have a tree growing in their heads, but the brain itself is much more a grass than a tree" (p. 15). The brain is not a circuit board with engraved pathways feeding through trunks to a central bus, but a self-configuring network of connections that spring up and grow spontaneously. So the electronic text, which allows multidimensional linking in the infinite plane that Jay David Bolter (1990) calls "writing space" (pp. 2–4), represents a closer approximation of the mind's native element.

But this attempt to affililate Wordsworth with post-structuralism and electronic literacy will not really stand up to scrutiny. Wordsworth was no lover either of irruptive disorder or of mechanical reproduction, and his concern about print's "frailty" may refer less to the fragility of paper than to his own legislative battles over copyright.[2] The social implications of electronic writing systems, to which we must now turn, would no doubt have horrified Wordsworth. But this attempt at a *discordia concors* illustrates an important ambiguity. Electronic writing systems are both the answer to Wordsworth's prayer and a print poet's nightmare. They are an evolutionary outcome of the codex itself, a response to our desire for a medium in which better to express the Mind; but at the same time they deeply threaten authorship, intellectual property, canonicity, and other pillars of Gutenberg culture.

Electronic writing does make a difference. Nelson's hypertext may not be identical with Barthes's text, but it is a much nearer approximation to that concept than anything achievable in print. True, hypertext still gives a discourse that we hold in our hands (or our hard disks) rather than in our language. A hypertextual document is still arguably a "work," at least at any given moment of its history—it remains limited by the facts of its material existence. But at the same time, no hypertext is ever an exclusive and unitary expression. The reader is free to find (or in some cases create) multiple pathways through the network of linkages. Hypertext thus reverses the paradox of printed deconstructions by inviting and enjoining the reader to participate actively in the assembly or extension of the discourse. While the medium of print silently reconfirms singularity against any argument for multiplicity, hypertext presents the possibility of alternatives even in the most hierarchical and determinist of writings. Hypertext thus nullifies the traditional defense against "rhizomatic" thinking, the tendency to limit such ideas to pure theory; it may thus open the first breach in the hothouse walls.

The consequences of such a breakthrough would be highly significant. Michel Foucault (1979) once characterized authorship as "the principle of thrift in the proliferation of meaning" (p. 159), a conservative hedge against the uncontrolled inflation of expression that occurs in nonpublished discourse. Hypertext would revise this economy of language, empowering every user of the writing system either to reconstitute a given discourse by drawing his or her own links, or to expand the range of the document (or as Nelson prefers, "docuverse") by introducing new information. In a limited but powerful way, electronic writing realizes Barthes's (1979) vision of the text as "that social space that leaves no language safe or untouched" (p. 81). As Deleuze and Guattari (1987) note, the text-as-hypertext is a field of language whose divisions and boundaries are always at issue, a discourse in which all forms of authority are provisional and contingent, the realization in linguistic practice of a "rhizomatic" form.

This feature of hypertext may pose acute problems for a society in which information is a primary manifestation of capital and intellectual property is a sacred trust. As Nelson (1987a) has warned, "Tomorrow's hypertext systems have immense political ramifications, and there are many struggles to come" (p. 3/19). In the military and business sectors, whose command trees do not bear uprooting, these struggles will no doubt be successfully suppressed and attenuated for many years to come. But in the humanities departments of colleges and universities, the situation is likely to be different. It was there, after all, that the theoretical revision of textuality got its start. Richard Lanham (1989) has enumerated the factors working toward change, and they are considerable:

> We conceive the humanities as a pickle factory preserving human "values" too tender and inert for the outside world. . . . But our students and the society from which they come will not permit this illusion to continue unchanged; nor will a technology which has volatilized print; nor will our own thinking, our "theory," about what we are and do. All these are asking us to think systematically about literary study, to model it from kindergarten through graduate school. They are asking us to reconceive literary study, to think of it as permeating society in the way literary rhetoric has always done in the West, but with new technologies and through new administrative arrangements. We are being asked to explain just how the humanities humanize. (p. 287)

As Lanham points out, the textual theorists of the seventies and eighties have envisioned a radical revision of writing and the teaching of texts. No doubt some of these visions are inconsistent with the purposes of liberal education—a university probably ought never become a pure informational anarchy. But academics of the nineties will be called upon to test these theories, and to put into practical effect those that stand up to scrutiny. Our choices must be defended. If we choose to preserve narrow notions of canon, authority, and discursive control, we must be prepared to answer charges of self-interest and hypocrisy. If hypertext makes a difference, it also seems likely to create divisions.

Lanham's forecast of change must be juxtaposed with Nelson's prediction of "struggle"—for our purposes, a struggle between academic cultures. The obvious set of oppositions to invoke here pits conservative champions of the printed word against enthusiasts of technology; but this is ultimately not the most interesting division likely to confront us. Of far greater importance for the future of writing pedagogy is the division between the "we" whom Lanham (1989) addresses in *New Literary History* (professors of literature) and the "we" of this essay (teacher/theorists of composition). For teachers of writing, the "political ramifications" of electronic text must inevitably involve the tension between expository writing programs and other elements of the humanities faculty, especially those concerned with literature and literary theory. In the power geography of many universities, literature departments and writing programs are related as metropolis to colony or center to margin. As we all know too well, the work of rhetoric and composition teachers is often regarded as ancillary or irrelevant to the main currents of intellectual discourse—a judgment confirmed in the eyes of some administrators when writing-across-the-curriculum programs are established outside English departments. Movements toward "interdisciplinary" studies, as Stanley Fish (1989) has recently observed, may only relocate the old territorial borders, having no real impact upon the academic power structure. When one's institutional existence is spread "across" multiple disciplines there seems to be even less hope of empowerment.

Changes in the technology of writing offer to uproot this dismal order. Their reverberations proceed from microcosm to macrocosm, technical transformations at the level of text production leading up to social transformations at the level of reception in the discursive community. As hypertext and other electronic writing systems are adopted in academia, the social structure of discourse—who writes and publishes, what they produce, on what occasions, and under whose review and auspices—will be open to change. Electronic textuality introduces what Jay David Bolter (1987) has called "topical writing" (p. 8), a conception of the text not as tree or hierarchy but as a rearrangeable, multidimensional discursive space. This innovation affects not just textual but social organization. The topography of writing space does not support the dichotomy of central and marginal. Having no absolutely defined outlines, a spatial text possesses neither center nor margins: readers are free to annotate or expand the "central" thread of the text by linking their own discourse to it. Thus, the collapse of distinctions in the formal space of the electronic text may produce a corresponding difference in its "social space." The printed page privileges exclusive and singular utterance. As Stanley Fish (1980) has pointed out, print fosters the illusion of an exhaustive, predetermined "content." Electronic text, on the other hand, lacks the singular authority of a discursive center. It presents itself as a field of linkage and associational play whose meaning depends upon its permutations. In reading as well as writing, electronic text thus erases the invidious distinction between process and product by allowing us to reformulate the text not as a limited artifact nor as a theoretical "heteroglossia," but as a medium for the actual intersection of discourses.

This is a difference with profound importance for teachers of writing. "The writing process" under hypertext can no longer be defined as the (minor) province of first-year rhetoric, because such a writing system unifies the encounter with discursive product (reading) and the activity of text production (writing). Writing as an activity in which language is recursively produced, circulated, and modified becomes everyone's business—a business far too important to be left solely to either literary or composition theorists.

The new textuality demands a renovation of rhetoric. This rhetoric would not be a catalogue of forms or models but would itself be an activity—an attempt to describe and assess the dynamic and socially constructed aspects of electronic writing, such as the interaction between the initial intentions of a hypertext's "scriptor" and its eventual reformulation at the hands of multiple reader/writers. For teachers of expository writing, accustomed to dealing with the emergence of discourse through recursive and interactive processes and with learning as a collaborative transaction, the outlines of this enterprise are quite familiar—they are the outlines of the modern expository rhetoric our profession has been evolving since the sixties. There can be little doubt that teachers of writing are among the members of the academic community best suited to understand and explore the world of electronic text.

If John Smith's prediction proves correct, we may well be living through the last days of our marginality. As Lanham (1989) wisely suggests, academia can only understand how the humanities humanize if it places reading and writing in a broader social context. This expanded vision demands the participation of those who understand writing as activity or process, i.e., teachers of rhetoric and composition. The digital revolution may well give teachers of writing the chance to become much more rewardingly integrated into the academic community.

But before we all rush off to negotiate new contracts, we had best consider a few sobering realities. First, technological change in academia is not a simple, linear process. It is more like what physicists call a "dissipative system"—an irregular alternation between order and chaos in which the difference is governed by essentially random factors. John Smith's prediction seems likely enough to come true, but there is always the possibility of reversal. In technological as in biological evolution, initial success is no guarantee of long-term survival. The vision of electronic textuality might fail—or worse, it might survive only in a travestied and abhorrent form such as "cultural literacy" databases and harsher, nastier avatars of programmed instruction (Joyce, 1988; Moulthrop, 1989). These darker reflections lead to a second reservation. As Cynthia Selfe (1989) has warned, there are advantages as well as disadvantages in marginality, and we should think the situation through very carefully before signing on with any new order. The politics of writing in academia may be in for changes just as sweeping as those in the technology of writing, but we had best advance into this future with caution. The past reminds us that revolutions do not always meet with instant success.

Déjà Vu

When teachers of writing and reading come face-to-screen with the technological future, we should remember that we have all been here before. Our current digital revolution is not the first of its kind: there was an earlier demand for a rethinking of educational goals in response to communications technology. In the midst of the sixties, Marshall McLuhan (1964) proclaimed that

> the young people who have experienced a decade of TV have
> naturally imbibed an urge toward involvement in depth that
> makes all the remote visualized goals of usual culture seem
> not only unreal but irrelevant, not only irrelevant but anemic.
> It is the total involvement in all-inclusive nowness that occurs
> in young lives via TV's mosaic image. . . . It is, of course, our
> job not only to understand this change but to exploit it for its
> pedagogical richness. (p. 335)

According to McLuhan, the mode of consciousness supported
by print technology was fated to collapse and dissolve under the
competitive pressures of radio and television. The linear, hierarchical, perspectival worldview of the Gutenberg era would yield
to "cooler" media in which the distinctions between perceiver and
object, process and product would be shattered. The echoes and
reverberations of this prophecy have gone on for twenty years.
Walter J. Ong (1982), extrapolating from McLuhan, has held that
we are moving into a period of "secondary orality" in which the
fluidity and openness of preliterate cultural forms will return to
the West (p. 153). Likewise, some readers of the postmodern
scene, like Jean Baudrillard and Arthur Kroker and David Cook
(Kroker & Cook, 1986) announce a "techno-primitivism" that
embraces the power and dynamism of technology but rejects its
cult of rationality (p. 15).

Print is "dead," but like the assorted poltergeists, ghouls, aliens,
and things-that-will-not-die in our horror movies (in fact, like the
endless sequels themselves), "Gutenberg technology" always rises
again. As Horowitz (1986) has noted, book sales in the United
States have steadily expanded in the decades since the Second
World War, unaffected by the introduction of television in the
fifties or the personal computer in the seventies. More to the point,
exposure to the depth-illusion of television did not trigger an
apocalypse of literate culture. Thus Lanham (1989) in his recent
forecast of change can begin by reassuring the conservatives that
"literature has continued to be taught in American schools and
colleges much as before"—though he adds that the "grace period"
of the seventies and eighties has now expired (p. 287).

Déjà vu is not the same thing as recollection, however. Lanham's
call for a new pedagogy may be reminiscent of McLuhan's, but
there is an important difference. At the end of the eighties, we

know print for what it is: the beast that cannot die. It is likely that McLuhan would be just as dismayed at the prospect of computer-mediated writing as would Wordsworth, though for opposite reasons. Typographic literacy, that demon of objectification, perspectivism, and dissociation of sensibility, is very much present in electronic writing. User interfaces like that of the Apple Macintosh replace alphanumeric strings with icons and spatial metaphors (the informational world as "desktop"); but in an academic context, this object-oriented conception still serves mainly as a staging platform for an encounter with print. This relationship is most clearly evident in INTERMEDIA, the academic hypertext program recently adopted by Apple for use with its version of UNIX.[3] Though INTERMEDIA supports combinations of text, graphics, and audiovisual material, its primary purpose is to deliver typographic discourse. From a strict McLuhanite point of view, products like INTERMEDIA are abominations. "Our official culture is striving to force the new media to do the work of the old," McLuhan complained (McLuhan & Fiore, 1967, p. 93). Print-based hypertext, it might be argued, is just the latest manifestation of this process. Print is print whether it appears on a sheet of paper or a phosphor plane. Despite the evanescent quality of electronic writing, one might object that hypertext enslaves the cathode ray tube to typography, cheating the video image of its revolutionary power. Taken to its most irrational conclusion, this line of thinking suggests a certain technological paranoia: it was perhaps not out of economy alone that the first personal computers were designed to plug into home television sets. To a firm believer in the video revolution, the microcomputer is an insidious retrofit designed to re-heat the electronic media and restore cultural control. Hypertext, to a McLuhanite paranoid, would represent Gutenberg's Revenge.

But if déjà vu reminds us that we have been here before, it also informs us that "here" is not the place it used to be. McLuhan's (1964) thermocline model of media has great polemical and analytical value, but it also has its limits. To assume that the world of audio/video and the world of print do not interpenetrate is to paint the universe in binary pixels, all on or off with no shades of gray. Such an approach can produce only a distorted image of reality, but an image with which we should nonetheless be familiar. It is just such a harsh two-cultures worldview that produces political metaphors like center versus margins, metropolis versus colonies, teaching of "disciplines" versus teaching of "skills." Symmetries of this type are indeed fearful, as Deleuze and Guattari (1987) point out. The problem with a binary or Manichaean system of thought, they declare, is that it "has never reached an understanding of multiplicity: in order to arrive at two . . . it must assume a strong principal unity" (p. 5). Under binary thinking, there can be no many without the presumption that everything reduces ultimately to one.

The reason McLuhan's call for pedagogical revolution failed (or as paranoia would have it, was encouraged to fail) may well lie in just such an erroneously exclusive logic. According to McLuhan (1964), the new technology had a linear destiny: it would come, be seen, and conquer. No provision was made for dialectical outcomes such as reciprocal modification or co-evolution. As we know from hindsight, this was a poor prophecy and a serious rhetorical bungle. Having defined the encounter between media as a struggle to the death, McLuhan made it all too easy for the print world to resist even incremental influence or change. The result of this programmatic division is a culture divided against itself—an outcome that is the same in academic politics as in media theory. In both instances a radically expansive and dynamic medium is carefully segregated from an older and (as Lanham has it) more "fragile" form.

Unifying the Academic Sensorium

A culture divided against itself cannot understand. Armed with McLuhan's condemnations of Gutenberg technology, the shamans of the global village gave up the allusive and analytical power of literacy. With the exception of work by avant-garde artists like Laurie Anderson and Nam June Paik, video has gone the way of the laugh track, the film clip, and the sound bite. Likewise, those who rallied to the cause of the book seem to have missed the point of electronic media, which challenge us to understand the world as a complex and contradictory system, not a chain of rational assertions. This blindness to the nature of media may account for statements like the following, taken from the introduction to an anthology of post-structuralist literary criticism:

> Each reading [in this collection] develops an insistent coherence of its own that drives toward conclusive and irrefutable assertions. But it does this while holding open the possibility of a multiplicity of competing meanings, each of which denies the primacy of the others. (Machin & Norris, 1987, p. 7)

A bound volume offers only so many words and pages. How, one may ask, can a printed essay "hold open the possibility" of opposed readings when the range of its expression is defined by the artifact that contains it? The tacit assumption, of course, is that the post-structuralist "opening" is a matter of implication, not necessarily of practice. The rhetoric of these self-deconstructing essays disclaims certainty, refusing the possibility of a final word just as firmly as it "denies the primacy" of other discourses. Presumably this recognition of unexhausted possibility is meant to stimulate the reader into the pursuit of other discourses. Readers with different views are implicitly invited to pursue their own insights, write them down, and find themselves a publisher.

But this trick of critical "openness" is done with mirrors. Printing and publishing, as Foucault (1979) accurately described them, are dedicated not to the proliferation but to the restriction of discourse. The fact of commercial or academic publication signifies a chain of affiliation: it transmits authority to the writer from editor, publisher, and ultimately some university, foundation, or multinational conglomerate. The bound volume is a commodity, produced and distributed (we are always reminded) on the slimmest of profit margins or at a scandalous loss. But we are not encouraged to connect the economics of publishing with questions of openness in academic discourse. All "important" work, we assure ourselves, will find its way into print. As we have seen, it seldom crosses our minds that print may be an inimical medium for some of the most important kinds of critical work.

In electronic text, matters are different. It is true that this mode of writing does not give us back an ear for an eye or free us from a dependence on artifacts. In fact, it mediates its discourse through a technology whose expensiveness, complexity, and unreliability are still highly problematic. But even with these limitations, electronic textuality accomplishes something that print can never manage: it unbinds writing. With discourse organized in hypertextual networks and with these networks integrated into a truly decentered "social space of writing," the possibility of open expression becomes more than a theoretical projection. Because in a fully developed hypertext any user is free to rearrange old links or create new ones, the old hierarchical model of textual authority must be rejected. Readers become writers and, by extension, eventually publishers as well.

The best new models of authority (or community) may not come from traditional literary theory, which for all its efforts at deconstruction still betrays a fatal affection for the definitive statement. Those who will understand electronic textuality most clearly are likely to be those who have been teaching and thinking about expository writing under the impact of electronic technology. Diane Pelkus Balestri (1988), an authority on academic computing whose expertise derives in part from teaching college composition, points out that

> most faculty across the academic disciplines define "writing" as hardcopy product, including (sometimes) the act of drafting it. But current theorists and teachers of composition take "writing" to mean the whole process of creating text, from the most formative thinking (which may or may not be "written down") to the last revision. In fact, they usually separate the terms "process" and "product," or even oppose them to one another. (p. 17)

The "word processor," Balestri notes, is an aptly named tool, because it makes available to pedagogy some aspects at least of the writing process itself. Balestri, therefore, suggests that teachers of composition make greater efforts to exploit "softcopy," writing in its fluid and malleable early stages where structures have not yet become rigid and connections may still be proposed and rejected. Balestri argues that the computer's ability to make this stage of composition open to examination (through network collaboration, for instance) represents its greatest value.

Balestri's remarks on "softcopy" provide the bridge between the static, product-centered conception of writing that still dominates academia (witness this essay and even this book) and the more fully evolved form of electronic discourse: hypertext. Michael Joyce, a writing teacher, novelist, and hypertext system designer, has taken the next step. Joyce (1988) distinguishes between two kinds of hypertext: "exploratory" texts, in which the user is mainly concerned with discovering or defining connections in a pre-defined system of information, and "constructive" texts, which are undefined, expansive models of developing conceptual structures (p. 11). Exploratory hypertexts, even though they are to some extent controllable by their users, are the closest thing to "hardcopy" in the electronic domain, and their value is accordingly limited. As Joyce sees it, it is the constructive hypertext, a provisional and necessarily unfinished product, that represents the greatest potential for enriching the writing process.

Empirical Questions

A number of empirical questions follow from these early approaches to computer-mediated writing. Balestri's and Joyce's speculations both suggest that our new understanding of textual authority must be centered not on singularity, consistency, and closure, but on difference, multiplicity, and community. They indicate that we must reconceive writing not as a private activity eventuating in a public product, but as a process of revision or construction that is itself shared between writer and readers, or among reader/writers. It would seem, then, that we need to know much more about the way readers, writers, and "scriptors" of hypertext work. George Landow (1989) has proposed a first step toward this understanding, a "rhetoric of arrivals and departures," a system of discursive conventions by which users of hypertexts can orient themselves and create coherent chains of discourse out of a combinatorial structure (pp. 333–35). Landow's initial sketch of a hypertextual rhetoric could be expanded productively in several ways.

We might begin, for instance, with the simple question of identity. What exactly do we mean by hypertext? There could be great value in a taxonomic description of existing hypertext projects, for instance in detailed, comparative analyses of texts that have been written in different hypertext schemes, such as the Association for Computing Machinery's three versions of *Hypertext on Hypertext* (Yankelovich, 1988). Various hypertextual rhetorics or systems of "navigation" will need to be described and investigated. Continuous, document-centered models (what Nelson [1987, p. 0/2] calls "smooth" hypertext) need to be contrasted with more disjunctive, spatially oriented, "chunk-style" conceptions. But as Catherine F. Smith points out in "Reconceiving Hypertext" in this collection, definitions proposed thus far have emphasized the technical at the expense of the social. Any taxonomic descriptions of hypertext ought to address the technical differences of systems as reflections of the different discourse communities in which the hypertexts function.

This emphasis on the reception of hypertext suggests a second direction in which practical discussion might move. Landow's (1989) rhetoric of arrivals and departures might be examined in its effect not on the scriptor or designer of the text, but on the reader/writer:

- What do readers expect on their "arrival" in a hypertextual space?

- How do strategies of interpretation based on printed texts succeed or fail in an electronic context?

- How might readers rationalize their "departure" from the text's existing or default structure should they decide to pass from an "exploratory" to a "constructive" role, becoming writers and scriptors themselves?

Investigations in this area might be more analytical than descriptive, probably involving some formal inquiry (by protocol analysis or some related method) into the cognitive processes underlying hypertext reception.

Political Questions

Empirical research into electronic writing systems will be essential, but we must not restrict ourselves to empirical questions alone. Any issues of form and expression that come up here are inextricably related to a more fundamental concern, one which is not rhetorical but ultimately political:

- What role will we have as writing teachers in this new world of academic discourse?

- How can we promote a post-"marginal" understanding of writing, one in which theorists of product and teachers of process can find common ground?

- How will notions of the text as "rhizome"—an evolving, unattributable, "unauthored" structure without central controls—be received by academic institutions that may be ambivalent or hostile to such concepts?

These are questions whose best response lies not in articles or research projects but in direct initiatives—for instance, proposing innovative courses and faculty seminars, setting up publication outlets for electronic text, and creating intellectual communities (perhaps on lines very different from existing professional organizations) to promote the development of electronic writing.[4] Though much more needs to be thought, said, and discovered about electronic writing systems, the most important contributions in the next decade will probably come only when we turn from speculation to action.

Notes

1. The best general survey of hypertext is E. J. Conklin's "Hypertext: An Introduction and Survey," *Computer* (1987), 20, pp. 17–41. See also Sueann Ambron and Kristina Hooper's (Eds.), *Interactive Multimedia: Visions of Multimedia for Developers, Educators, and Product Information Providers* (1988), Redmond, WA: Microsoft Press.

2. I am indebted here to Susan Eilenberg's work on Wordsworth, copyright, and the language of appropriation. See her article, "Mortal Pages: Wordsworth and the Reform of Copyright," *ELH*, 56(2), pp. 351–374.

3. For a description of intermedia and its applications, see Landow (1987).

4. The last two options are already being explored. Electronic conferences like Megabyte University provide an important impetus for the formation of alternative academic communities. There has been discussion on several of these forums recently of a refereed on-line journal to focus on the pedagogy of writing. For more information about this project, contact Edward M. Jennings at EMJ69 @ ALBNYVMS.Bitnet or c/o Department of English, State University of New York at Albany, Albany, NY, 12222.

References

Balestri, D. P. (1988, February). Softcopy and hard: Wordprocessing and the writing process. *Academic Computing*, 14 ff.

Barthes, R. (1979). From work to text. In Josué Harari (Ed.), *Textual Strategies* (pp. 73–81). Ithaca: Cornell University Press.

Bolter, J. D. (1990). *Writing space*. Hillsdale, NJ: Erlbaum.

Deleuze, G., & Guattari, F. (1987). *A thousand plateaus: Capitalism and schizophrenia* (Brian Massumi, Trans.). Minneapolis: University of Minnesota Press.

Fish, S. (1980). *Is there a text in this class?: The authority of interpretive communities*. Cambridge, MA: Harvard University Press.

Fish, S. (1989). Being interdisciplinary is so very hard to do. *Profession '89*, 15–22.

Foucault, M. (1979). What is an author? In Josué Harari (Ed.), *Textual Strategies* (pp. 141–60). Ithaca: Cornell University Press.

Horowitz, I. L. (1986). *Communicating ideas*. New York: Oxford University Press.

Joyce, M. (1988, November). Siren shapes: Exploratory and constructive hypertexts. *Academic Computing*, 10 ff.

Kroker, A., & Cook, D. (1986). *The postmodern scene: Excremental culture and hyper-aesthetics*. New York: St. Martin's.

Landow, G. P. (1987). *Hypertext in literary education, criticism, and scholarship*. (IRIS Research Rep.). Providence, RI: Institute for Research in Information and Scholarship, Brown University.

Landow, G. P. (1989). Relationally encoded links and the rhetoric of hypertext, *Hypertext '87 Proceedings*. New York: Association for Computing Machinery.

Lanham, R. (1989). The electronic word: Literary study and the digital revolution. *New Literary History*, 20(2), 265–90.

Machin, R., & Norris, C. (1987). *Post-structuralist readings of English poetry*. Cambridge: Cambridge University Press.

McLuhan, H. M. (1964). *Understanding media: The extensions of man*. New York: McGraw-Hill.

McLuhan, H. M., & Fiore, Q. (1967). *The medium is the massage*. New York: Random House.

Moulthrop, S. (1989). In the zones: Hypertext and the politics of interpretation. *Writing on the Edge: A Multiperspective on Writing*, 1(1), 18–27.

Nelson, T. H. (1987a). *Literary machines*. Self-published.

Nelson, T. H. (1987b). *Computer lib/Dream machines*. Redmond, WA: Tempus Books.

Ong, W. J. (1982). *Orality and literacy: The technologizing of the word*. New York: Methuen.

Selfe, C. (1989). *Notes from the Margins*. Paper presented at the Fifth Computers and Writing Conference, Minneapolis.

Smith, J. B. (1989). Keynote address. Fifth Computers and Writing Conference, Minneapolis.

Yankelovitch, N. (1988). *Hypertext on hypertext*. New York: Association for Computing Machinery.

Part Four

The Politics of Computers: Changing Hierarchies

Introduction

> The question of how we adopt and use the computer is in fact part of a larger question that asks what the future of society itself will be. . . . Will we see a gradual erosion of tradition and the realignment of power?
>
> —Eugene Provenzo,
> *Beyond the Gutenberg Galaxy*

How computers are introduced into our society and, particularly, into our schools is ultimately a political question with serious implications for us as teachers, as members of school or university communities, and as citizens. The move from an industrial culture to an information culture has also shifted the ways in which power is distributed and controlled. Power now belongs, to a great extent, to those members of our society who can use technology to access and manipulate the expanding world of information.

This fact becomes increasingly important when we consider computers as cultural artifacts of our information society and, in an historical sense, of our military-industrial complex. These tools, like any others, embody the values, biases, and ideologies of the tool-makers. Hence, computers come with "built-in" values, and these values mirror those inherent in our educational system, which itself reflects the belief systems of our culture. Given this situation, our use of computers in English classrooms must be carefully considered and monitored to ensure that we are achieving those goals we deem most important as humanists and teachers.

If, for instance, our culture privileges competition and individual achievement, our educational system, left to its own natural tendencies, will unwittingly employ computers to further these same ends. Hence, educational decision-makers who are *not* deliberately critical in their thinking about technology may purchase stand-alone workstations to be placed at the back of classrooms so that individual students can be encouraged to achieve mastery of particular tutorial programs or other individual projects. Students who succeed best in such learning spaces will be those who thrive on challenge and individual achievement, the same students who now succeed most often on standerized tests, the same students who now succeed most readily in the college and university systems. The students who might be set up for failure within such learning spaces—minority students, nontraditional students, students raised in cultures that do not value competition or individual achievement, disabled students, women—might be handicapped within such electronic environments and be required to work unduly hard to excel.

Teachers and farsighted administrators, however, who *do* understand the power associated with technology may be able to make a difference by using computers to precipitate educational change. Our greatest hope is that these educators, by thinking critically and with an eye toward the humanistic use of computers, can employ technology, whenever possible, to tie humans together in expanding networks of information and resources, joining teachers and students, providing electronic spaces for collaborative as well as individual electronic projects, and creating new online forums that are not constrained by the same hegemonies that characterize traditional classrooms. If this vision is to prove true, we must create generations of educators who see both the problems and the potential associated with technology, and who are committed to critical thinking about computer use within our educational system.

In this section, we look at computers in the context of the learning spaces we inhabit—schools, departments of English, writing programs, and writing classes. In chapter 12, Ruth Ray and Ellen Barton argue that we must examine the use of technology in both the workplace and the university if we are to extend the study of computers in the next decade. They maintain that it should be people rather than institutions who control the language and discourse of technology. Turning to college writing programs, James Strickland, in chapter 13, examines the use of computers within the institutional context of English programs. Throughout the chapter, Strickland argues that the success with which programs can use computers to promote learning is ultimately a political rather than an empirical question. In chapter 14, our view shifts to individuals caught up in the political contexts of schools: students of every age and color. Mary Louise Gomez points to the inequitable distribution of computer use in schools in which the supposedly brighter and whiter of children are treated to computer software for "cognitive enrichment" rather than to the workbook-like drill-and-practice programs reserved for the poor and students of color. Finally, in chapter 15, Emily Jessup calls our attention to gender issues surrounding computer use. Specifically she looks at college writing classes and asks us to examine carefully our practices, for we may unknowingly privilege males over females in subtle ways.

In scrutinizing the politics of computers, then, these four chapters point not only to ways that electronic technology can abet our students' writing abilities but also to ways that these abilities can be abused. If we are to succeed as teachers and as computer-using professionals, we must remain constantly vigilant of these issues.

References

Provenzo, E. F. Jr. (1986). *Beyond the Gutenberg Galaxy*. New York: Teachers College Press.

Chapter 12

Technology and Authority

Ruth Ray and Ellen Barton
Wayne State University

One possible direction for research on computers in the 1990s is to explore technology in its larger social and political contexts. In this paper, we show how the discourse of technology can be interpreted from two perspectives: a perspective favoring an institutional imperative, in which the making of meaning is subject to the authority of the institution, and a perspective supporting an institutional interaction, in which individuals establish authority over the making of meaning through technology. We argue that university English departments should play a central role in challenging the institutional imperative that currently dominates the role of technology.

During the 1980s, the computer entered the composition classroom as a tool for creating flexibility in language and texts, an additional means for the making of meaning. The ensuing body of research has focused on word processing, text analysis, networked conferences, long-distance communication, and other ways technology contributes to the development of student writers (see Collins & Sommers, 1985; Gerrard, 1987; Hawisher & Selfe, 1989). This research, though, has been largely discipline-specific, investigating computers primarily within the context of composition studies. As Hawisher and Selfe point out, however, researchers and teachers need to broaden their study of computers to encompass "the wider arena of the study of discourse" (p. xi) that typically takes place in university English departments. For us, this broader study of discourse, following current research in the social construction of knowledge (Bartholomae, 1985; Berlin, 1987, 1989; Bizzell, 1982, 1986; Cook-Gumperz, 1986; Cooper & Holzman, 1989; Kintgen, Kroll & Rose, 1988), requires a study of the social and political contexts in which technology is used and promoted. Thus, in this chapter, we consider the discourse of technology in two contexts: that of the workplace and that of the university. Specifically, we look at various discourses on authority—how people in workplaces and universities talk about technology in terms of power and control. Our purpose in this chapter is to examine ways of interpreting this discourse and to argue for an interpretation that encourages individual authority over technology.

Understanding the relationship between technology and authority is especially important for teachers and researchers in the next decade because computers now represent our cultural age. From the intellectually rarified views of postmodernist critics of culture (Jameson, 1984; Mandel, 1978) to the generally accepted views of best-selling authors (McLuhan, 1962; Wurman, 1988), computers have become the signifier of the twentieth century. The phrases used to name the twentieth century attest to the importance of the computer: the Electronic Age, the Information Age, the Third (or Fourth, or nth) Machine Age, or, simply, the Computer Age. America's schools are constantly exhorted to produce trained workers for our information and computer age and are criticized publicly for not meeting the challenge. *Time* magazine, for instance, estimates that between 20 and 27 million adults—one quarter of the labor force—lack the reading, writing, math, and computer skills for today's high-tech job market ("Literacy Gap," 1988). For these reasons, the Carnegie Commission (1986) has called for major changes in the American educational system, suggesting that schools have a responsibility to produce workers who can use technology in ways that will help America compete in the global economy:

> Advancing technology and the changing terms of international trade are remolding the basic structure of international economic competition. . . . In the future, the high-wage-level societies will be those whose economies are based on the use of a wide scale of very highly skilled workers, backed up by the most advanced technologies available. . . . We do not believe the educational system needs repairing; we believe it must be rebuilt to match the drastic changes needed in our economy if we are to prepare our children for productive lives in the 21st century. (p. 44)

Rightly or wrongly, technology is touted as the crucial connection between schools and society, the classroom and the workplace (Aronowitz & Giroux, 1985; Olson, 1987).

There are at least two interpretive perspectives from which we might examine the relationship between technology and the people who use it. One perspective, which we call the "institutional imperative," asserts that all meaning and the making of meaning is subject to the authority of the institution (be it a school or a particular workplace). Under this view, the individual has little or no personal authority over the ways technology is used or over the language of technology; patterns of meaning are strictly constituted by the institution in which computers are used. The second perspective, which we call "institutional interaction," asserts that, though meaning and the making of meaning through computers reflect the authority of the institution, this authority can be defined, analyzed, resisted, and changed by the individual user. Though both perspectives see all institutions as political—ideological constructs in which there is no such thing as a "neutral" technology, "neutral" uses of that technology, or "neutral" language about technology—the two differ considerably in terms of the authority and personal control granted the individual user of technology.

In the first section of this paper, we show that the institutional imperative is the dominant perspective from which computers are promoted and understood in the workplace. We argue against this interpretation of technology, pointing to its negative results on the individual in the workplace. In the second section, we argue that university English departments are in a position, both theoretically and pedagogically, to encourage institutional interaction, developing the authority of the individual over technology by analyzing the discourse of technology. At the end of each section, we raise questions for further research on the relationships among technology, institutions, and authority.

Technology, Authority, and the Workplace

Many researchers have assumed that computers are a politically neutral technology, always contributing positively to social and intellectual progress. A typical example is Walter Ong (1977), who asserts that computers, like other technologies of literacy, "enable men to . . . shape, store, retrieve, and communicate knowledge in new ways . . . enabling the mind to constitute within itself . . . new ways of thinking" (pp. 44–47). Recently, however, this position has been challenged. As an example, Bowers (1988) names the implicit set of beliefs—which he labels "technicism"—underlying positions such as Ong's:

> The cultural orientations that are strengthened [by technology] generally relate to the technological consumer domain of society: attitudes toward technological innovation, the progressive nature of change, measurement and planning as sources of authority, a conceptual hierarchy that places abstract-theoretical thought at the highest, a competitive-remissive form of individualism, and the definition of human needs in terms of what can be supplied by a commodity culture. (p. 6)

Technicist thinking typically leads to the institutional imperative, in which technology contributes to the authority of the institution by dictating what and how things will be done and how people and things will be evaluated. For this reason, C. A. Bowers (1988), Richard Ohmann (1985), Michael Holzman (1984), and Shoshana Zuboff (1988) all have argued strongly against technicist thinking in the workplace.

Zuboff describes the dual nature of computer-generated information in the workplace, explaining that technology not only automates but also "informates," providing continuous information on the way people perform jobs. Zuboff sees a possible negative potential for "informating" in terms of Michel Foucault's discussion of the Panopticon as a sign of our cultural age. The original Panoptican was a design for a prison with a central tower allowing potential observation of every cell even though actual surveillance is sporadic. The effect of *potential* surveillance, Foucault argues (1979), is enough to maintain the central authority of the observers:

> Hence the major effect of the Panopticon: to induce on the inmate a state of conscious and permanent visibility that assures the automatic functioning of power. So to arrange

things so that the surveillance is permanent in its effects, even
if it is discontinuous in its action . . . sustaining a power
relation independent of the person who exercises it. (p. 201)

Technology, Zuboff argues, has the potential to create a
Panopticon in the workplace. Bowers vividly describes how this
has already happened:

> 20,000 [computer surveillance] systems were sold in the United
> States that have the capacity to record such information as
> what telephone is used to make a call, what user identification
> code and extension is used, where the call goes, what time it
> is made, and how long it lasts. . . . Similar technology used
> by an airline company collects data on how long each of its 400
> reservation clerks spends on each call and how much time
> elapses before they pick up their next one. Workers earn
> negative points if they repeatedly use more than 109 seconds
> in handling a call or take more than 12 minutes in bathroom
> trips. . . . Even the keystrokes of the typist can be electronically
> recorded, so that compensation can be exactly calibrated to
> performance. In one data-processing firm, for example, an
> employee who performs five keystrokes a second (18,000 per
> hour) earns the top salary. (p. 17)

Ohmann also asserts that our information-based economy has
ceded too much authority to the computer, with the consequences
that the computer not only perpetuates but also strengthens
traditional lines of authority. He argues that computers in our age
of monopoly capital simultaneously increase the literacy of the
privileged managerial and professional class and decrease the
literacy of the less-privileged working class through the "deskilling"
of labor (p. 683). Holzman makes much the same argument. In
response to observations that most workers will use computers on
the job in the 1990s, he points out that electronic workstations with
pictures of fast food on the keys merely allow workers to be both
illiterate *and* computer-illiterate. Holzman describes some other
negative consequences of the computerization of particular workplaces:

> A common path for advancement in the middle part of the
> twentieth century was through clerical work, the most basic
> type of which might be taken as that of a bank teller. Even a
> recent emigrant with basic English skills could stand at a bank

counter eight hours a day, accepting deposits, certifying withdrawals. Eventually this might lead to the possibility of the acquisition of other, more complex skills, of other, more highly paid work. In just the last two years many of these positions have been eliminated by the introduction of machines to perform those basic tasks. Very soon, for all practical purposes, there will be no entry level positions for unskilled white collar workers in banking. One can see that similar changes will occur in other service industries. (p. 225)

These institutional perspectives on technology perpetuate unequal distribution of authority and divest the individual of any control over technology.

In many workplaces, these uses of computers enhance management capabilities. This is evident in a comment made by John Sununu (now chief of staff to President George Bush) when he was elected governor of New Hampshire in 1983. Sununu, who had instituted a computerized budget system that was inaccessible to members of the State Legislature, justified the closed system by saying, "When things take a long time to come out, you're in more control. That's power a governor can use" ("When Data," 1989). This, too, is the case with technology in the workplace: when management implements a computer system that is inaccessible to workers, it wields more control over them.

Case studies from our own research on computers in the workplace (Barton & Ray, 1989) reflect the concerns of Zuboff, Bowers, and Ohmann, and raise further questions about the relationships between people and technology. The following cases raise crucial issues for teachers and researchers who are studying the effects of technology on language, learning, and the making of meaning in the workplace and other institutional contexts.

Mary Jo, owner of a small research-consulting business, uses her computer mostly for word processing. She thinks of it as an "expensive typewriter." Because she considers the instruction manuals for more advanced software "no help at all," she frequently finds herself at the computer store, waiting for a salesperson to answer her questions. A highly independent and accomplished woman, Mary Jo finds herself dependent on outsiders to tell her how to run her business with a computer.

Mary Jo's frustration at her dependence on others to learn to use her computer raises questions about the nature and purpose of learning in a technological age:

- What approaches to learning about computers empower and enable?

- What approaches intimidate and frustrate?

- How is learning about computers best accomplished?

- Are learning styles altered through computer use?

- What are the consequences—personal, intellectual, economic—of a learner's inability or resistance to learning about computers?

Colleen, a hospital administrator, trains staff to use the new computerized record-keeping system. A recent controversy has involved the housekeeping staff, who must enter data into the computer when they have made a bed or cleaned a room. Colleen says, "There's a real fear [among other hospital workers and administrators] that 'we don't think these people can do that' and 'those people shouldn't be touching [the computer].' "

Colleen's description of the controversy over computer users in a hospital illustrates the non-neutrality of technology and raises questions of access:

- Who uses computers and for what purposes?

- Who decides who uses computers and on what basis?

- How are computers used to exclude or include groups, to deny or permit access to information?

- How are computers used to strengthen existing lines of authority?

- How might broadened access threaten these lines of authority?

- How are issues of access resolved in various institutions?

Colin, an insurance adjuster, doesn't know much about computers, but says,

> I took it upon myself—for the job I have now—to under-
> stand the computer, because the girls in the office pretty much
> run it, and I don't want to appear too ignorant around them
> about what's going on.... Other [adjusters] in the office really
> have no idea what the computer can and cannot do for them,
> and I think that puts them at a disadvantage.

Colin's view of himself in relation to the computer and his
coworkers raises issues of status and gender:

- How does knowledge of computers situate a person among
  colleagues and peers?

- When and how does knowledge of computers perpetuate or
  challenge hierarchical relationships in an institution?

- How is status achieved and maintained through the use of
  computers?

- Does people's language about computers indicate gendered
  thinking?

- Does computer use perpetuate traditional gender relations?

- How might knowledge and use of computers challenge these
  relations?

- What are the consequences in the workplace of integrating
  computers into jobs traditionally held by women?

Claudia, a computer consultant, has taught employees to use
new computer systems. Often, she says,

> The employers resented that the computer was not going to be
> an instant productivity bonus, and a lot of times the people
> who were being given the computers to use resented it.
> [Why?] Because they were [already] real efficient, they
> thought, doing what they were doing on devices that they felt
> like they could control and understand.

Claudia's description of expectations about and attitudes toward
computers raises questions of resistance:

- Under what circumstances do people feel compelled to use
  computers?

- What are the reasons people resist using computers?

- How is this resistance related to people's perceptions of their own authority versus institutional authority?

- What are the consequences in the workplace of this resistance?

- How is resistance to computers acknowledged and addressed in various institutions?

These case studies raise issues of learning, access, status, and resistance—all significant issues for teachers and researchers, who must begin to examine critically the ways they will interpret and promote the relationships between people and technology in the 1990s. The work of Zuboff, Bowers, Ohmann, Holzman, and Barton and Ray argues that interpreting technology from the perspective of an institutional imperative has negative consequences for the individual and society. The result is a work force that is subject to the authority of the institution and workers who often view computers as an imposition on and a restriction of individual growth and development.

Technology, Authority, and the University English Department

Zuboff (1988) discusses the integration of computers in the workplace in terms of a textualizing of the work: what was once concrete and physical (e.g., checking vats and solutions in a paper mill, reviewing the history of a patient on a handwritten chart) is now abstract and electronic (e.g., checking readings in the paper mill, pulling up the electronic record of a patient). Although Zuboff notes that computers often contribute to what we have termed the institutional imperative, she also sees a positive potential for computer-based informating to introduce a new cooperation and development in the workplace:

> [An] approach to technology deployment that emphasizes its informating capacity uses technology to do far more than routinize, fragment, or eliminate jobs. It uses the new technology to increase the intellectual content of work at

> virtually every organizational level, as the ability to decipher
> explicit information and make decisions informed by that
> understanding becomes broadly distributed among
> organizational members. (p. 243)

This interactive use of technology, Zuboff argues, can only arise through analysis of the "text" created by the computer, an analysis that leads to the use of new information to develop jobs rather than de-skill them. Within this interactive perspective, technology can be interpreted so as to involve computer users in negotiating meaning and altering traditional lines of power and control.

We see university English departments, which study texts as their primary activity, as potentially influential in developing an analysis and critique of the discourse on technology, an analysis that promotes an interaction between people and technology. Recent research in literary theory allows us to view the two interpretive perspectives we have been discussing—the institutional imperative and the position of institutional interaction—in terms of text. In English departments, as in other workplaces, the institutional imperative historically has been dominant in the form of a textual imperative which asserts that text and author are the sole sources of authority. A more recent position explores textual interaction, assuming that readers and texts negotiate meaning and that authority is established through this negotiation. Both positions have clear implications for teaching with technology and for research on the ways language is used and meaning is made through technology.

The position of textual imperative, firmly established over the last sixty years by proponents of the New Criticism (Richards, 1929; Wellek & Warren, 1962) is based on the following central tenets: the text is an esthetic object to be appreciated and preserved; an author's intentions are encoded in the words of a text (i.e., meaning is "in" the text); and the purpose of the critic/researcher, carefully schooled in exegesis and endowed with special sensibilities, is to decode for the less discerning reader the author's intentions and the meaning in the text. The textual imperative regards the text as the primary authority over meaning, and the critic/researcher as the primary authority over interpretation. This New Critical perspective, though currently on the wane among literary critics, is firmly established in the English classroom and is the perspective from which several generations of students were schooled.

Some implications of the textual imperative with respect to technology can be found in the work of Michael Heim (1987), a philosopher who argues from a position similar to that of the New Critic in his emphasis on text as esthetic object and on authorial status. Heim argues that the traditional status of text is seriously challenged by the word processor and expresses concern about the future of text as esthetic object: "With the advent of digital writing and digital text reproduction, will literature—and the culture based on respectful care for the word—be eroded?" (p. 3). In decrying the loss of the traditional book culture, Heim also notes the decline of "meaning in the text" and authorial status: "Because its symbolic element is impermanent, flimsy, malleable, contingent, the word processor has provided a new metaphor for the eclipse of all absolutes. . . . The definiteness that was once the prize attribute of written symbols now shimmers on the flickering screen" (p. 212). Further, with the loss of "permanent" encoded meaning comes the loss of authorial control:

> The glut of possibilities opened by word processing . . . may lead to the disappearance of the authentic and determinate human voice or personal presence behind symbolized words. . . . It becomes possible to treat the entire verbal life of the human race as one continuous, anonymous code without essential reference to a human presence behind it, which neither feels it must answer to anyone nor necessarily awaits an answer from anyone. (pp. 212–213)

From Heim's perspective, educators must counter the negative influences of computers and restore the status of the written word. This argument, however, puts educators in the position of working against technology rather than helping students negotiate their own authority in terms of it.

In direct contrast to the New Critical position, current literary theory offers an alternative position focused on a more interactive view of text and reader. From the perspective of post-structuralists, feminists, and reader-response critics, text and author have little or no status. The central tenets that unify these positions are that the text is indeterminate, created anew by each encounter with it; the meaning of a text is not encoded in the words, but in the interaction between text and reader; and the purpose of the critic/ researcher is to name and examine the extra-textual conditions— linguistic, social, psychological, political—under which particular readers construct particular meanings. Current literary theory, then, undermines the permanence and authority of both text and critic by making the reader the primary focus of critical attention. Crucial to this position are drastically altered concepts of text and interpretation. No longer privileging the written text, post-structuralists broadly define "text" as "whatever is articulated by language" (Culler, 1982, p. 8), and the interpretation of text as "an account of what happens to a reader: how various conventions and expectations are brought into play, where particular connections or hypotheses are posited, [and] how expectations are defeated or confirmed" (p. 135).

Post-structuralists (deconstructionists) look for ways in which any search for meaning is subverted by the texts themselves (Foucault, 1969, 1970; Derrida, 1968, 1977). Deconstructive criticism, which includes critiques of sign, of representation, and of subject, looks to the "perverse, apoetical moments of the text," identifying the paradoxes that arise in pursuit of meaning (Culler, 1982, p. 22). Thus, the deconstructive critic concentrates on the critical enterprise rather than on authorial intentions or text, looking for sources of conflict—for anything that counters an authoritarian interpretation. From this perspective, neither text, author, nor critic has "authority" over meaning. Instead, meaning is a philosophical, political, and intellectual construct negotiated by a reader in response to other readings.

Reader-response critics (Fish, 1980; Holland, 1975; Bleich, 1978, 1988; Iser, 1978; Rosenblatt, 1938, 1978) also grant the reader a central role in the interpretation of meaning, but vary considerably among themselves in characterizing the reader and positing the role of the text. Stanley Fish argues that a literary work is a temporal experience, discovered "bit by bit, moment by moment" (p. 44) rather than sentence by sentence or page by page . Meaning is an event (rather than a static entity) embedded in a text and evoked by an experience of reading. Norman Holland argues that readers adapt a text to their own "identity theme" or personality:

> Some readings take close account of the words-on-the-
> page and some do not, but no matter how much textual,

"objective" evidence a reader brings into his reading, he structures and adapts it according to his own inner needs. (p. 40)

From Holland's perspective, the text is just "so many 'words-on-a-page' " (p. 12) without an analysis of the reader who brings meaning and purpose to those words.

Contemporary feminist critics, drawing on both deconstructive criticism and reader-response theory, as well as Freudian and Lacanian psychoanalysis, begin with the premise that meaning is in the experience of the reader, and they problematize that premise by adding the variable of gender. Of particular interest is how meaning is affected when the reader is a woman. Elaine Showalter (1979) asserts that feminist criticism examines "the way in which the hypothesis of a female reader changes our apprehension of a given text, awakening us to the significance of sexual codes" (p. 25). Feminist critics have begun to identify the "gendered" position of the reader by demonstrating that women are trained to read as men and by arguing that women must become "resisting readers" rather than assenting readers in order to overcome the male perspective that has dominated them and to validate their own interpretations (Fetterly, 1978). Feminists also critique the position and authority of text, the literary critic, and traditional criticism by exposing the androcentric nature of the literary canon and interpretations of that canon, as well as the ways those interpretations serve to exclude women from the critical enterprise. Thus, feminist scholarship is both a critical and political movement; while identifying the procedures and assumptions underlying readers' interpretations of texts, it also seeks to displace androcentric modes of interpretation and validate alternative modes.

These post-structuralist, feminist, and reader-response perspectives, despite their differences in emphasis, share the belief that author and text have limited authority in determining meaning; it is the reader—either as individual or member of a community of readers—who exerts control over the text and authorizes meaning. This general perspective can be characterized as textual interaction because meaning arises out of encounters between readers and texts.

Reader-centered perspectives on text have significant implications for teaching with technology and for researching the effects of technology. Much work needs to be done in this area in the next decade, and researchers and teachers can gain useful insights and formulate further questions by looking at the initial work of Stuart Moulthrop (1989), Catherine Smith (1989), Cynthia Selfe (1990), and Richard Lanham (1987).

In contrast to Heim, Moulthrop embraces computerized text over the "old textual model of the bound volume" because he sees it as a powerful way to access what Culler calls the "story of reading." Of particular interest to Moulthrop is interactive fiction, a computerized narrative that can be determined and altered by readers' decisions and responses. In his analysis of students' reading of interactive fiction, Moulthrop found that, although initially students were bound by their traditional expectations of textual authority, they later became deeply engaged in interactive fictions. Moulthrop's work raises questions for both teachers and researchers about the changing nature of reading in an electronic classroom:

- How do electronic texts differ in form and function from traditional texts?

- Do electronic texts require different methods of reading and interpretation? If so, how do readers learn these methods?

- Do readers transfer their methods for reading electronic texts to their reading of traditional texts?

- What forms of authority over texts do students develop as a result of interacting with electronic texts?

- Do these forms of authority differ among individual students or groups of students? (That is, how are they affected by race, class, and gender?)

- Does electronic reading affect writing? If so, in what ways?

- How can studies of electronic reading inform reader-response criticism?

Catherine Smith's work considers recent developments in hypertext, focusing particularly on the connections between electronic experience and everyday physical and social experience. Smith sees relationships between feminist phenomenology, in particular, and types of thinking augmented by hypertext. Drawing upon work in cognitive psychology which shows that there are various kinds of thinking that are valued differently (Belenky, Clinchy, Goldberger, & Tarule, 1986; Polanyi, 1958), Smith argues that what theorists have learned about gendered thinking, the composition of personal knowledge, and the basis of experiential thinking should be related to the development and analysis of hypertext (see also Smith in this collection). Smith's work is significant because it is the first to place the reader/knower, as opposed to the computer or text, at the center of research on hypertext. For teachers and researchers, it raises questions about the use and implications of hypertext in an electronic classroom:

- What are the assumptions—intellectual, social, political— underlying the development of hypertext environments?

- In what ways are students' reading, writing, and thinking affected by hypertext resources?

- Do students develop more awareness of their own thinking processes as a result of exploring hypertext environments?

- Do students or groups of students develop different styles of using hypertext? (That is, how are styles related to race, class, and gender?)

- How can research on hypertext inform theories on the inter- action of reading, writing, and thinking?

Drawing on feminist theory, Selfe (1990) questions the academic status quo that privileges some groups over others, and she suggests how technology can extend privilege, provide more egalitarian access to reading and writing communities, and alter power relationships between readers and writers. From this perspective, computers in education are tools for political and social reform as well as tools for communication. One purpose of this work is to open up the possibilities for textual interpretation by encouraging alternative views. Selfe, in contrast to Heim, suggests that the anonymity available through computerized texts "can help us de-marginalize those individuals who have been excluded from our discussions by more traditional approaches to the teaching of literacy" (p. 122). In Selfe's vision, computers can significantly change patterns of information sharing and power relationships among students and between students and faculty because of the emphasis on what is said rather than on who says it. Cooper and Selfe (1990) discuss the potential of computerized class discussions for realizing this objective, arguing that the anonymity of computers provides "forums [that] should encourage students to use language to resist as well as to accommodate, and should enable individuals to create internally persuasive discourse as well as to adopt discourse validated by external authority" (p. 847). This work raises questions about the development of electronic pedagogy:

- How can the use of technology, such as electronic discussions and conferences, break down traditional forms of authority between teacher and student?

- How can these electronic discussions and conferences break down traditional forms of authority among students themselves?

- How can electronic discussions encourage students to develop and articulate their own perspectives on reading and writing?

- How is the teaching of reading and writing altered by the electronic classroom?

- How can research on electronic classrooms inform theories of teaching and learning?

Moving beyond the text and the classroom, Richard Lanham (1987) suggests that the personal computer, "the ultimate Post-Modern work of art" (p. 9), has the potential to transform English departments and their place within the university. In a 1987 address to English department chairpersons, Lanham argued that because electronic text is "insistent in its pressures for the democratization of art," it forces English departments to come to terms with rhetoric, "away from the purity of Arnoldian seriousness toward the mixed-motive world of present dangers where rhetoric has always dwelt" (p. 8). Further, Lanham argues that technological and social changes require a different administrative structure based on new relationships between the humanities and the social sciences, literary study and the fine arts, English and other disciplines. These areas need to be realigned in the university so as to avoid intellectual fragmentation. Lanham's argument suggests further questions for research on the effects of technology in the 1990s:

- How is technology integrated within English departments? Within other departments?

- Do departments differ significantly in their attitudes toward and uses of technology? If so, how and why?

- How do individual faculty and departmental attitudes toward computers affect student attitudes?

- How does technology challenge or maintain traditional lines of status and authority in departments and in the university at large?

- How might technology promote further communication among departments and foster interdisciplinary perspectives on teaching and research?

- How does the university see its role in teaching and researching with technology?

- How and to what extent does the university's perspective on technology affect the perspective in the workplace and vice versa?

In this paper, we have demonstrated two approaches to interpreting the discourse of technology—the institutional imperative and institutional interaction. We have tried to show that the most effective interpretive frame is that of institutional interaction, whereby computers are a means of encouraging greater participation by more people. Further, we have suggested that this perspective favors the use of technology in ways that can open up avenues for positive change in the institution, in the individual, and in the interaction of the two. We have also suggested that university English departments can play a major role in developing, modeling, analyzing, and discussing the interactive role of technology in an institution, which opens up a challenging direction for research on computers in the next decade.

References

Aronowitz, S., & Giroux, H. (1985). *Education under siege: The conservative, liberal and radical debate over schooling.* South Hadley, MA: Bergin & Garvey.

Bartholomae, D. (1985). Inventing the university. In M. Rose (Ed.), *When a Writer Can't Write: Research on Writer's Block and Other Writing Process Problems* (pp. 134–165). New York: Guilford.

Barton, E., & Ray, R. (1989). *Computer literacy from bottom to top.* Paper presented at the Fifth Computers and Writing Conference, University of Minnesota, Minneapolis.

Belenky, M. F., Clinchy, B. M., Goldberger, N. R., & Tarule, J. M. (1986). *Women's ways of knowing: Developing self, voice, and mind.* New York: Basic Books.

Berlin, J. (1987). *Rhetoric and reality: Writing instruction in American colleges, 1900–1985.* Carbondale: Southern Illinois University Press.

Berlin, J. (1989). Rhetoric and ideology in the writing classroom. *College English, 50,* 477–494.

Bizzell, P. (1982). Cognition, convention, and certainty. *Pre/Text, 3,* 213–243.

Bizzell, P. (1986). What happens when basic writers come to college? *College Composition and Communication, 37,* 294–301.

Bleich, D. (1978). *Subjective criticism.* Baltimore: Johns Hopkins University Press.

Bleich, D. (1988). *The double perspective: Language, literacy and social relations.* New York: Oxford University Press.

Bowers, C. A. (1988). *The cultural dimensions of educational computing: Understanding the non-neutrality of technology.* New York: Teachers College Press.

The Carnegie Commission. (1986). *A nation prepared: Teachers for the 21st century.* Excerpts from the Report by the Carnegie Forum's Task Force on Teaching as a Profession. (Reprinted in *Chronicle of Higher Education,* 21 May 1986, pp. 43–55.)

Collins, J., & Sommers, E. (Eds.). (1985). *Writing on-line: Using computers in the teaching of writing.* Upper Montclair, NJ: Boynton/Cook.

Cook-Gumperz, J. (Ed.). (1986). *The social construction of literacy.* Cambridge: Cambridge University Press.

Cooper, M., & Holzman, M. (Eds.). (1989). *Writing as social action.* Portsmouth, NH: Boynton/Cook.

Cooper, M., & Selfe, C. (1990). Computer conferences and learning: Authority, resistance, and internally persuasive discourse. *College English, 52,* 847–869.

Culler, J. (1982). *On deconstruction: Theory and criticism after structuralism.* Ithaca: Cornell University Press.

Derrida, J. (1968). Différance. In H. Adams & L. Searle (Eds.), *Critical theory since 1965* (pp. 120–136). Tallahassee: Florida State University Press.

Derrida, J. (1977). *Of grammatology.* Baltimore: Johns Hopkins University Press.

Fetterly, J. (1978). *The resisting reader: A feminist approach to American fiction.* Bloomington: Indiana University Press.

Fish, S. (1980). *Is there a text in this class?* Cambridge: Cambridge University Press.

Foucault, M. (1969). What is an author? In H. Adams & L. Searle (Eds.), *Critical theory since 1965* (pp. 138–148). Tallahassee: Florida State University Press.

Foucault, M. (1970). *The order of things: An archaeology of the human sciences.* New York: Random House.

Foucault, M. (1979). *Discipline and punish: The birth of the prison.* New York: Vintage Books.

Gerrard, L. (Ed.). (1987). *Writing at century's end: Essays on computer-assisted instruction.* New York: Random House.

Hawisher, G. E. & Selfe, C. L. (Eds.). (1989). *Critical perspectives on computers and composition instruction.* New York: Teachers College Press.

Heim, M. (1987). *Electric language: A philosophical study of word processing.* New Haven: Yale University Press.

Holland, N. (1975). *5 readers reading.* New Haven: Yale University Press.

Holzman, M. (1984). Teaching is remembering. Reprinted in M. Cooper & M. Holzman (Eds.), *Writing as social action* (pp. 221–232). Portsmouth, NH: Boynton/Cook.

Iser, W. (1978). *The act of reading: A theory of aesthetic response.* Baltimore: Johns Hopkins University Press.

Jameson, F. (1984). Postmodernism, or the cultural logic of late capitalism. *New Left Review, 146,* 53–73.

Kintgen, E., Kroll, B., & Rose, M. (Eds.). (1988). *Perspectives on literacy.* Carbondale: Southern Illinois University Press.

Lanham, R. (1987). *Convergent pressures: Social, technological, theoretical.* Paper presented at The Future of Doctoral Studies in English Conference, Spring Hills Center, Wayzata, MN.

The literacy gap. (1988, December). *Time*, pp. 56–57.

Mandel, E. (1978). *Late capitalism.* London: Verso.

McLuhan, M. (1962). *The Gutenberg galaxy: The making of typographic man.* Toronto: University of Toronto Press.

Moulthrop, S. (1989, May). *Sharing the fantasy: Creating a discourse community with interactive fiction.* Paper presented at the Fifth Conference on Computers and Writing, University of Minnesota, Minneapolis.

Ohmann, R. (1985). Literacy, technology, and monopoly capital. *College English, 47,* 675–689.

Olson, C. (1987). Who computes? In D. Livingstone (Ed.), *Critical pedagogy and cultural power* (pp. 179–205). South Hadley, MA: Bergin & Garvey.

Ong, W. (1977). *Interfaces of the word: Studies in the evolution of consciousness and culture.* Ithaca: Cornell University Press.

Polanyi, M. (1958). *Personal knowledge: Toward a post-critical philosophy.* Chicago: University of Chicago Press.

Richards, I. A. (1929). *Practical criticism.* London: Kegan Paul.

Rosenblatt, L. (1938). *Literature as exploration.* New York: Modern Language Association.

Rosenblatt, L. (1978). *The reader, the text, the poem: The transactional theory of the literary work.* Carbondale: Southern Illinois University Press.

Selfe, C. (1990). Technology in the English classroom: Computers through the lens of feminist theory. In C. Handa (Ed.), *Computers & community: Teaching composition in the twenty-first century* (pp. 118–139). Portsmouth, NH: Boyton/Cook-Heinemann.

Showalter, E. (1979). Towards a feminist poetics. In M. Jacobus (Ed.), *Women writing and writing about women* (pp. 22–41). London: Croom Helm.

Smith, C. (1989, May). *Reconsidering hypertext.* Paper presented at the Fifth Computers and Writing Conference, University of Minnesota, Minneapolis.

Wellek, R., & Warren, A. (1962). *Theory of literature* (3rd ed.). New York: Harcourt Brace Jovanovich.

When data rains and reigns. (1989, February 19). *The Detroit Free Press*, pp. B1, B6.

Wurman, R. (1988). *Information anxiety.* New York: Doubleday.

Zuboff, S. (1988). *In the age of the smart machine: The future of work and power.* New York: Basic Books.

Chapter 13

The Politics of Writing Programs

James Strickland
Slippery Rock University

The computer has come to be regarded by writing programs as a serious academic component. However, the academic use of comput- ers is often determined—constrained or supported—by politics. To what extent do theoretical and pragmatic politics influence the role of computers and the changing status of rhetoric and composition studies, computers and the empowerment and authority of writers, decision making about computers in writing programs, and com- puters and support from outside interest groups? How do politics determine whether or not computers make a difference in writing programs?

A friend wrote me a letter, observing that he was writing while sitting under a poster quoting A. J. Liebling: "Freedom of the press belongs to those who have one." Tom was writing with a Mac Plus, and the scene seemed an epiphany. The power of the computer belongs to those who have one.

Recently, a graduate student in my seminar "Teaching Writing with Computers" received a part-time position at a local commu- nity college, one with a computer lab. She found, however, that she would have to petition to use the room because it was designated for business students and the software was available only for limited use. As an alternative, she investigated the college's library, where she found only one computer available and no software. My brother Don has experienced similar frustration trying to teach his English classes in the high school computer lab because the math classes have scheduling priority.

The power of the computer belongs to those who have one, and to those who control who may use it and to what purpose.

Writing programs, whether broadly defined within a curriculum, such as a first-year composition program, or within a location encouraging writing, typically a writing center, have come to regard computers as a serious academic component. However, various non-instructional factors determine the extent to which computers make a difference in classrooms and writing centers. This chapter will investigate how politics—non-instructional issues and considerations—influence the academic use of computers.

Pragmatic Politics and Theoretical Politics

A useful approach to take in this investigation is to consider the distinction between pragmatic politics and theoretical politics, although the distinction is often blurred. For the purposes of this chapter, "pragmatic politics" refers to concerns of educational policies and policymakers—the secretary of education, school board members, teachers' unions, superintendents, school administrators, and principals. Even teachers are policymakers in this pragmatic political sense. However, these pragmatic politics of education—the daily decisions and actions—are directly related to theoretical politics—theories of language, literature, and pedagogy. Thus, to operate politically we must also understand the theoretical context in which current computers in writing programs function. This current context, as many composition specialists agree, regardless of how fully we understand its philosophical entanglements, is largely post-structuralist criticism—Marxism, reader-response theory, and deconstruction. Marxist criticism examines the political and cultural contexts shaping literary texts. Reader-response criticism challenges the authority of New Criticism readings, asserting that the reader brings meaning to the text. Deconstruction denies determinate meaning altogether, each reader constructing an indeterminate text within which there are only variable meanings.

For a more detailed example of the relationship between pragmatic politics and theoretical politics in educational settings, we can consider how Marxism influences our current use of computers in classrooms. The Marxist view cautions that the machine itself is political. As Marcuse (1941) reminds us, computers, as a device of technology, "can promote authoritarianism as well as liberty, scarcity as well as abundance, the extension as well as the abolition of toil" (p. 139). The machine as an agent of repression profits those within the power structure, the hegemony. The computer enforces or reinforces conformity. Marcuse continues, "In manipulating the machine, [we learn] that obedience to the directions is the only way to obtain desired results. Getting along is identical with adjustment to the apparatus" (p. 144).

Within such a setting, there is political pressure to conform to whatever choices have been made—the extent to which commitments have been made to computers in the writing programs, what machines are used (IBM, Macintosh, or other Apple environments), and what software is adopted. Deborah Holdstein and Tim Redman (1985), for instance, caution that results in the computer classroom may be influenced by factors outside the teacher's control: the choice of an awkward word-processing program, an inefficient mainframe or writing lab, or a noisy writing environment. Hence, practical political decisions about using the technology to support literacy—informed choices made by teachers knowledgeable about language theories—are also constrained by theoretical political decisions about using the technology to create consumers—choices made by the hegemony, the corporate power structure of the university or school district, influenced by what Richard Ohmann (1985) calls "monopoly capitalism." Although teachers may make practical political decisions designed to support the use of computers in an educational setting that respects diversity, other forces outside the classroom may be making theoretical political decisions that support the use of computers in writing programs in ways that promote conformity.

As a second example of theoretical politics that currently affect our pragmatic political decisions about computer use, we can explore the case of reader-response theory. Reader-response criticism empowers the reader through a theoretical position grounded in phenomenology, in opposition to logical positivism. In a political sense, it transforms readers from the role of consumers to that of producers of meaning. In this sense, reader-response criticism may be liberating. The computer, in such a framework, may be used by teachers, not as the "state apparatus" of Louis Althusser (1971) but as the "symptomatic technology" of Raymond Williams (1975)—value-neutral, capable of being used, in O'Shea and Self's (1984) terms, "to enhance the educational process and equip each learner with an exciting medium for problem-solving and individual tuition" (p. 1). In this vision, teachers can use computers to facilitate the notion that readers/writers create text, allowing the text to be manipulated on the screen, although readers cannot usually manipulate a computer's program. (Machine code, a deep structure, is unavailable to the nontechnical user.) Readers in the act of reading on-screen text bring meaning to that text, as reader-response theory maintains.

Finally, we can consider the influence of theories of deconstruction upon computer use in the classroom. Crowley (1989) notes, "On a deconstructive model of textuality, literary texts do not hold still and docilely submit themselves to repeated identical readings; they can be read and reread, and each reading differs from the last" (p. 20). As a student reads and deconstructs text on the computer screen, it is the rare writer who can avoid making changes. The fluid text in computer memory will not "hold still" for reading; it constantly invites its reader to massage the text, regardless of whether or not the reader is the original writer (although we might put the entire notion of an original writer "under erasure," after Derrida). Some might criticize these variations in the fluid text as being mere changes in surface features, but to the deconstructionist, even the smallest change is one of "différance," one of significance (Derrida, 1982).

Using the perspectives of these post-structuralist theoretical contexts allows us to envision, to "see," how pedagogy can help us politicize ourselves and our students, how it can help make us and them aware of constraints imposed by culture and language on the activity of learning as well as on the politics of class, sex, and race. As Ohmann (1985) says, "The technology is malleable; it does have liberatory potential. Especially in education, we have something to say about whether that potential is realized. But its fate is not a technological question; it is a political one" (p. 685). As teachers of composition, most of us would support efforts to inform our use of computers with the "vision" of one or more post-structuralist theories, would welcome the influence of such theories on pragmatic decisions we make about computers. Yet, because technology is so much a part of our conceptual world, forces of pragmatic and theoretical politics often work in opposing ways to inform, constrain, and shape our use of these machines as we integrate them into our classrooms and writing programs.

The Issues

In the case of technology, theoretical politics and pragmatic politics often intersect at "sites" of controversy involving economic matters, power/control concerns, and democratic movements. Within these sites we encounter those issues most vigorously contested in the profession today: the changing status of rhetoric and composition studies, the empowerment and authority of writers, the way decisions are made about computers in writing programs, and the politics of support from outside interest groups. As Schilb (1989) notes, "Post-structuralists can remind [us] that vulnerable presuppositions underlie even the most avowedly pragmatic stance (p. 437). These issues show the power that both pragmatic and theoretical politics have in the application of computers to writing programs. In the remainder of this chapter, we can examine each of these issues to reveal how the dynamics of computers in writing programs result from the interplay between political theory and pragmatics.

The Changing Status of Rhetoric and Composition Studies

An obvious site at which theory and practice intersect to affect the use of computers in our profession is found within our discussions of the changing status of writing programs. As Maxine Hairston (1982) has documented, a theoretical shift in the way writing programs are viewed yields pragmatic division within the profession. When a senior member of our English department turned to a junior member and said, "We've hired enough of you people," my female colleague was both speechless and confused, unsure to whom the remark referred: women? writing specialists?

computer advocates? One's theoretical politics not only shapes the choice of teaching practices but informs one's status within the department/the institution/the profession.

The notion that the study of the composing processes of student writers could be scholarship worthy of tenure and promotion consideration, enhancing the researcher's prestige, can be traced to research following the Dartmouth Conference of 1966, specifically to research such as Janet Emig's (1971), focusing on the composing process of individual writers. Research in composition gained additional esteem when the discipline began to share research techniques with cognitivists, such as Linda Flower and John R. Hayes (1981), and ethnographers, such as Shirley Brice Heath (1983). During the same period, we shaped our notion of composition as a discipline by tracing its origins from Aristotle and classical rhetoric (Corbett, 1965) to nineteenth-century rhetoric (Berlin, 1984). Currently, we are moving toward a self-reflexive conceptualization of our discipline, with some scholars discounting the classical trace as a "myth of origins" while admitting that this theoretical focus is motivated by a pragmatic desire to establish scholarly respectability for rhetoric and composition studies (Hatlen, 1988).

Whether the introduction of computers and word processing into the equation has contributed to or detracted from this effort of identifying the discipline's perceived worth is a valid question. There are some, like that senior colleague, who see the machine exposing the utilitarian nature of composition scholarship, and regard the discipline as too pedestrian for full membership in the academic community. These literary historians and critics discount scholarship published by composition journals, and certainly by computer journals, and refuse to count software authorship as the equivalent of scholarly publication (Bourque, 1983). It is no coincidence that these literary historians show equal contempt for post-structuralist literary criticism.

Others in the profession of teaching take just the opposite view, such as those in the hard sciences or computer science, who regard the machine as strengthening what is otherwise perceived as very subjective research in the humanities. Computers have been observed to confer prestige upon writing programs by association. The business, mathematics, and science departments—those granted the most opportunities for new labs, new machines, new hirings, course load reductions, and priority in scheduling and location considerations—once saw allocating computers to the writing program as a poor use of resources. Ironically, the very fact that writing programs are now competing for these computers has raised the status of these programs in the eyes of competing departments. The machines command attention, giving writing programs credibility because what occurs is observable; on the surface, computer writing facilities are like science labs, where experiments take place. Computers make writing programs seem more researchable, more like computer science than like literature classes. Unfortunately, these colleagues in other disciplines, as much as the literary historians, often have theoretical foundations that encourage them to see computers and technology as tied to skill reinforcement and mechanical problem solving. Hence, on a pragmatic level, the people in business, mathematics, and science might lend support for computers in writing programs, but given their theoretical politics they would generally have no use for the computer unless, as Frank Smith (1988) warns, it were

> used as a mechanical taskmaster to drill or test . . . according to someone else's prescription . . . presenting the most trivial, decontextualized, and fragmented drills in endless variation. (p. 83)

It would be easy to dismiss these observations of our profession's perceived worth in a department/institution/profession if it were not for one thing: status and prestige determine tenure, promotion, and sabbaticals for individuals; budgets and hiring authorizations for departments; and grants and outside funding for institutions—a very pragmatic concern indeed. Professional recognition is needed for the advancement of research in the use of computers in writing programs (Holdstein, 1987), and yet, in an ironic twist, status will only be realized when the research can demonstrate a positive correlation between computers and improvement in writing (Thiesmeyer, 1989).

The Empowerment of Writers

The second site of intersection between practical and theoretical politics concerns the changes that occur when computers become part of writing programs that seek to empower student writers as meaning makers in the post-structuralist sense. In such programs, computers can be used at several levels to give pragmatic support to post-structuralist theory.

At a basic level, computers can help teachers change the concept of authority, shifting it away from the front desk in the classroom where authority was once conferred by the teacher, toward students who earn authority by their prowess on the machine. And yet, that oversimplifies the theoretical shift. At a deeper level, the computer in the classroom gives authority to the reader as the reader, in constructing meaning, becomes the author. A theoretical change in politics occurs in the classroom when a pragmatic tool—the computer—radically alters the meaning of author, text, reader, and teacher. Writing programs using computers can no longer pretend to operate from a theory that is text-centered and product-oriented, or even one that is author-centered and process-oriented. Writers using computers move toward an interactive model of writer-text-reader-teacher relationships (Hawisher, 1989). As Hawisher notes,

> Partially as a result of the use of computers, instructors can begin to relinquish [some of their] traditional authority . . . over students' texts, their conversations, [and] other readings. (p. 4)

Authority changes as the concept of authorship changes (Foucault, 1969). The machine, a political agent of liberation, allows those who use it to feel empowered in a new way (Sudol, 1985). Users become writers, sharing a sense of themselves as authors with published, "real" writers. One of the children studied by Lucy Calkins (1983) perceived the difference this perspective makes: "Before I ever wrote a book," this seven-year-old observed, "I used to think there was a big machine, and they typed a title and then the machine went until the book was done. Now I look at a book and I know a guy wrote it and it's been his project for a long time" (p. 157). Although this revelation had nothing to do with computers—all writers are capable of this realization—imagine the child's sense of power when given the "big machine": a computer with desktop publishing capability. Writing is empowering, and computers are enabling, whether they are used for simple word-processing or desktop publishing.

It is in this sense that the pragmatic reality of writing with the "big machine" has begun to compel a theoretical change. Writing, once conceived of as a text created by the writer in isolation and given to an instructor to be read/returned, is now being seen as a text in fluid form, in an electronic medium, often produced in a room with other people engaged in similar activities, and displayed for others to read at their own or the author's invitation. Hard copy is only a trace, fixed in time, of a text that may or may not still be evolving on the screen. The reader/instructor may make comments on the hard copy, but that is not the text—the text maintains its own authority, remaining in its own form, quite separate from a reader's remarks or suggestions. The theoretical concept of authority/authorship has been changed, and the notion of a text is completely deconstructed by the computer. An author has only an intended text, approximated by the text created in the act of writing. On its most surface level, a text created with a computer has little of the author's person about it; there is no individual handwriting, no hand-stricken typeface, no coffee cup rings on the page. Instead, uniform symbols glow on a luminescent screen, corresponding to binary code according to an ASCII standard.

The pragmatic presence of computers in writing programs changes the essential political balance within a classroom in other ways as well, and it is these changes most people intend when they speak of changing authority and empowering students. Schools and their classrooms, to use the categories of Margaret Mead (1970), are primarily post-figurative, where "children learn primarily from their forebears," rather than pre-figurative, where "adults learn . . . from their children" (p. 1). In the traditional school, the notion that teachers in the classroom learn from their students is unthinkable. An exception that Shirley Brice Heath (1988) noticed, one that changes the post-figurative political relationship, is the situation created when computers are in the classroom. In this case, learning becomes pre-figurative and the classroom nontraditional. In these nontraditional classrooms, as well as computer showrooms, adults repeat the same stock phrase, "My kids know more about these things than I do." In the shift from a post-figurative model of learning to a pre-figurative one, as Frank Smith (1988) notes,

Computers constitute a new culture. To live with [computers] requires a new language. To understand them demands individuals without fear or preconceptions who can rapidly learn to make sense of a new language and to feel quickly at home in a new culture. Fortunately such individuals exist in large numbers every generation . . . [They are known as] children. The time has come in education when we must at last acknowledge that the greatest source of learning for teachers must be children. (p. 89)

In a classroom equipped with computers, students learn from each other, and often they teach the teachers (Bruce, Michaels, & Watson-Gegeo, 1985). Students, as computer hackers, take control of their learning and what they need to know.

What happens to the writing produced, once the classroom politics have changed? Students have the power of the press: writing with computers gives them a forum for ideas that adds force to their writing. Networks allow students and faculty to distribute their writing across campus and community. Desktop publishing allows small presses, and even individuals, to present products similar to those produced by publishing houses. Many educators project that blacks, females, and other minority students can find, in such a setting, an increasing freedom of expression.

The Politics of Decision Making

A third site at which theoretical and practical politics intersect involves curricular decision making. In the case of technology, the instructional use of computers is limited by pragmatic non-instructional decisions made in the absence of theory or under the influence of reactionary politics. Although the public pressures schools to prepare students to use the technology of the future, as Andrea Herrmann (1989) notes, decision-makers charged with these preparations are school administrators or school board members with little understanding of computers or the instructional use of computers in English composition. In fact, when the educational impact of computers is discussed at a gathering of teachers, everyone seems to have a story about how decisions about a computer lab or classroom at their school were made or influenced by someone in administration, someone in another department, or an outside interest group—parents, community agencies, the federal government. Rarely are decisions about instructional technology made by the teachers themselves.

Why is there so much interference? Computers do necessitate the investment of large resources that writing programs never received previously: additional staff (faculty and aides knowledgeable about computers), service contracts, and supplies (ribbons, disks, and paper). Computers also require software, a major expense to buy, maintain, or develop. Few English teachers are given the power to control such large budgets. Generally, these fiscal decisions are made by people outside of writing programs—people who are uninformed about the theory of language and composition instruction and are often politically reactionary. And, unfortunately, as Herrmann (1989) notes, "Decisions [made about computers] are costly; mistakes are expensive and usually have long-lasting consequences" for writing programs (p. 118).

On the other hand, computers can protect writing programs when budgets get cut. According to Marcuse (1941), for instance, the "principle of competitive efficiency favors the enterprises with the most highly mechanized and rationalized industrial equipment" (p. 141). To keep the equipment running in times of economic austerity and budget crunches, writing programs, under the guise of offering occupational training for students, have often called upon the powerful alliance of the business and technology community to support them—a connection applauded by administrators who are pragmatically aware that schools with computers are perceived as more prestigious and receive better ratings.

Forces outside the classroom also end up making crucial political decisions about software development and the ownership of software developed by faculty. Some institutions, operating in a "monopoly capitalism" framework, feel justified in claiming that software authored by faculty in their employ, who use machines on their campus to design software for students, is the property of the institution. In such situations, sale of the software, locally or nationally, is prohibited unless the royalties are surrendered to the institution. It matters little that faculty who write software are often given no released time to support their work and no money through institutional grants or future financial rewards, such as promotion and sabbaticals. This politically pragmatic decision has a powerful inhibiting effect upon the development of theoretically informed software for computers in writing programs.

The Politics of Support

As we have already noted, a final site of intersection between practical and theoretical politics occurs in computer-supported writing programs funded by outside interests. Many school systems and universities regularly seek the support of corporations, federal agencies, and the Defense Department as a way to fund the expense of computers. Programs dependent upon these institutions of "monopoly capitalism" for support find it hard to maintain a post-structuralist political perspective—one that is liberating, anti-authoritarian, and consumer-based. In these situations, the power of the computer belongs to those who have one, and more so to those who control its cost and support its expense.

Corporations, for instance, control how computers are used in writing programs because they control software prices, site licenses, software demonstrations, support services (not required of textbooks), presentations at professional conferences, and the marketing of educational versions of software (an oxymoron if ever there was one—"crippled versions" would be more appropriate). The companies also control what is on the market, selling inappropriate software to unwary teachers, producing what Smith (1988) calls "drill and kill" software (p. 85) dressed up as "process" or "whole language" material. Often these companies price better software beyond the means of departments, faculty, and students, and continue policies that limit the return of software once it is purchased. Yet it is difficult to support writing curricula without software. The power of the computer belongs to those who control the software.

Nor is the control of software the only way in which capitalism influences educational computing. As Richard Ohmann (1985) states, "There are now about 500,000 computers in American schools, many of them gifts or nearly so from the manufacturers and other companies. The motives for such generosity are not hard to imagine" (p. 685). Students who learn to use computers in school become consumers who buy computers when they graduate. As Ohmann continues, "Most likely, the technology of classroom computers—especially software—will serve [the] purposes [of monopoly capitalism]" (p. 685). He admonishes, "Computers are a commodity for which a mass market is being created in quite conventional ways" (p. 684).

Individual teachers, too, are not exempt from the politics of support. I know of at least one colleague who is creating on-line handbooks for publishing companies, not because he believes in the value of these programs but because the corporations are paying well. He reasons that if he did not produce them, the publishers would get someone else to do it. Assuming he may be right, that the product would have been produced anyway, endorsement of the software is nevertheless implicit, given his status in the profession, his association with movements such as the National Writing Project, and his professional publications. Our theoretical politics, our beliefs, and our knowledge about writing make tacit demands about what type of support we seek and accept in writing programs.

The Questions

In considering the political consequences of computers in writing programs, we must identify those questions that address both pragmatic and theoretical issues.

We must, for instance, ask questions concerning the power and status connected with the use of computers:

- Precisely why and how does the introduction of computers affect the status of writing programs in some departments, schools, or districts and not in others? Do computers affect a program's status? Does this effect last? What are the long-lasting effects of computers on the status of writing programs?

- How does computer involvement affect teachers in literature and writing programs? Do these colleagues enjoy an increase in professional returns or merely an increase in responsibilities—training new faculty, monitoring computer lab use, and taking inventory of supplies? What incentives do schools offer, for instance, to faculty who conduct research on computer use or develop computer software?

We will also want to investigate how computers in writing programs have changed course design, textbook selection, choice of preferred genres, and the nature of the assignments:

- Which features of computer use support a post-structuralist perspective on learning? Which features hinder such an approach? How do such features affect course design? textbook selection? genre study? assignments? What educational goals are linked to a post-structuralist approach?

- What particular kinds of computer use will foster pre-figurative learning in the classroom? How will this use manifest itself in classroom configurations? assignments? activities? computer labs?

- Given the political constraints under which teachers labor, can they use computers in writing programs to help transform education into "a continuing dialogue in which the young, free to act on their own initiative, can lead their elders in the direction of the unknown" (Mead, 1970, p. 3)? If so, what political activities must teachers engage in in connection with computers? If not, what are the political forces keeping them from achieving their goals and how do these forces exert pressure within our education system?

The relationship between post-structuralist politics and power as it is situated in and around computer use suggests other important considerations:

- What happens when computers are provided for teachers, students, or programs that were previously powerless to acquire computers? Do pragmatic policymakers allow "the direct participation of those who, up to now, have not had access to power and whose nature those in power cannot fully imagine" (Mead, 1970, p. 3)? We will want to investigate more critically the claim of Ted Nelson (1987) that the pragmatic politics of personal computers, standing alone or connected in a democratic network topology, liberate writers in a way that password access to the mainframe never could.

Conversely, we need to ask,

- What happens when forces outside of writing programs control the use of computers and manipulate activities? Do the political maneuverings of "monopoly capitalism" and the "state apparatus" conspire to keep certain people computerless?

- In what ways is the impact of computers at specific educational sites shaped by the pragmatic politics of "monopoly capitalism" policymakers? By the theoretical politics of post-structuralism? How do such political considerations affect computer purchases? computer labs? computer-supported curriculum? students composing on-line?

- In what ways can we, as a profession, influence software development and selection? the equitable allocation of computer resources?

In addition, we need studies that look at how pragmatic decisions shape theory and how theoretical politics drives practice:

- What are teachers' expectations for computers in writing programs? What are the expectations of administrators? of funding sources?

- What are the long-term outlooks for funding in computer-supported writing programs? Where have specific schools gone for such funding? What do their experiences tell us as educators?

- Can business-education partnerships be productive both politically and intellectually for writing programs and our students? What models for such relationships do we have?

Finally, we must realize that political questions, as most politicians quickly discover, have little to do with statistics and research. Most political issues are settled by narratives about "the way it is" at home. As Pat Hartwell (1987) says, we organize our literate lives around metaphors and narratives. Most of us tell stories to fix our place in the cosmos and our place in the profession. These narratives are a political device, shaping our expectations about what is and what is not possible in writing programs with computers. We need to listen to each other and our stories about writing programs and what each program has done with computers.

Acknowledgments

My thanks to those who have helped me look at the educational politics of writing programs: Diana Dreyer of Slippery Rock University, Pennsylvania; Tom Falkner, The College of Wooster, Ohio; Gail Hawisher, University of Illinois at Urbana-Chanpaign; Wendy Paterson, Buffalo State College, New York; Dave Roberts, Samford University, Birmingham; Kathy Simmons, Hempfield High School, Greensburg, Pennsylvania; and Bill Williams, Slippery Rock University. A special thanks to my wife, Kathleen, for editorial help, and much more.

References

Althusser, L. (1971). *Lenin and philosophy*. London: New Left Books.

Berlin, J. A. (1984). *Writing instruction in nineteenth-century American colleges*. Carbondale: Southern Illinois University.

Bourque, J. H. (1983). Understanding and evaluating: The humanist as computer specialist. *College English, 45*, 67–73.

Bruce, B., Michaels, S., & Watson-Gegeo, K. (1985). How computers can change the writing process. *Language Arts, 62*, 143–149.

Calkins, L. M. (1983). *Lessons from a child: On the teaching and learning of writing*. Exeter, NH: Heinemann.

Corbett, E. P. J. (1965). *Classical rhetoric for the modern student*. New York: Oxford University.

Crowley, S. (1989). *A teacher's introduction to deconstruction*. Urbana, IL: National Council of Teachers of English.

Derrida, J. (1982). *Margins of philosophy* (A. Bass, Trans.). Chicago: University of Chicago.

Emig, J. (1971). *The composing processes of twelfth graders*. Urbana, IL: National Council of Teachers of English.

Flower, L., & Hayes, J. R. (1981). A cognitive process theory of writing. *College Composition and Communication, 32,* 365–387.

Foucault, M. (1988/1969). What is an author? (J. V. Harari, Trans.). In D. Lodge (Ed.), *Modern criticism and theory: A reader* (pp. 197–210). New York: Longman. (Original work published 1969)

Hairston, M. (1982). The winds of change: Thomas Kuhn and the revolution in the teaching of writing. *College Composition and Communication, 33,* 76–88.

Hartwell, P. (1987). Creating a literate environment in freshman English: Why and how. *Rhetoric Review, 6,* 4–19.

Hatlen, B. (1988). Michel Foucault and the discourse[s] of English, *College English, 50,* 786–801.

Hawisher, G. (1989, July). *The changing writing class: Computers and composition instruction.* Paper presented at annual Penn State Conference on Rhetoric and Composition. State College, PA.

Heath, S. B. (1983). *Ways with words: Language, life, and work in communities and classrooms.* Cambridge, England: Cambridge University Press.

Heath, S. B. (1988, November). *Will the schools survive?* Paper presented at annual convention of the National Council of Teachers of English, St. Louis, MO.

Herrmann, A. (1989). Computers in public schools: Are we being realistic? In G. E. Hawisher & C. L. Selfe (Eds.), *Critical perspectives on computers and composition instruction* (pp. 109–125). New York: Teachers College Press.

Holdstein, D. H. (1987). The politics of CAI and word processing: Some issues for faculty and administrators. In L. Gerrard (Ed.), *Writing at century's end: Essays on computer-assisted composition* (pp. 122–130). New York: Random House.

Holdstein, D. H., & Redman, T. (1985). Empirical research in word-processing: Expectations vs. experience. *Computers and Composition, 3*(1), 43–55.

Marcuse, H. (1982/1941). Some social implications of modern technology. In A. Arato & E. Gebhardt (Eds.), *The Marxist position from The Essential Frankfurt School Reader* (pp. 138–162). New York: Continuum. (Original work published 1941)

Mead, M. (1970). *Culture and commitment.* Garden City, NY: Doubleday.

Nelson, T. (1987). Computer lib/Dream machines (2nd ed.). Redmond, WA: Tempus Press.

Ohmann, R. (1985). Literacy, technology, and monopoly capital. *College English, 47*, 675–689.

O'Shea, T., & Self, J. (1984). *Learning and teaching with computers.* Englewood Cliffs, NJ: Prentice-Hall.

Schilb, J. (1989). Composition and post-structuralism: A tale of two conferences. *College Composition and Communication, 40*, 422–443.

Smith, F. (1988). *Joining the literacy club: Further essays into education.* Portsmouth, NH: Heinemann.

Sudol, R. A. (1985). Applied word processing: Notes on authority, responsibility, and revision in a workshop model. *College Composition and Communication, 36*, 331–335.

Thiesmeyer, J. (1989). Should we do what we can? In G. E. Hawisher & C. L. Selfe (Eds.), *Critical perspectives on computers and composition instruction* (pp. 75–93). New York: Teachers College Press.

Williams, R. (1975). *Television: Technology and cultural form.* New York: Schocken.

Chapter 14

The Equitable Teaching of Composition with Computers: A Case for Change

Mary Louise Gomez
University of Wisconsin–Madison

Schooling in the United States reflects inequitable practices of teaching and learning with computer technology. Curriculum and instruction remain differentiated by students' race, social class, language background, and gender. As the number of diverse learners grows, teachers and researchers are challenged to develop new pedagogies and practices to meet all learners' needs. How can schools, community centers, and other locations incorporate the best possible practices of teaching and learning for all participants regardless of their race, class, gender, or language background? How can we move beyond equality of opportunity to equity of opportunity to learn with and about computers? How can we broaden the focus of teaching and learning with technology from the individual student to encompass the family and the community?

Microcomputers have been installed in United States classrooms for over a decade now, yet access to, and use of, the hardware and software remains inequitably differentiated by students' race, social class, language background, and gender. Such differentiation serves to further marginalize students already pushed to the periphery of the United States' social and economic order. This chapter discusses issues and poses questions about equity and teaching in computer-supported classrooms that affect a broad range of America's diverse student learners. Although the use of computers could be instrumental in implementing improved practices of teaching and learning writing, technology has not yet accomplished these aims. Dramatically changing demographics in the United States, as well as dilemmas posed by our concern that equitable opportunities exist for all students, make our profession's consideration of these topics an urgent one.

Demographic data indicate that America's population is becoming more diverse. United States classrooms are increasingly filled with children who are poor (Kennedy, Jung & Orland, 1986), children who have limited English proficiency (Hispanic Policy Development Project, 1988), and children who are not white (National Center for Education Statistics, 1987a, 1987b). For example, estimates of the growth of the nonwhite[1] school population include a rise from 24% in 1976 to 30–40% in the year 2000 (National Center for Education Statistics, 1987a, 1987b). Many children in the United States also come from non-English-language background (NELB) homes. Currently, 2.5 million school-age children speak a language other than English or come from homes where English is not spoken (Romero, Mercado, & Vazquez-Faria, 1987). These numbers will increase, as the total NELB population in the United States is expected to grow to 39.5 million by the year 2000. Although the largest percentage of these children speak Spanish or Chinese, there are increasing numbers of children entering U. S. schools who speak different languages.

Many of these children also live in poverty. Although data show that one in four children in the United States lives in poverty, a breakdown of these figures for race shows much higher rates of poverty for blacks (50%) and for Hispanics (40%). Of the 80 million school-age children in the United States in 1988, nearly 10 million came from homes headed by a single female parent (Strong, 1989). For children living in female-headed households, rates of poverty are high, rising to 47.6%, 68.5%, and 70.5% for whites, blacks, and Hispanics (Kennedy, Jung, & Orland, 1986). In 1988, only 4% (in contrast to 60% in 1955) of American families represented our traditional image of one mother, one father, and two children (Strong, 1989).

What are the implications of these figures for our educational system? Poverty, living within single-parent families, and limited English proficiency are key variables contributing to the high secondary school dropout rates of nonwhite students within this country. Of students who were enrolled as sophomores in our public secondary schools in 1980, 12.2% of whites had dropped out of school by the autumn of 1982, while in the same period, 17% of black students, 18% of Hispanic students, and 29.2% of Native American students left school (Wheelock & Dorman, 1989). Clearly, our schools are failing to meet the needs of vast numbers of our youth.

Although classrooms will be increasingly populated by diverse learners, their growing numbers alone do not make the case for changing teaching practices. Rather, it is this growth combined with concerns for equity that has spurred teachers and researchers to action. Educators now frankly acknowledge the critical necessity of addressing in this decade the distribution of opportunity. And in connection with technology, this need has become all the more clear. As C. Paul Olson (1987) writes,

> Otherwise, both educationally and materially, we are likely to experience in our own society the anomaly of our time so pronounced in Third World contexts—aggregate increases in real wealth, but dramatic increases in the very wealthy and poor. Our new knowledge in information processing should serve all our children. As the maker of opportunities, this is what schooling ought to be about. (p. 204)

As makers of opportunities, teachers and researchers must be concerned with issues of equity as they relate to computer access and use for all learners.

How Might We Think about Equity?

Equitable teaching constitutes just practices; that is, equitable teaching transcends any set of rules when the outcome of those rules may be unjust. Secada (1989) writes,

> Equity gauges the results of actions directly against standards of justice, and it is used to decide whether or not what is being done is just. Educational equity, therefore, should be construed as a check on the justice of specific actions that are carried out within the educational arena and the arrangements that result from these actions. (pp. 60-61)

What does this mean in reference to educating students about composing with the aid of computer technology? Equitable teaching with computers means providing some students more than equal time to work with hardware and software; more than equal opportunities to sign up for after-school, club, or free time with computers; more than equal opportunities to enroll in coursework; and more than equal occasions to engage in drill-and-practice and/or remedial activities with the computer—especially students from lower-income families, nonwhite students, women students, and students with limited English proficiency. Teaching and learning activities for these students must provide more than mere access to technology. These activities must actively recruit students to use computers. These students need teaching and learning activities that move beyond the traditional activities of drill, practice, and remedial tutorials in so-called basic skills. Our best and most innovative practices in teaching students how to use computers will be required if teachers are going to reach these students.

Inequitable Teaching Practices with Computers

Unfortunately, there exists a large body of evidence documenting inequitable school practices related to computer use by students who are not white males. In *Contextual Factors in Education: Improving Science and Mathematics Education for Minorities and Women* (1987), Michael Cole and Peg Griffin argue that

- more computers are being placed in the hands of middle- and upper-class children than poor children;

- when computers are placed in the schools of poor children, they are used for rote drill and practice instead of the "cognitive enrichment" that they provide for middle- and upper-class students;

- female students have less involvement than male students with computers in schools, irrespective of class and ethnicity. (pp. 43–44)

Why does such disparity exist? Educators alone cannot assume the blame for these dilemmas. Data suggest (Linn, 1985a, 1985b; Lockheed & Frakt, 1984; Marrapodi, 1984; Miura & Hess, 1983) that parents appear unwilling to allocate as many resources to females as they allocate to males who want to learn with and about computers. Further, the beliefs of community members, including teachers, about females, about poor children, and about nonwhite children, as well as these groups' perceived ability to learn with and about computers, replicate existing models of teaching and learning with traditional resources. That is, members of the public and private sector perpetuate stereotypic assumptions regarding the superior abilities and greater interests in technology, science, and mathematics of males, whites, and students of higher socio-economic status. These assumptions guide teachers' expectations of students. In turn, teachers' assumptions about learners' abilities and interests guide the development of activities for students. Different learners, then, receive different and inequitable treatment.

Current research documents that schools offer differential access to computer hardware and software and different instruction with computers to students in their classes, and that access and instruction are varied according to students' race, social class, and gender (Cohen, 1983; Miller, 1983). The reasons for such varied treatment of students are complex. In part, funding sources for computers help to determine who uses computers and for what purposes. For example, the Computer Use Study Group (CUSG) of San Diego conducted a study in twenty-one schools in five California school districts and found a strong correlation between the source of funding for microcomputers, the sorts of students educated with the computers, the types of instruction offered to the students, and the rationale for computer use in the districts studied. The CUSG (1983) reports,

> Money available for gifted and talented youngsters, economically and culturally disadvantaged students, school improvement programs, and the desegregation effort purchased 93% of the computers in these districts. (p. 52)

The CUSG found that funding directed to particular groups, assumed to have particular characteristics and needs, led to differential access to the hardware and software and to different instruction. Students of color and those of low socioeconomic status received instruction of a classic compensatory nature—practice in discrete "basic" skills—while their middle- and upper-class white counterparts received instruction in programming and problem solving that required them to construct, as well as receive, knowledge.

Karen Sheingold and her colleagues (1987) also found disparities in teaching and learning with computers for different groups of students:

> Surveys of computer use in schools reveal that in schools with large minority enrollments, computers are used primarily to provide basic skills instruction delivered by drill-and-practice software. . . . In contrast, computer use in majority schools is characterized by its emphasis on the use of computers as tools to develop higher order literary and cognitive skills and as objects of study (e.g., instruction focused on computer literacy and programming). . . . (p. 89)

In an analysis of data from the 1985 second National Survey of Instructional Uses of School Computers (commissioned by the U.S. Department of Education), Henry Jay Becker (1987) also noted differentiated opportunities for learning with computers in schools. He reported that while 60% of activities in high-ability middle-grade classrooms were focused on programming, computer literacy, and problem-solving activities, these activities accounted for only 40% of the mixed-ability classes and less than 20% of the time for low-ability classes (p. 156).

Although funding sources may drive some of the placement of hardware and uses of computers, Asa Hilliard of Georgia State University reminded educators at the 1989 meeting of the Association for Supervision and Curriculum Development that our assumptions about learners ultimately shape the development of curriculum. Hilliard (ASCD, 1989) stated,

> Educators must raise expectations for minority youth [often those in low-ability classes] and reject certain killer assumptions. These assumptions, which color much educational thinking, suggest that students are either born with educational aptitude or aren't; that low achievers need remedial drills of "more of the same"; that low achievers can't do higher order thinking; and that after falling behind, it will take years for low achievers to catch up. (p. 2)

Similar diminished expectations for females' potential to learn with, and about, computers have resulted in fewer opportunities for girls and women to use computer technology. A gender gap in computer use exists for three reasons. First, there are, as mentioned earlier, cultural biases regarding females' use of technology.

For example, females view television and print advertising of technology that reflects and sustains cultural biases. This advertising depicts few women in roles of power (Fisher, 1984). Second, there is limited existing instructional software with female-oriented topics and formats. The available software often contains competitive game formats more familiar and often more appealing to males than to females (Fisher, 1984; Gilliland, 1984; Miura & Hess, 1983). Third, the content and structure of programming as a focus of entry-level computer literacy courses provides an additional barrier to some females as programming sustains an image similar to mathematics as male turf. Combined with the scarce resources of technology for which students must compete, these factors act as barriers to females' access to and participation in a wide range of activities with computer technology (Gomez, 1986; Lockheed & Frakt, 1984; Sanders, 1989).

Additional barriers to computer access and use exist for females as well as for students of low socioeconomic status and students of color because inequitable models of curriculum and instruction in mathematics, English, and other subject areas have been transferred to the teaching of those subjects with computer technology. The clearest examples of such transfers of pedagogy from the medium of paper and pencil to that of computers may be found in the heavy emphasis on skill-and-drill computer programs for those students (often nonwhite students, students with low socioeconomic status, or students of limited English proficiency) enrolled in lower-ability classes. (Secada [1988] includes a discussion of barriers related to students' race, social class, and language in learning mathematics, and Nystrand & Gamoran [1988] include a discussion of the correlation of students' ability grouping with writing instruction focused on "clerical" editing and fill-in-the-blank type tasks—rather than on "compositional" tasks.)

Although classroom practices continue to differentiate curriculum and instruction—with and without computers—for students in differing ability groups (Becker, 1987; Cole & Griffin, 1987; Nystrand & Gamoran, 1988; Sheingold, Martin, & Endreweit, 1987), researchers of effective teaching strategies (e.g., Hillocks, 1984, 1986; Nystrand, in press; Secada, 1988) argue that *all* students require similar opportunities to acquire skills of mathematical reasoning and composing. Recent research (Hillocks, 1984, 1986;

Nystrand, in press) about how students learn to write has high-lighted the importance of purposeful writing activities linked to opportunities for feedback from genuine audiences of peers, parents, and others. In a recent paper, Martin Nystrand (1990) focused on the significance of this activity for students learning how to write. Nystrand concludes:

> Perhaps the most important insight from recent research on composition is that effective writing instruction is less a matter of teaching knowledge about composition, rhetoric, or grammar to students and more a matter of promoting and refining the process of writing. English teachers need to think of writing as a verb, not a noun. In any case, information about writing (e.g., parts of speech, principles of rhetoric, types of paragraphs, etc.) makes best sense to students only in the context of the activity itself. That is why writing teachers' primary responsibility concerns initiating and sustaining appropriate writing activities and arranging for effective feedback. (pp. 154–155)

Although Nystrand and others (Donovan, 1978; Graves, 1983; Taylor & Dorsey-Gaines, 1988) argue for teaching writing as an active, meaning-making craft, Susan Florio-Ruane and Saundra Dunn (1987) make the case that current school-based models of teaching writing remain teacher- and product-centered and leave little time for students to draft or revise their work. Gail Hawisher (1989) believes the transfer of such instructional strategies from writing with paper and pencil to writing with computer and word-processing packages may be responsible for the lack of empirical evidence regarding students' improved writing with computers. Hawisher speculates that "an appropriate pedagogy has not yet been devised to accompany computers when word processing is used to teach writing" (p. 90). Because a focus on teacher- and product-centered writing is heightened in classrooms where learners are perceived to be of lower ability (Nystrand & Gamoran, 1988), it is imperative that new models of instruction with computers be devised if these additional curriculum barriers to learning for nonwhite students, students of low socioeconomic status, and students of limited English proficiency are to be broken.

Three Model Projects

Three exemplary projects designed specifically to provide equity of access to, and excellent instruction with, computers are presented here as a means of posing questions for the 1990s to teachers and researchers. Each project represents an effort to target a distinct group of students—students of non-English-language background, students of color, or females—for instruction using computers. The projects are described in the sections that follow, and the descriptions are used to identify questions for future consideration.

The Computer Chronicles

An innovative telecommunications publishing project, called The Computer Chronicles, linking students in California with students in Mexico, Alaska, and Hawaii was designed by Hugh Mehan and his colleagues (Mehan, Moll, & Riel, 1985) as part of a project to investigate how "the availability of one or very few microcomputers in classrooms has an influence on (a) the arrangement of the classroom, and (b) the curriculum" (p. 48). Four elementary classrooms were studied: one bilingual program class, two classes that included many students who spoke Spanish as a first language, and one class for educationally disadvantaged students.

Funded by the National Science Foundation, this project combined writing activities with peer cooperative learning activities and the integration of computers into existing classrooms (Riel, 1983). Students in the California classrooms exchanged disks of news stories with peers in distant locations. Children at each site chose from stories written by students at all sites to publish their site-specific version of *The Computer Chronicles*. The project emphasized purposeful reading and writing activities intrinsically interesting to students, activities in which a real audience of peers and parents provided feedback. Researchers found gains in students' reading and writing skills following their participation in this project.

South Madison Neighborhood Center

A second project targeting predominantly black students of low socioeconomic status and their families is currently under way at the South Madison (Wisconsin) Neighborhood Center (DeVault, personal communication). A city with a total population of 200,000 people, Madison, Wisconsin, has a nonwhite school population that has doubled in the last decade, growing to 17.9% of the total school population in 1988. An area at the southern edge of Madison, with a number of low-income housing complexes, is home to many poor black families. Many black students who live in South Madison have lower school achievement rates and higher dropout rates than their Asian and white peers.

Recently, partnerships were formed between the University of Wisconsin–Madison, the Madison Metropolitan School District, and community groups (e.g., the Urban League) to raise the achievement (as measured by student tests and demonstrated by portfolios of student work) of nonwhite students in the schools. Among the projects begun by this alliance is one linking several departments in the university with the Madison Children's Museum and the South Madison Neighborhood Center to provide instruction about, and with, computers to black students and other neighborhood residents. Begun in 1988 with a donation of used computers, the project is staffed primarily by volunteer teachers and administrative staff from the university, the museum, the neighborhood center, and the community. Although elementary, middle, and secondary school students are the primary focus for instructional groups, classes have also been offered for youngsters in a neighborhood preschool, for retirees, and for mothers of young children. The use of volunteer teachers from the university provides unique dilemmas and opportunities: that is, teachers are experts in their fields (e.g., university faculty and graduate students who serve as volunteer teachers share their expertise in computer science, educational technology, and education), yet these people have busy schedules. This situation often places constraints on the number of classes that can be offered and the timing of these classes.

Students in this project engage in three primary activities: writing on topics and in modes of discourse of their choice in a workshop setting; participating in computer literacy–type activities (programming and learning about computers); and using instructional software across subject-matter areas of their interest. A major goal of this work is to offer the best practices of teaching and learning to students. For example, when a writing class was opened after school for primary-grade students, the volunteer university professor and graduate-student teachers provided students with direct instruction in how to use a word-processing program, but went on to focus on developing a writing workshop. Students wrote on topics, and in forms, of their choice and regularly conferred with the teachers concerning their intentions. Teachers, peers, and the recipients of their writing (often parents and school friends) provided real and interested audiences for their work. Despite the labor of typing with small hands, and the difficulties with spelling and mechanics that many students experienced, the workshop consistently drew students who relinquished opportunities for other after-school play activities to come and write.

Although a formal assessment of this project is ongoing and as yet incomplete, the teachers volunteering at the neighborhood center are encouraged by the positive responses of area families to the opportunities offered their children and by feedback from teachers of neighborhood students regularly attending the computer writing workshops. Elementary school teachers have remarked that keyboarding skills and general knowledge of computer operations are greater for those children who frequently attend the neighborhood center's computer activities than they are for these children's peers who do not participate in these activities.

Computer Equity Training Project

A third exemplary effort is the work of the Computer Equity Training Project of the Women's Action Alliance, a two-year project of national scope. This project was developed in response to the comparatively low numbers of females engaging in voluntary activities with computers in American schools (Sanders, 1986). Pilot-tested in three middle schools in different geographic regions in the country, this program was then further tested in five middle and junior high schools. Female students were targeted for special activities, such as software selection and collaborative work with peers at computers. The project also used specially prepared materials to distribute information about computers to girls, their teachers, and their parents. The project also brought parents to school for presentations concerning computer technology and its potential for use by females.

Girls' voluntary computer use at schools using the project materials showed dramatic gains over the course of a school term. On average, at schools participating in the project, 26% of the girls were voluntary computer users at the beginning of the experimental period, and 48% of the girls used computers for optional activities at the end of the experimental period.

Questions to Guide Our Future Teaching

All of these projects pose questions for the design of equitable curricula and instruction:

- How can projects in schools, as well as other locations, focus on using the best practices of teaching and learning for all participants, regardless of race, class, gender, or language background? Despite their deficiencies in spelling, mechanics, and grammar, the black students participating in the South Madison Neighborhood Center writing workshop constructed stories, letters, and raps for real audiences of parents and peers and received genuine feedback. What combination of factors made this possible in a neighborhood center? How might schools and teachers create similar environments in classrooms?

- How do we move beyond equality of opportunity, inviting all students to participate in learning with and about computers, to equity of opportunity, targeting specific groups with activities specially designed to meet their needs, skills, or interests? The Computer Equity Training Project, for example, focused on determining females' preferences in software, classroom interaction with computers, and time spent on computers, then acted on these findings to make computer use more inviting for female students. How can classroom teachers and curriculum specialists work with individuals to provide similar experiences for poor children or students of limited English proficiency?

- How do we broaden the focus of attention from the individual student to encompass the family and community? In the exemplary neighborhood center project, families provided audiences for student writing, and in the exemplary computer project for females, the families of females were participants in learning about and with computers and were educated about the potential benefits of using technology. How can schools, families, and neighborhoods collaborate to educate students with the aid of technology? What funding, leadership, or other resources are necessary for such collaboration to occur?

Although these projects' practices are commendable, the constraints of each also pose questions for future work. Two related flaws mark each project: each project took place in what Simmons (1987) terms "learning sanctuaries," laboratories or special-project classroom environments outside of, or added on to, the ongoing daily life of schools. Do these projects subtly give the message that such activities are not possible in "regular" classrooms without special consultants or extra funding? Second, all of these projects were begun by persons concerned with schools and schooling, yet these persons were not paid members of the schools' staff responsible for students' ongoing instruction and achievement. If the diverse populations of students coming to American schools are to be well served, how can their teachers also become invested in translating theories about equitable curriculum and instruction into practice? This is difficult work, as Mehan, Moll, and Riel (1985) note:

> The computer easily becomes an intruder whose potentials are outweighed by the inconveniences they create (some of which we have already described). The strategy of choice then becomes, not by design, but by necessity, to accommodate the machine to the prevailing constraints. This decision, although pragmatic in the short run, is fatal, especially for language minority students, because it assumes uncritically that the

status quo is the appropriate context for computer use; inevitably, existing curricular practices become the model for computer use. Why should we expect that the same practices that have produced widespread academic failure will create propitious environments for computer use? (p. 226)

We can expect that the use of computers will contribute to students' school achievement, rather than their failure, only if the conditions under which technology is used and the assumptions which guide its use are changed. The successful outcomes of the three creative projects described here point the way to innovations that can become a part of the daily life of schools if skilled and caring teachers—questioning, planning, and acting with the support of school administrators and community members—tackle the challenges of schooling with technology.

Additional questions exploring the relationship between equity and technology use in public schools also suggest themselves:

- Currently, workplace literacy projects are under way in large U.S. cities (see, for example, Collins, Balmuth, & Jean, 1989) that use computers to teach job skills as well as reading and writing skills to employees. How will such projects influence and/or empower the parents of female students, students of low socioeconomic status, nonwhite students, or students of limited English proficiency? Will participation in such projects cause parents and other community members to question the activities in which students participate in school if these activities are related to teaching and learning with computer technology?

- The plight of urban school systems combined with current outcries for community-responsive schooling have led to the creation of local governing boards for neighborhood schools in large U.S. cities (e.g., Chicago). How will such groups, composed of parents, community members, and school personnel, view the role of computers in teaching students composing and other skills?

- Current uses of computer technology in schools frequently reflect the power relations and attitudes of our society. Is it possible for *individual* teachers or parents to work to effectively change such inequitable teaching and learning practices? Is collective action a more effective goal and tool for changing the status quo? How might such collective initiatives be developed at the school, neighborhood, or community levels?

Black Boston civil rights activist Mel King (*Harvard Educational Review*, 1989) speaks of the human capacity for "transformation." Critical theorist Henry Giroux (McLaren, 1989) speaks of developing a "language of opportunity" for schooling. In both cases, there is an underlying assumption that teachers and community organizers must be willing to be transformed as well as to transform others, that they must build opportunities for others, not only speak of how individuals might accomplish these goals for themselves. Is it possible that schools, the bastions of cultural transferral, can also become institutions that provide opportunities for cultural transformation? If this is possible, what role can computer technology play in such an enterprise? How can teachers, students, and community members harness technology for transformation?

Note

1. In this paper, the terms *nonwhite* and *student of color* are used interchangeably.

References

Association for Supervision and Development. (1989, May). Equity expert faults "choice" plan. *ASCD Update, 31*(3), 2.

Becker, H. J. (1987). Using computers for instruction. *Byte, 12*(2), 149–162.

Cohen, M. (1983). Exemplary computer use in education. *Quarterly Newsletter of the Laboratory of Human Cognition, 5*(3), 46–51.

Cole, M., & Griffin, P. (1987). *Contextual factors in education: Improving science and mathematics education for minorities and women.* Madison, WI: Wisconsin Center for Education Research, University of Wisconsin–Madison.

Collins, S. D., Balmuth, M., & Jean, P. (1989). So we can use our own names, and write the laws by which we live: Educating the new U.S. labor force. *Harvard Educational Review, 59*, 454–469.

Computer Use Study Group. (1983). Computers in schools: Stratifier or equalizer? *Quarterly Newsletter of the Laboratory of Comparative Human Cognition, 5*(3), 51–55.

DeVault, V. (1988). Personal communication.

Donovan, T. (1978). Seeing students as writers. *Composition and Teaching, 1*, 13-16.

Fisher, G. (1984). Access to computers. *The Computing Teacher, 11*(8), 24.

Florio-Ruane, S., & Dunn, S. (1987). Teaching writing: Some perennial questions and some possible answers. In V. Richardson-Koehler (Ed.), *Educator's handbook: A research perspective* (pp. 50–83). White Plains, NY: Longman.

Gilliland, K. (1984, April). Equals in computer technology. *The Computing Teacher, 11*(8), 42.

Gomez, M. L. (1986). Equity, English, and computers. *Wisconsin English Journal, 29*(1), 18–22.

Graves, D. H. (1983). *Writing: Teachers and children at work.* Exeter, NH: Heinemann Educational Books.

Harvard Educational Review. (1989). On transformation: From a conversation with Mel King. *Harvard Educational Review, 59*, 504–519.

Hawisher, G. E. (1989). Computers and writing: Where's the research? *English Journal, 78*(1), 89-91.

Hillocks, G. (1984). What works in teaching composition: A meta-analysis of experimental treatment studies. *American Journal of Education, 93*, 133–170.

Hillocks, G. (1986). *Research on written composition: New directions for teaching.* Urbana, IL: National Conference on Research in English and ERIC Clearinghouse on Reading and Communication Skills.

Hispanic Policy Development Project. (1988). *Closing the gap for U. S. Hispanic youth: Public/private strategies.* Washington, DC: Author.

Kennedy, M. M., Jung, R. K., & Orland, M. E. (1986, January). *Poverty, achievement and the distribution of compensatory education services.* (An interim report from the National Assessment of Chapter I, OERI). Washington, DC: U. S. Government Printing Office.

Linn, M. (1985a). Gender equity in computer learning environments. *Computers and the Social Sciences, 1*(1), 19–27.

Linn, M. (1985b). Fostering equitable consequences from computer learning environments. *Sex Roles, 13*, 229–240.

Lockheed, M., & Frakt, S. B. (1984, April). Sex equity: Increasing girls' use of computers. *The Computing Teacher, 11*(8), 18.

McLaren, P. (1989). *Life in schools*. White Plains, NY: Longman.

Marrapodi, M. (1984, April). Females and computers? Absolutely! *The Computing Teacher, 11*(8), 57–58.

Mehan, H., Moll, L., & Riel, M. (1985). *Computers in classrooms: A quasi-experiment in guided change*. San Diego, CA: University of California–San Diego.

Miller, J. J. (1983). *Microcomputer use in San Diego/Imperial County school districts*. San Diego, CA: San Diego County Department of Education.

Miura, I., & Hess, R. D. (1983). *Sex differences in computer interest, access, and usage*. Paper presented at the annual meeting of the American Psychological Association, Anaheim, CA.

National Center for Education Statistics. (1987a). *The condition of education*. Washington, D C: U. S. Government Printing Office.

National Center for Education Statistics. (1987b). *Digest of education statistics*. Washington, D C: U. S. Government Printing Office.

Nystrand, M. (1990). On teaching writing as a verb rather than a noun: Research on writing for high school English teachers. In G. E. Hawisher and A. O. Soter (Eds.), *On Literacy and its teaching: Issues in english education*. Albany, NY: SUNY Press.

Nystrand, M. & Gamoran, A. (1988). *A study of instruction as discourse*. Madison, WI: National Center for Research on Effective Secondary Schools.

Olson, C. P. (1987). Who computes? In D. Livingstone (Ed.), *Critical pedagogy and cultural power* (pp. 179–204). Smith Hadley, MA: Bergin and Garvey.

Riel, M. (1983). Education and ecstasy: Computer chronicles of students writing together. *Quarterly Newsletter of the Laboratory of Comparative Human Cognition, 5*(3), 59–67.

Romero, M., Mercado, M., & Vazquez-Faria, J. A. (1987). Students of limited English proficiency. In V. Richardson Koehler (Ed.), *Educator's handbook: A research perspective* (pp. 348–369). White Plains, NY: Longman.

Sanders, J. S. (1986, Jan./Feb.). The computer gender gap: Close it while there's time. *The Monitor*, 18–26.

Sanders, J. S. (1989). Equity and technology in education: An applied researcher talks to the theoreticians. In W. G. Secada (Ed.), *Equity in education* (pp. 158–179). New York and London: Falmer Press.

Secada, W. G. (1988). *Student diversity and mathematics education reform.* Paper presented at the Symposium Sponsored by the Southwest Center for Equity: Equity Issues in Mathematics and Science Achievement, Culver City, CA.

Secada, W. G. (1989). Educational equity versus equity of education: An alternative conception. In W. G. Secada (Ed.), *Equity in education* (pp. 68–88). New York and London: Falmer Press.

Sheingold, K., Martin, L. M. W., & Endreweit, M. W. (1987). Preparing urban teachers for the technological future. In R. D. Pea & K. Sheingold, (Eds.), *Mirrors of minds: Patterns of experience in educational computing* (pp. 67–85). Norwood, NJ: Ablex Publishing.

Simmons, W. (1987). Beyond basic skills: Literacy and technology for minority schools. In R. D. Pea & K. Sheingold (Eds.), *Mirrors of minds: Patterns of experience in educational computing* (pp. 86–102). Norwood, NJ: Ablex Publishing.

Strong, L. A. (1989). The best kids they have. *Educational Leadership, 46*(5), 2.

Taylor, D., & Dorsey-Gaines, C. (1988). *Growing up literate: Learning from inner-city families.* Portsmouth, NH: Heinemann Education Books.

Wheelock, A., & Dorman, G. (1989). *Before it's too late.* Boston: Massachusetts Advocacy Commission.

Chapter 15

Feminism and Computers in Composition Instruction

Emily Jessup
University of Michigan

A gender gap in computer use appears as early as elementary school, and persists in some form into our college writing classes. What impact has the computer gender gap had on the use of computers in composition? How has the computer gender gap affected teachers of writing? What are the consequences of this gap for our students? What can we do in our classrooms to try to minimize its effect? What can we do to try to close the computer gender gap?

The land of computing is a frontier country, and, as in the development of most frontier territories, there are many more men than women. Indeed, it appears that at all levels of learning about computers—in school, in higher education, in further education, in training, in adult education classes, and in independent learning—women tend to be strikingly underrepresented. The extent of their underrepresentation varies from sector to sector and to some extent from country to country, but the fact of it is so ubiquitous that the evidence tends to become monotonous (Gerver, 1989, p. 483).

In 1980, Cindy Selfe and Billie Wahlstrom visited a computer store in Houghton, Michigan. Five years later, they described their experience of trying to join the "computer revolution." Selfe and Wahlstrom (1985) discovered that

> We couldn't even read the enlistment material. . . . [T]he variety of English spoken by the computers, the people who talked to them, and those who ministered to their needs were as foreign to us as the untranslated *Aeneid* is to most first-year college students. Indeed, these people had taken the same

language we used every day in our scholarly pursuit of the humanities and transformed it into a language of mechanistic violence. (p. 64)

Selfe and Wahlstrom appear to attribute their lack of comfort in this technological world to their training as humanists. They contrast their experience using computers with that of "a skinny lad . . . [who] tippity-taps his way through a paper for first-year English; the machine seems friendly enough to him" (p. 67). In this article, Selfe and Walhstrom do not discuss gender explicitly; however, they do identify the computer-using student as a skinny *lad*, not a *lass*, while describing themselves as (female) outsiders. Ten years after Selfe and Wahlstrom's foray, many more women are participating in the "computer revolution." Unfortunately, most of the people in the vanguard of this revolution appear to be men. For example, according to *Women Computing* (1988, p. 2), women constitute a relatively small percentage of the readers of popular computing magazines:

Magazine	% of women readers
Lotus	19.6%
Personal Computing	19%
PC Resource	15%
InfoWorld	10%

The "gender gap" in computer use is visible as early as elementary school. For instance, a participant in EDU:WIT, a computer conference focusing on women in technology that grew out of the 1989 EDUCOM conference, reported in November 1989 that her daughter was encouraged to play with computers but was discouraged from programming them in her elementary classroom. The child's teacher explained that because girls are not as good in math as are boys, it made more sense to let the boys try their hands at programming. Reviewing the results of several different research projects, Hawkins (1985) claims that "sex was the most obvious factor affecting differential use of the machines at all grade levels across sites" (p. 171). Gerver (1989) describes a pattern in which the age of females in both the United Kingdom and the United States is inversely proportional to their computer use. At the elementary level, the percentage of girls and boys using computers is approximately equal. By high school, girls make up only one-third of computer users. In higher education, far more men than women pursue degrees in computer science; the more specialized the degree, the lower the percentage of women (p. 484).

The gender gap in computer use in school is not simply a quantitative one. For instance, use of word-processing software does not appear to be linked to sex (Hawkins, 1985; Becker, 1987). Girls in elementary school are as likely as boys are to play computer games, although this changes in middle and high school (Becker, p. 152). The difference in computer use appears to be greatest in after-school and self-sponsored use. More boys than girls use computers before and after school; more boys than girls use computers at home; more boys than girls attend computer camps (Peer Computer Equity Report, 1984; Hawkins, 1985; Elmer-DeWitt, 1986; Sanders, 1986; Becker, 1987; Gerver, 1989). Girls also have less confidence in their abilities to use computers than boys do (Peer Computer Equity Report, 1984; Gerver, 1989). Hawkins argues that to understand sex differences in computer use, investigators need to look deeper, to "examine functional uses of the material in particular situations" (p. 178). Stephen Marcus (1987) argues that the sociocultural context of computers leads to the dominance of white middle-class males as computer users:

> Gender, race, and socioeconomic status profoundly influence the experience students have with computers before they reach college classrooms, and these experiences establish the foundation of what students (and faculty) think computers are for. What our students think about computers (their prethinking and their patterns of thinking) and how they think with computers are conditioned by their early experiences with computers. (p. 134)

Some researchers believe that this situation is changing. Strickland, Feely and Wepner (1987) believe that the gender biases surrounding computers are a function of this particular time:

> Our experience suggests that the sexual stereotypes surrounding the use of computers are gradually eroding. In schools where computers are used extensively for word

processing as well as other types of activities, students readily
see the usefulness of the computer in their lives.... We agree
that as the computer is given wider and more personal use in
the curriculum it is less likely that these sexual distinctions
will persist. (pp. 179–80)

Others disagree, claiming that expanding the uses of the computer in the classroom does not do enough to challenge traditional
images of sex-appropriate behavior and sex-linked abilities
(Sanders, 1986; Stanworth, 1983; Gerver, 1989).

Concerted efforts to make computers more appealing to girls
and women have been successful. Some schools, looking for ways
to upset the social stereotype of the computer as a "boy's toy,"
have tried to encourage girls to use computers by initiating clubs
and summer sessions for girls, by hiring female computer teachers, and by screening software for gender bias (Elmer-DeWitt,
1986; Sanders, 1986). Other good examples of this effort are
Deborah L. Brecher's (1985) book, *The Women's Computer Literacy
Handbook* and the computer literacy project for women from which
it grew. After working in the computer industry as an "insider,"
Brecher founded the National Women's Mailing List using a PC
and a commercial software package. As she traveled across the
country meeting with representatives of women's groups, she
found that women who were outside the computing world were
having trouble finding a way in. Brecher (1985) states, "There was
nothing available that made it easy for women to gain these skills
without being patronized, put down, or paralyzed by unnecessary
fears" (p. 2). Brecher opened a computer school in San Francisco
and began The Women's Computer Literacy Project. The premise
of the project is that the language of the computer industry is
deliberately exclusive; the goal of the project is to make this
language accessible. Before using a technical term, Brecher defines
the term, often by making an analogy to something—like cooking—
with which women are likely to be more familiar. The Women's
Computer Literacy Project's goal is to help women break into the
world of computers.

Despite efforts like these, a gender gap in attitudes toward
computers and in computer use persists. Without careful scrutiny
of gender issues in the area of computers, we in composition risk
replicating this gender gap. Unfortunately, composition teachers

appear to be doing just that. Seventeen panels at the 1989 annual convention of the Conference on College Composition and Communication focused on computers and composition. Approximately three-fifths of those presenting papers in that area were men, and two-fifths were women (i. e., 30 men, 21 women). On ten of the panels, men and women presented papers together; on seven panels, the speakers were the same sex. Five of the seven same-sex panels were comprised of men; only two same-sex panels were comprised of women. The numbers are significant in themselves, for they reinforce a wider cultural stereotype that links computers with the realm of science and math—a traditionally masculine area. The topics of these same-sex panels are also telling: men spoke about computers and composition with an emphasis on the technology—two panels discussed hypertext, one panel discussed computers and text analysis, one panel discussed the technology of networked computers, and one panel discussed the national project on computers and writing. Women spoke about teaching with computers, emphasizing the social implications of using computers in composition classes—one panel discussed computers and basic writers, and one panel discussed the "social rhetoric of empowerment in computer-supported writing communities."

Clearly, when gender differences are so acute among the most computer-literate members of our field, we need to ask ourselves about the ways in which the fact of gender has been and is influencing composition instructors' use of computers in classrooms. We also need to ask ourselves about the implications of this gender gap for our students. How and when do writing faculty and students begin using computers for writing? What kinds of formal support do male and female composition students and teachers receive for using computers? What kind of informal networks facilitate or hinder teachers' and students' work with computers? What kinds of mentoring go on for men and women, students and teachers, as they use computers for writing? We need to ask questions about the access male and female students and teachers have to computers, at school and at home. We need to learn more about the ways academic and nonacademic computer experts interact with novice male and female students and faculty as they attempt to learn more about using computers in composition classes. We need to ask questions about the attitudes teachers and students have toward the use of computers for writing, as well as ask questions about the origins of those attitudes.

An Epistemological Approach to Feminism and Computers

Feminist research in other disciplines suggests that because we live in a patriarchal society, men and women tend to develop different epistemological frameworks that shape the way they think about the world as well as the way they learn. These frameworks will inevitably influence the way men and women conceptualize computers. In *Women's Ways of Knowing: The Development of Self, Voice, and Mind*, Belenky, Clinchy, Goldberger, and Tarule (1986) argue against claims for universal stages in intellectual development. Based on their interviews with 135 women, Belenky et al. take issue with William Perry's scheme for intellectual development:

> In Perry's (1970) account of intellectual development, the student discovers critical reasoning as "how They (the upper case "T" symbolizing authority—here, the professors) want us to think," how students must think in order to win the academic game. The student uses this new mode of thinking to construct arguments powerful enough to meet the standards of an impersonal authority. (p. 101)

Belenky et al. characterize this way of knowing as "separate knowing" (p. 98), and contrast it with the "connected knowing" (p. 100) described by women:

> The focus is not on how They want you to think, as in Perry's account, but on how they (the lower case "t" symbolizing more equal status) think; and the purpose is not justification but connection. (p. 101)

In *Learning Styles: Implications for Improving Educational Practices*, Claxton and Murrell (1987) suggest that the distinction between separate and connected knowing resonates with distinctions other researchers have made: separate knowers, like the "splitters, field independents, serialists, and abstract, analytical learners are more in the objectivist mode of knowing" while connected knowers, like "lumpers, field sensitives, holists, and concrete learners are more in the relational mode" (p. 75). Claxton and Murrell claim that to improve current educational practice,

> teaching practices are needed that honor both analytic and relational knowing . . . . By honoring both analytical and relational ways of knowing, we may make our greatest contribution—not only to effective learning but also to building a greater sense of community as well. (p. 76)

Sherry Turkle's (1984) research suggests that the computer can play a special role in legitimizing this relational way of knowing when students are allowed to develop their own approaches to computers. In a study of children, Turkle observed differences in programming styles which she characterized as "hard" and "soft." Hard mastery "is the imposition of will over the machine through the implementation of a plan" (p. 104); soft mastery envisions the computer's formal system "not as a set of unforgiving 'rules,' but as a language for communicating with, negotiating with, a behaving, psychological entity" (pp. 108–109). Soft mastery exemplifies an alternative approach, Turkle observes, providing "a model of how women, when given a chance, can find another way to think and talk about the mastery not simply of machines but of formal systems" (p. 118). To what extent are we encouraging students to find their own ways of using computers in our classrooms? Are we doing enough to ensure that computers act as catalysts for a range of learning styles and writing processes, or are we unwittingly using computer applications to reinforce a single way of approaching tasks?

The research on learning styles and on epistemology is also important for composition teachers and students because the kinds of thinking we value get translated into specific kinds of writing. To date, at least one strand of composition studies has resisted the dominant objectivist epistemology that emphasizes a clear separation between subject and object, through its emphasis on the importance of personal writing. As Elizabeth Flynn (1988) writes,

> James Britton . . . reverses traditional hierarchies by privileging private expression over public transaction, process over product. In arguing that writing for the self is the matrix out of which all forms of writing develop, he valorizes an activity and a mode of expression that have previously been undervalued or invisible. (p. 424)

The emphasis on the self as the matrix, on subjectivity, creates tension, for even though composition teachers and researchers recognize the need to reverse the traditional hierarchies, as a field they also wrestle with trying to legitimize their work in the eyes of the rest of the academic community, and composition teachers are terribly conscious that their students need to "master" objectivist prose. Importing the computer from its traditional home in analytic culture may tip the balance. The computer can easily become merely a tool to help teachers help students become assimilated into the dominant academic culture if, for example, composition teachers relinquish journal writing to spend more time writing essays with the computer; if the layout of computer labs makes it easier for teachers to focus on the production of texts rather than on the creation of community; and if teachers are not comfortable using available technology to create electronic settings for genuine collaboration. Composition teachers need to ask about the kinds of thinking computers are used to support. For instance, when teachers or researchers develop tutorials, do they focus on academic arguments that assume the stance of a separate knower? Do they develop programs that build on relational knowing, that encourage students to make connections between themselves and their material, between themselves and their audience? Do they work as hard to develop programs that facilitate collaborative writing as they do to develop (more marketable) programs that guide individuals through a process of writing with a special emphasis on editing?

Computers can help make connections between students and between teachers and students through collaborative writing and computer conferencing. Gerrard (1988) argues that

> For women, computers in the writing course may be particularly congenial: research has shown that while many female students dislike the isolation typical of programming, they enjoy collaborative uses of computers. (p. 8)

Computers can have this effect when they are used for collaboration, but composition teachers need to ask questions about how computers are used. Some writing instructors are finding that classes meeting in computer labs without local area networks may do more individual work and less collaborative work than classes in traditional classrooms. Are teachers and researchers developing software and designing computer labs that facilitate interaction among students? Are teachers training male and female writing instructors to use the technology to promote collaboration? Are teachers making certain that both male and female students are confident about using the technology?

Research on Feminism and Computers in Composition Instruction

Very little research on feminism and computers in composition has been done, but at least one study supports the general observations made by Marcus and Gerver. Selfe, Ruehr, and Johnson (1988) report that their modified case study of twenty-three computer lab users at Michigan Technological University confirmed both of their initial hypotheses:

> Age and gender determine the amount of computer-related experience individuals bring to the task of learning a word-processing package and, thus, the attitude with which they approach this task and the instructional methods they prefer to use in learning the package. (p. 75)

> Age and gender influence the instructional methods individuals prefer to use when they learn a word-processing package. (p. 75)

According to this study, younger subjects had more experience with computers than did older ones and male subjects had a more positive attitude and less apprehension about using computers than did females. Men also found on-line instruction more effective and enjoyable than did women. Selfe, Ruehr, and Johnson conclude that "teachers cannot expect learners of different ages and genders to approach word processing with the same experience, attitudes, or skills" (p. 82).

Other studies (Selfe, 1990; Cooper & Selfe, 1990) that directly address feminist issues in computers and composition focus on the potential of computers to subvert traditional classroom hierarchies. Selfe (1990) argues that the "value of computers in our classrooms is due as much to their power as tools for social and political reform of literacy education as it is to their power as tools of communication" (p. 121). Her emphasis is on the power of computer networks to facilitate interactions among people when standard markers—sex, age, race—are invisible, and when conventional patterns of turn-taking no longer exist. As Selfe states,

> In this vision, computer networks become human networks, electronic circles that support alternative, non-traditional dialogue and dialect, communities that value re-vision and reinterpretation of traditional educational structures. (p. 123)

The potential of computers to reform education is limited, however, as long as the visions of those who have power to make decisions remain limited. Selfe goes on to say,

> School boards and administrators, privileging individual achievement over group communication, will pay for computers but not the essential software and cables needed to link them together. (pp. 131–132)

The research on feminism and computers in composition instruction completed to date has focused on two central areas: the potential of computers to subvert traditional hierarchies and to enfranchise diverse populations of learners, and on different attitudes among actual computer users. As we enter the 1990s, more research needs to be done that self-consciously asks questions about the impact of gender on computer development and use, and on the sociocultural context surrounding computers. As we consider the place of computers in our society, researchers or teachers of composition might ask what impact computers are having on women, and what the implications of this are for education? What roles are women in the computer industry playing? What are the implications of this for us and for our students? As we think about computers within our own institutions, we might ask how decisions about computers get made, and who makes them. What influences those decisions? As we think about computers within the context of our writing programs, we need to ask whether female teachers and students are as confident in their abilities to use technology as male teachers and students are. Is this true across applications (i.e., word processing, computer conferencing, data retrieval, CAI)?

The Research Agenda for the 1990s

Among the necessary questions we need to ask in the 1990s are a set of questions that focus on the institutional contexts of computers in composition. Researchers or teachers of composition need to ask questions about institutional hierarchies and decision-making processes. Andrea W. Herrmann (1989) argues that because most school systems are paternalistic in the full sense of the word—the administrators still predominantly male, the teachers female—women are being excluded from making decisions about incorporating technology into the curriculum (p. 113). Within the realm of academia, conversations about computers— about the development of new products, about adopting already-developed state-of-the-art products, about applications of new products, and about access to new developments—quickly establish an elite group of insiders and a much larger group of outsiders. Men are more likely to have the background needed to participate in these conversations, and men without a formal background in technology may find it easier to bluff their way into this realm of techno-talk than women will. (See Herrmann in this collection.) Specific questions we need to ask include the following:

- We need to explore the decision-making processes of institutions with respect to technology: Who makes decisions about technology? How are decisions made? Whose values do those decisions represent? To what extent are women excluded from making institutional decisions about the kinds of technology that will be available for writing instruction, and the uses to which the technology may be put?

- What steps can we take to ensure that women will be involved in these institutional decisions in increasing numbers?

- What can we do to ensure that women gain both the technical background and the self-confidence it takes to have access to decision-making circles?

We need to look more carefully at teachers as users of technology, and we need to ask ourselves what the repercussions are for not using (or for using) computers. As status begins to accrue to instructors using technology, those most likely to be penalized are those with the most limited background in technology (older women) and those with the fewest opportunities for using computers outside the writing classroom itself (teachers with family responsibilities—likely to be women; underpaid writing instructors—also likely to be women). Herrmann (1989) suggests that "until they feel confident using [word-processing] technology for themselves, teachers are unlikely to teach others to use it" (p. 115). Selfe, Ruehr, and Johnson (1988) report that women, especially older women, are less likely to feel comfortable with a range of instructional modes in learning to use technology. Questions we need to ask about teachers as users of technology include:

- Within our writing programs, are we inadvertently creating a caste system of elite technology users and lower-status computer avoiders?

- How can we develop teacher-training programs that enable women and men of different ages with different experiences to become comfortable using technology in a variety of ways?

- How can we change the statistics in our Conference on College Composition and Communication program, so that women are as likely to be presenting papers on the programs they are developing, the networks they are building, the conferences they are running, as men are to be presenting papers on the social dynamics in the computer classroom, or the rhetoric of empowerment?

We need to think more about the impact of the computer gender gap on the students in our classes. Margaret Benston (1988) claims that

> Men and women have different access to training, knowledge
> and confidence about technology. One result of this difference
> is that men have access to much more of the technological
> realm than women have and their potential for action is
> correspondingly much larger. (p. 19)

We are likely to teach students the rudiments of the computer
applications we use in our classrooms, but in many cases what we
teach students to do represents only a fraction of available computing resources. Therefore, we must ask the following:

- What "potential for action" do our male and female students
  have? Students who explore the technology on their own are
  likely to benefit from it—who are the explorers?

- What can teachers do to ensure that female students are as
  likely to investigate computer resources as male students
  are?

- What kinds of role modeling go on in computer classrooms?
  What kinds of attitudes toward computers and themselves as
  users of technology do female and male teachers intentionally or unintentionally portray?

Communication about technology is also likely to be influenced
by gender. As Benston says, "The information flow is almost
entirely one-sided: men may explain a technological matter to
women but they do not discuss it with them; that they do with
other men" (p. 26).

- What happens in classrooms as teachers talk about technology? Do teachers talk with male and female students about
  technology in similar or different ways? Do teachers discuss
  with males, explain to females? Do teachers make more eye
  contact with males when they talk about technology?

- How do students talk with each other about technology in
  classrooms?

- Are the people to whom students turn with technical questions explaining or discussing ideas with them? Does this
  vary? According to what variables?

Further questions arise as teachers consider the kinds of software and hardware we are using or developing for use in writing classes:

- Are teachers affirming the epistemological frameworks students bring into the classroom, or are they using computers in ways that reinforce an "objectivist" epistemology?

- Are teachers privileging one way of knowing over another, or are they finding ways to use computers to help students (women and men alike) develop their abilities to think in different ways?

Teachers tend to assume that teaching in computer labs can help them change the social dynamics of their classes in constructive ways, by increasing the emphasis on collaborative learning.

- Are teachers using computers in ways that disrupt the conventional academic emphasis on the individual? that disrupt traditional patterns of teacher-student and student-student interaction? Does the use of the computer make class participation more equitable across sexes, or is it privileging those who feel more confident about using the technology?

- As teachers relinquish authority in the classroom, who assumes power?

- Are female students as likely as male students to assert their authority in the classroom? For instance, as students use, or teachers assign, computer conferences, are women as active as men? Are women assuming a wide spectrum of roles in their responses on computer conferences (i.e. initiating topics as well as supporting other students' contributions)?

- As teachers consider student participation, they need to consider students' access to technology. For example, the need to travel across campus at night to get to a computer may seriously limit women's willingness to use technology. Teachers need to consider other physical aspects of computer use as well; a pregnant woman trying to avoid sitting in front of a video display terminal for long stretches of time will not participate in a computer-intensive course to the extent that her male peer will.

As teachers learn more about addressing the gender gap within their own classrooms, they need to ask questions about the kinds of experiences with computers students have had before coming to college. Teachers also need to learn more about efforts being made to narrow the gender gap among computer users outside institutions of higher education:

- What kinds of programs are being established in K–12 class-rooms to achieve computer equity? What can teachers learn about teaching from those efforts? For instance, what can teachers learn from publications like *The Neuter Computer: Computers for Girls and Boys* (Sanders & Stone, 1986)? What have teachers learned from their experiences that might support those efforts? What mechanisms need to be developed to ensure that conversations about computer equity in schools cross age and institutional boundaries?

- What kinds of efforts are going on outside schools to achieve computer equity? What can writing teachers learn from programs like the Women's Computer Literacy Project in San Francisco, and publications like *Women Computing*? What can teachers learn from the women who formed a special-interest group at the 1989 EDUCOM to meet and discuss "strategies to deal with issues facing women in higher education and information technology" (p. 12) at a time when all nine speakers at general sessions were men, and men outnumbered women as speakers in other sessions by a ratio of nearly 2.5 to 1? What kinds of links can teachers forge with groups like these, combining efforts to make the gender gap smaller?

Feminist Methodology

The set of questions writing teachers decide to explore in the 1990s is important; of equal importance, however, are the ways they go about exploring them. Teachers cannot use traditional research methodologies without examining the origins of these methodologies and their underlying assumptions, if they hope to uncover insights into the field of computers and composition. One of the most important tasks facing such researchers in the 1990s will be to develop feminist research methodologies. Although no one research methodology is inherently "more feminist" than any other, all feminist research is likely to share certain characteristics. The first feature will be a shared concern with effecting genuine social change. Feminism began as a social movement, not an academic vantage point. Feminist work begins with the premise that we live in a patriarchal society that privileges some groups (most frequently white, wealthy men) at the expense of others. The intent of feminist work is to change this inequality. Feminist perspectives on computers in composition instruction will be informed by issues of power and shaped by the desire to disrupt conventional social hierarchies. The questions researchers ask will necessarily include considerations of how to use knowledge to make changes—to open up the world of computers and the power it holds to more people, particularly women, and to make use of computers to explore previously discounted ways of thinking and learning. Sandra Harding (1987) argues that

> The class, race, culture, and gender assumptions, beliefs, and behaviors of the researcher her/himself must be placed within the frame of the picture she/he attempts to paint . . . [because] the beliefs and behaviors of the researcher are part of the empirical evidence for (or against) the claims advanced in the results of the research. (p. 9)

The beliefs and behaviors of the researcher shape the questions they ask, the evidence they consider, and the relationships they establish with the group they are studying. This fact is particularly important for people working in computers and composition because of the striking differences in teaching situations in terms of instructors' access to and comfort with technology. Some teachers will be running writing centers equipped with only a few computers, while others will be working with advanced work-stations; some teachers will be learning about computers from their students, while others will be collaborating with computer scientists and computer engineers. What teachers learn about computers and composition will invariably be deeply tied to specific contexts because these contexts determine the kinds of questions they can ask. Teachers need to understand these contexts, and work to appreciate the differences that context—including differences between teachers, students, hardware, software, access, even writing programs—makes.

A third characteristic of feminist research in the 1990s will be an interactive and honest relationship between the researcher and the "researched." By refusing to accept an androcentric perspective that posits white middle-class male experience as the norm, teachers can create situations in which both the researcher and the researched can formulate and reformulate their stories. In computers and composition, this reformulation is particularly important. Computers make people vulnerable because while they are associated with power and status in our culture not everyone has equal access to them. It may be "too costly" for a teacher or a student to speak frankly about being fearful of computers. Conversely, the student who loves computers because of the fonts and the laser printer might fear sounding "not serious" if he or she were to report this. Consequently, as Klein (1983) notes, feminist researchers need to develop methodologies that

> open ourselves up to using such resources as intuition, emotions and feelings both in ourselves and in those we want to investigate. In combination with our intellectual capacities for analyzing and interpreting our observations, this open admission of the interaction of facts and feelings might produce a kind of scholarship that encompasses the complexity of reality better than the usual fragmented approach to knowledge. (p. 95)

Cooper and Selfe (1990) claim that computer technology may provide a liberating set of tools:

> We can draw on the revolutionary potential of computer technology to create nontraditional forums that allow students the opportunity to re-examine the authoritarian values of the classroom, to resist their socialization into narrowly conceived forms of academic discourse, to learn from the clash of discourses, to learn through engaging in discourses. (p. 867)

Teachers can draw on that revolutionary potential, but they won't be able to unless they look carefully at the whole configuration before them—at the technology itself, at the users of the technology, and at the ways teachers of writing go about trying to understand both.

References

Becker, H. J. (1987, February) Using computers for instruction. *Byte*, pp. 149–162.

Belenky, M. F., Clinchy, B. M., Goldberger, N. R., & Tarule, J. R. (1986). *Women's ways of knowing: The development of self, voice, and mind*. New York: Basic Books.

Benston, M. L. (1988). Women's voices/men's voices: Technology as language. In C. Kramarae (Ed.), *Technology and women's voices: Keeping in touch* (pp. 15–28). New York: Routledge & Kegan Paul.

Brecher, D. (1985). *The Women's Computer Literacy Handbook*. New York: New American Library.

Claxton, C. S., & Murrell, P. (1987). *Learning styles: Implications for improving educational practices*. College Station, TX: Association for the Study of Higher Education.

Cooper, M., & Selfe, C. L. (1990). Computer conferences and learning: Authority, resistance, and internally persuasive discourse. *College English, 52*, 847–869.

EDUCOM '89 (program book). (1989). Ann Arbor, MI: The University of Michigan.

Elmer-Dewitt, P. (1986, November 3). From programs to pajama parties. *Time*, p. 88.

Flynn, E. A. (1988). Composing as a woman. *College Composition and Communication, 39*, 423–435.

Gerrard, L. (1988). *The politics of computer literacy*. Paper presented at the 39th annual convention of the Conference on College Composition and Communication, St. Louis, MO.

Gerver, E. (1989). Computers and gender. In T. Forester (Ed.), *Computers in the human context: Information technology, productivity, and people* (pp. 481–501). Cambridge: The Massachusetts Institute of Technology Press.

Harding, S. (1987). Introduction: Is there a feminist method? In S. Harding (Ed.), *Feminism and methodology* (pp. 1-14). Bloomington, IN: Indiana University.

Hawkins, J. (1985). Computers and girls: Rethinking the issues. *Sex Roles 13*, 165–180.

Herrmann, A. W. (1989). Computers in public schools: Are we being realistic? In G. E. Hawisher & C. Selfe (Eds.), *Critical perspectives on computers and composition instruction* (pp. 109–121). New York: Teachers College Press.

Klein, R. D. (1983). How to do what we want to do: Thoughts about feminist methodology. In G. Bowles & R. D. Klein (Eds.), *Theories of women's studies* (pp. 88–104). London: Routledge & Kegan Paul.

Marcus, S. (1987). Computers in thinking, writing, and literature. In L. Gerrard (Ed.), *Writing at century's end* (pp. 121–138). New York: Random House.

Peer Computer Equity Report. (1984). *Sex bias at the computer terminal—How schools program girls*. Washington, DC: National Organization for Women Legal Defense and Education Fund.

Sanders, J. (1986, January/February). The computer gender gap: Close it while there's time. *The Monitor*, pp. 18–20.

Sanders, J., & Stone, A. (1986). *The neuter computer: Computers for boys and girls*. New York: Neal–Schuman.

Selfe, C. L. (1990). Technology in the English classroom: Computers through the lens of feminist theory. In C. Handa (Ed.), *Computers and Community: Teaching Composition in the Twenty-first Century* (pp. 118–139). Portsmouth, NH: Boynton/Cook-Heinemann.

Selfe, C. L., Ruehr, R. R., & Johnson, K. E. (1988). Teaching word processing in composition courses: Age, gender, computer experience, and instructional method. *The Computer-Assisted Composition Journal 2*(2), 75–88.

Selfe, C. L., & Wahlstrom, B. J. (1985). Fighting in the computer revolution: A field report from the walking wounded. *Computers and Composition 2*(4), 63–68.

Stanworth, M. (1983). *Gender and schooling: A study of sexual divisions in the classroom*. London: Hutchinson Education.

Strickland, D. B., Feely, J. T., & Wepner, S. B. (1987). *Using computers in the teaching of reading*. New York: Teachers College Press.

Turkle, S. (1984). *The second self: Computers and the human spirit.* New York: Simon and Schuster.

Women Computing. (1988). San Diego, CA: Women Computing.

Editors

Gail E. Hawisher is an associate professor of English and director of the newly established Center for Writing Studies at the University of Illinois at Urbana-Champaign. Before returning to the University of Illinois, where she completed her Ph.D., she held faculty positions at Illinois State University and Purdue University, and was also head of a large high school department of English in Columbus, Ohio. Her recent publications are *On Literacy and Its Teaching* (with Anna Soter), *Critical Perspectives on Computers and Composition Instruction* (with Cynthia Selfe), and articles in *Research in the Teaching of English, English Journal,* and *Collegiate Microcomputer.* Other professional activities include the coeditorship of *Computers and Composition* and membership on CCCC's Committee on Computers. She is also currently serving as chair of the NCTE Committee on Instructional Technology.

Cynthia L. Selfe is an associate professor of composition and communication at Michigan Technological University, where she serves as assistant head of the Humanities Department. She has chaired both the NCTE Assembly on Computers in English and the NCTE Committee on Instructional Technology. She has served as a member of the NCTE College Section Steering Committee, the CCCC Executive Committee, the CCCC Committee on

357

Computers, and the MLA Committee on Emerging Technologies. In addition to her journal articles and book chapters on computer use in composition classrooms, Selfe is the author of *Computer-Assisted Instruction in Composition: Create Your Own* (NCTE) and *Creating a Computer-Supported Writing Facility (Computers and Composition)*. Selfe has also coedited several collections of essays on computers, including *Computers in English and the Language Arts: The Challenge of Teacher Education* (with Dawn Rodrigues and William Oates, NCTE), *Critical Perspectives on Computers and Composition Instruction* (with Gail Hawisher, Teachers College Press), and *Computers and Writing: Theory, Research, and Practice* (with Deborah Holdstein, MLA). In 1983, Selfe founded the journal *Computers and Composition* with Kate Kiefer; she continues to edit that journal with Gail Hawisher.

Contributors

Ellen L. Barton is an assistant professor in the Department of English at Wayne State University, holding a joint appointment in the Linguistics Program and the Composition Program. In linguistics, her research interests are in syntax, discourse, and pragmatics, and recent publications include *Nonsentential Constituents: A Theory of Grammatical Structure and Pragmatic Interpretation* (John Benjamins). In composition, Professor Barton's research interests are in discourse analysis and in computers and writing; recent publications, coauthored with Ruth Ray, include "Changing Perspectives on Summary through Teacher-Research" (*Journal of Teaching Writing*) and "Developing Connections: Computers and Literacy" (*Computers and Composition*).

Janis Forman is the director of management communication for the Anderson Graduate School of Management at UCLA. From 1986 to 1989, she conducted IBM-sponsored research on computing and collaborative writing, and she has published widely on this topic, including publications in *Computers and Composition*, *The Journal of Business Communication*, and *The Journal of Business and Technical Communication*. She is currently editing *New Visions of Collaborative Writing*, a collection of critical essays on collaborative writing, for Boynton/Cook Publications. She makes presentations regularly at CCCC conventions and at meetings of the Association for Business Communication.

Mary Louise Gomez is an assistant professor of English education in the Department of Curriculum and Instruction at the University of Wisconsin–Madison, where she is also associate director of the Wisconsin Writing Project. From 1986 to 1990, she was a senior researcher at the National Center for Research on Teacher Education at Michigan State University. Currently, she codirects an experimental program of teacher education designed to educate elementary teachers to become more effective teachers of low-income children of color, and she is conducting a qualitative longitudinal study of these teachers' development. She teaches courses focusing on the teaching of writing to diverse learners, on emergent literacy, and on the use of computers for literacy education. She has been a K–6 teacher and language arts resource specialist in midwestern and southern schools and has published articles and book chapters on the preservice and inservice education of teachers.

Andrea W. Herrmann is an associate professor, the graduate coordinator, and director of the MA Program in Technical and Expository Writing in the Department of English at the University of Arkansas at Little Rock. She teaches courses in writing with computers, the art of teaching writing, sociolinguistics, and qualitative research methods. Prior to receiving an Ed.D. in applied linguistics from Teachers College, Columbia University, she taught high school English and French. Recent publications include "Computers in Public Schools: Are We Being Realistic?" (in *Critical Perspectives on Computers and Composition Instruction*, Teachers College Press), "Computers and Writing Research: Shifting Our 'Governing Gaze'" (in Computers and Writing: Theory, Research, Practice, MLA), and "Anxious, B-L-O-C-K-E-D, and Computer Phobic: A Writing Teacher's Memoirs" (in *Writer's Craft, Teacher's Art: Teaching What We Know*, Heinemann-Boynton/Cook).

Emily Jessup is a lecturer in the English Composition Board at the University of Michigan, Ann Arbor. She has taught introductory composition and women's studies courses. Currently she is teaching practicum, a pre-composition course, as well as teaching in the writing workshop. As part of a multidisciplinary team, she has developed software programs for biology and history. She has served on the CCCC Committee on the Status of Women, led workshops and presented papers on feminist issues in composition studies, and is writing a book on that subject for the Prentice Hall Literacy and Culture series.

Nancy Kaplan is a senior lecturer in the John S. Knight Writing Program and director of the Writing Workshop at Cornell

University. She has taught computer-based literature and composition courses since 1984 both at Cornell and at Carnegie Mellon University, where she was a Dana Fellow in Computers and the Humanities in 1989–90. Together with Stuart Davis and Joseph Martin, she developed PROSE (Prompted Revision of Student Essays), an award-winning computer program enabling students and teachers to exchange and comment on writing electronically. A member of the CCCC Committee on Computers, she regularly presents papers at national conferences and conducts workshops on computers and writing.

Kate Kiefer is a professor of English at Colorado State University. She has written extensively on the application of computers to composition instruction and has trained teachers to use computers effectively to teach composition since 1982. She edited *Computers and Composition* from its inception until 1987 and now serves on its editorial board. She is the author of two basic writing rhetorics and coauthor of *Writing, Brief, 3e.*

Elizabeth Klem received her master's degree from Rutgers University in Camden, New Jersey, and is currently finishing her doctoral work at the University of Massachusetts at Amherst. She has taught freshman composition for several years, most recently in the Writing Program's computer-equipped facility. She has conducted several research projects on the ways in which the introduction of computers changes a writing environment and has collaborated with Charles Moran on an extended study of how instructors adapt to the computerized writing classroom.

John McDaid is an instructor of English at the New York Institute of Technology. He has taught computer-based composition courses at New York University and at NYIT. He is currently completing his dissertation, "Breaking Frames: Toward an Ecology of Hypermedia," at NYU. A cofounder of TINAC (Textuality, Intertextuality, Narrative, and Consciousness), a collective of researchers involved with hypertext and fiction, he has been a visiting hypermedia resource person for schools and colleges. He regularly makes presentations at both academic and computer industry conferences.

Charles Moran is a professor of English at the University of Massachusetts at Amherst. He is past director of the university's Writing Program and has been a principal player in the design and operation of the university's computer-equipped writing classrooms. In addition to his journal articles and book chapters, he collaborated with Elizabeth Penfield in editing *Conversations: Contemporary Critical Theory and the Teaching of Literature*, recently published by NCTE, and he is now coediting, with Anne Herrington, a collection of essays on writing to learn. He has served on NCTE's College Section Committee.

Stuart Moulthrop is an assistant professor of English at the University of Texas at Austin. He received his doctorate from Yale University, where he also served as codirector of the Bass Writing Program. He has published a number of articles on hypertext and electronic writing and recently completed a book on contemporary American fiction. His current project is "Creatures and Creators," a multimedia resource on *Frankenstein* combining Mary Shelley's novel with the 1931 film.

Ruth Ray is an assistant professor of English and director of composition at Wayne State University in Detroit. She has collaborated with Ellen Barton on several conference papers examining the nature and purpose of computer literacy. Professor Ray teaches a graduate seminar on computers and writing in which she and her students collaborate on classroom-based research. She is currently writing a book entitled *The Practice of Theory: Teacher-Research in Composition*, to be published by NCTE.

Donald Ross is a professor of English and composition at the University of Minnesota, where he is director of the upper-division composition program. His writings include several articles and chapters on computer-aided composition, along with studies of Thoreau and narrative technique. With David Hunter, he has recently revised the EYEBALL program for the microcomputer, and has been using it to contrast student and professional writing in the disciplines.

Henrietta Nickels Shirk is an assistant professor in the Department of English at Northeastern University. Prior to joining the

Northeastern faculty, she was employed for over fifteen years as a technical communication professional and manager in the computer software industry. Dr. Shirk teaches graduate-level courses in technical and professional writing, and she serves as coordinator of the Computer Writing Lab for the Department of English and assistant coordinator for the Technical Writing Training Program. Her research interests are related to computers and technical writing. Dr. Shirk is editor for *The Bulletin* of the Association for Business Communication, and she has published essays in *Text, ConText and HyperText* (MIT Press), *Data Training, The Journal of Technical Writing and Communication, Collaborative Technical Writing: Theory and Practice* (ATTW), and numerous conference proceedings.

Catherine F. Smith is an associate professor of writing and English and coordinator for computing in the Writing Program at Syracuse University. She is coauthor, with John B. Smith, of *A Strategic Method for Writing*, an instructional approach implemented in an experimental writing environment, WE, developed for research use at the University of North Carolina. She is a frequent consultant to organizations in government, business, and industry for training in technical and professional writing and speaking.

James Strickland is an associate professor of English at Slippery Rock University of Pennsylvania. He has taught first-year composition courses, as well as other writing and literature courses, for over twenty years—using computer-assisted instruction for the last ten. He is the editor of *English Leadership Quarterly*, an NCTE publication of the Conference on English Leadership, and a member of the NCTE Committee on Instructional Technology. In addition to journal articles and presentations at NCTE/CCCC conventions, he contributed a chapter on "Prewriting and Computing" to *Writing On-Line* (Boynton/Cook, 1985).

Patricia Sullivan, who received her Ph.D. from Carnegie Mellon University, is an associate professor and director of technical writing at Purdue University. A longtime advocate of the use of computers in the teaching of technical and professional writing, she has studied the impact of computers on writing and publishing and also the usability of interfaces and documentation. Professor Sullivan has published in journals such as *Computers and Composition, IEEE Transactions on Professional Communication,* and the *Journal of Technical Writing and Communication.* She chairs the NCTE Committee on Technical and Scientific Communication and has won, with Peggy Seiden, the NCTE award for Best Article in the Teaching of Technical and Scientific Communication (1987, "Designing User Manuals for the On-Line Public Access Catalog").

Index

Evolving Perspectives on Computers and Composition Studies was composed on a Macintosh IIci using MICROSOFT WORD 4.0. The text was set in 11/13 Palatino, with heads in Palatino and Avant Garde. Page makeup was done with PAGEMAKER 4.0, and figures were created using FREEHAND 2.02. Proof pages were output from a LaserWriter II NTX at 300 dots per inch, and final pages were produced on a Linotronic 300 at 1270 dots per inch.